思想史

Intellectual History

專號：明清思想史

5

2015 年 9 月

目錄

【論著】

王昌偉　王心敬續《關學編》與康乾之際關中理學傳統的建構：
兼論清代學術的區域化進程 ……………………………………1

劉　勇　晚明理學「止修」學派之宗旨與師承 ……………………39

張藝曦　明代陽明畫像的流傳及其作用——兼及清代的發展 …………95

Ying Zhang（張穎）　Confucian Principles and Representations of a
Scandal: Writing about Zheng Man in the
Seventeenth and Eighteenth Centuries ……………… 157

Harry T. Dickinson　Later Reflections on the Revolution in France:
Changing British Interpretations from 1815 to
the Present ………………………………………………215

【論壇】

金觀濤、劉青峰、邱偉雲　〈《新青年》的數位人文研究〉……………283

David Der-wei Wang　Talks at "New Reflections on *New Youth*:
Liberalism and Radicalism in Modern China" ……311

Yoshizawa Seiichio　Political Ideals of *New Youth*: Chen Duxiu and
Republicanism …………………………………………321

Jeu Jenq Yuann　Scientific Life View: Personal or Human …………333

【論著】

王心敬續《關學編》與康乾之際關中理學傳統的建構：
兼論清代學術的區域化進程

王昌偉

新加坡國立大學中文系副教授，研究領域爲宋代至清代的思想史。

王心敬續《關學編》與康乾之際關中理學傳統的建構：
兼論清代學術的區域化進程

摘要

　　過去學者談到明清兩代學術的時候，一般傾向於把經世之學與考據學的興起視爲知識界對理學的否定，並認爲到盛清時期，理學基本上已失去了生命力，其地位也已被考據學所取代。這個自晚清以來就占主導地位的觀點，致使學術界在過去一百年來對清代理學的重視不夠。這樣的情況近年來已有所改變，尤其是不少從區域文化入手的研究，爲我們展示了清代理學在地方上的生命力。

　　本文也是一次從區域入手，探討社會文化和理學義理之間的互動的嘗試。以往大多數以諸如「閩學」、「關學」、「徽學」、「湖湘學派」等等爲題的研究，都把地域性的理學學派視爲一不證自明的界定範疇，重點則放在分析學派成員的學術和思想。不過，這一類的研究傾向於比較草率把來自同一地區的思想家都視爲同一固定「學派」的成員，而忽略所謂的「學派」，其實是一經過各種思想與學術競爭的場域。而且，在這樣的討論框架之下，地域除了提供一個便於研究者勾勒理學家的社會網絡的範圍之外，並沒有其他更爲實質的意義，該地域的社會文化也因此變得可有可無，讀者一般也難以從中理解理學家的義理內涵與他們所處的特定社會文化環境之間的關係。

　　有鑑於此，本文將通過對生活於康熙、乾隆之際的關中理學家王心敬（1656-1738）對關學學統的重新建構，論證王心敬所處的社會環境，以及他個人對如何才算是正學的理解，如何具體影響他對關學的塑造。本文因此會採取思想史的進路，從思想家的時代、所處的地域環境、面對的思想文化傳統，以及其義理之學的內涵入手，一窺他重構一個地方學派的歷史與思想動因。

關鍵詞：王心敬、關學、清代學術、體用全學

一、前言

　　我們一般提起宋明理學的發展與流傳，都會以「濂洛關閩」為周敦頤、二程、張載與朱熹所代表的「學派」命名。似乎理學從一開始，理學內部就存在含有地域色彩的學派的分野。實際上，「濂洛關閩」作為一組固定的詞組出現得相當晚，大概不會早於宋末元初。[1]換言之，從周子到朱子，都沒有要創立一內涵與外延皆明確的地域性學派的意圖。然而，受宋末以來傳統論述的影響，不少現代學者經常會以這幾位宋代大儒作為其「學派」的開山鼻祖，并強調某一「學派」在學術思想與學風方面的特殊性與延續性。關於這一點，從學界對關學的界定與討論中即可見一斑。如陳俊民認為：「關學是宋明理學思潮中由張載創立的一個重要獨立學派，是宋元明清時代今陝西關中的

1　這個結論是通過對《四庫全書》網絡版的搜索所得。「濂洛關閩」這個詞組最早出現於胡炳文（1250-1333）致吳澄（1249-1333）的書信，見胡炳文，《雲峰集》，卷1，〈與草廬吳先生書〉，收入《文淵閣四庫全書》（臺北：臺灣商務印書館，1983），集部別集類，第1199冊，頁3a。在胡炳文之前的黃仲元（1231-1312）文集中，其原序雖有這個詞組，但此序實為宋濂（1310-1381）所作。見黃仲元，《四如集》，收入《文淵閣四庫全書》（臺北：臺灣商務印書館，1983），集部別集類，第1188冊。另外，稍早有方逢辰（1221-1291）的「濂洛關西武夷之學」之說。見方逢辰於1276年左右所寫的《蛟峰集》，卷5，〈芳潤堂記〉，收入《文淵閣四庫全書》（臺北：臺灣商務印書館，1983），集部別集類，第1187冊，頁8b。亦有王應麟（1223-1296）和湯漢（約1198-1275）於1260年代「隣牆居，朝夕講道」時，關於「關洛建上江西」異同之討論。見袁桷，《延祐四明志》，卷4，〈絜齋袁先生〉，收入《文淵閣四庫全書》（臺北：臺灣商務印書館，1983），史部地理類，第491冊，頁24a。由陳思編，陳世隆補的《兩宋明賢小集》記載此事，則作「比屋而居，朝夕講道，論關洛濂閩江西之同異」。見陳思編，陳世隆補，《兩宋明賢小集》，卷378，〈王尚書遺稿〉，收入《文淵閣四庫全書》（臺北：臺灣商務印書館，1983），集部總集類，第1364冊，頁2a。

理學。」[2]此一學派雖無不間斷的師承，卻有獨特的學術思想的承傳，具備有別於其他學派的特點。[3]

　　然而，事實卻與陳俊民的看法有出入。儘管活動於宋孝宗時期的劉荀（生卒年不詳）已有「橫渠張先生名載，字子厚，居鳳翔郿縣之橫渠鎮，學者稱橫渠先生。倡道學于關中，世謂之關學」之說，但劉荀並沒有把橫渠之關學視爲一獨立的，有別於濂學、洛學或閩學的學派。[4]更何況從金元至明初，關中學者對張載及其學術并不重視。[5]在這幾百年間，關中理學主要是程朱之學的餘緒。一直要到明中葉，才有學者開始因爲張載的關中人身份，而把他的地位抬到創派祖師的高度。即便如此，晚明的關中理學最關注的，並非傳承張載極有特色的學說，而是回應朱子學與陽明學的衝突。有鑑於此，林樂昌認爲我們有必要區分北宋時期及明清時期的關學：

　　　相對於明清關學，我們還可以把北宋關學視作「原始關學」或「原生關學」，其創始人是北宋理學家張載，張載之學是此時關學學派傳承的惟一對象。而相對於北宋關學，則可以把明清關學視作「次生關學」。所謂次生關學，是指產生於「後張載時期」的關學，具體指明清關學

2　陳俊民，《張載哲學思想及關學學派》（北京：人民出版社，1986），頁24。
3　陳俊民，《三教融合與中西會通：中國哲學及其方法論探微》（西安：陝西師範大學出版社，2002），頁236-237。
4　劉荀，《明本釋》，卷上，收入《文淵閣四庫全書》（臺北：臺灣商務印書館，1983），子部儒家類，第703冊，頁3a。
5　關於張載在明清時期的接受史，見呂妙芬，〈明清之際的關學與張載思想的復興：地域與跨地域因素的省思〉，收入劉笑敢主編，《中國哲學與中國文化》，第7輯，《明清儒學研究》（南寧：廣西師範大學出版社，2010），頁30。

作爲若干小學派的集合，無論其思想根源還是其傳承對象
都已經不再僅限於張載之學了。[6]

在具體操作的時候，林樂昌認爲應該更進一步把明清兩代的關學
區分開來，那麼在關學的發展史上，就可分爲北宋、明代與清代三個
時期：

與北宋張載關學作爲單一的理學學派不同，明代關學在朱
子學、陽明學、甘泉學以及西學等時代思潮的影響下，呈
現多學派共存的格局，包括三原學派、河東學派、甘泉學
派，以及以王徵爲代表的關學別派；清代關學則在維新運
動和西學的影響下逐漸完成了向近代的轉型，從而終結了
關學。這樣，就形成了關學歷史演化的三個階段，即：北
宋張載創建關學階段、明代關學學派多元共存階段、清代
關學近代轉型階段。在這三個不同階段的關學之間，是有
較大差異的。基於從北宋關學至明清關學三個階段之間的
差異性，我們對不同時代的「關學」不應當滿足於使用泛
稱，將其統稱爲「關學」；而應當使用特稱，將其分別稱
爲「北宋關學」、「明代關學」、「清代關學」。這可能更
符合北宋至明清關學演化脈絡的實際。[7]

林樂昌提醒我們，宋代以還的關學並非統一的概念，研究者更應
該注意不同時段的差異性，無疑是很有見地的。但林樂昌的觀點卻有
兩點值得商榷。首先，林樂昌認爲清代關學一方面受西學的影響，在

6　林樂昌，〈論「關學」概念的結構特徵與方法意義〉，《中國哲學史》，1
　　（北京，2013），頁63。
7　林樂昌，〈論「關學」概念的結構特徵與方法意義〉，頁65。

晚清則更與維新思潮發生關係，經歷了近代轉型，結果促成了關學的
終結。在清代「受西學影響」的名單中，林樂昌列舉了清中葉撫陝總
督陳宏謀（1696-1771）的幕僚楊屾（1699-1794）。可是楊屾在清末
關中學者有關關學譜系的討論中完全缺席，似乎當時有資格左右關學
史的編寫的關中大儒們，都不知道此人的存在，或者是不願意讓他占
有一席位置。

　　另外，林樂昌此處列舉了同樣具爭議性的王徵（1571-1644）作
爲晚明關學的「別派」，[8]也同樣存在問題。首先，林樂昌沒有說明是
以什麼標準把王徵劃入關學的別派。另外，王徵是否應該被列入關學
的譜系，在清代也是關中學者爭論的焦點（見下文）。這也說明雖然
林樂昌注意到并不存在一個能用以概括和解釋從北宋到明清的關中學
術的統一範疇，他卻仍然以關學爲一不證自明的概念，所以才會直接
以王徵與楊屾爲關學人物，而沒有注意到歷史上關學譜系的建構者，
經常都會爲了如何界定關學以及誰才算是關學人物而展開辯論。

　　有鑑於此，筆者曾撰文考察晚明著名陝西學者馮從吾（1556-
1627）所編纂的《關學編》，目的就在於說明關學其實是一個在特定
的歷史脈絡中被建構出來的範疇。唯有認識到這一點，我們才能眞正
擺脫以往離開歷史語境去試圖定義關學的誤區。[9]本文擬在這個基礎之

8　林樂昌，〈論「關學」概念的結構特徵與方法意義〉，頁63。關於王徵的
　　研究，見黃一農，《兩頭蛇：明末清初的第一代天主教徒》（上海：上海
　　古籍出版社，2006）。關於楊屾的研究，見呂妙芬，〈楊屾《知本提綱》
　　研究——十八世紀儒學與外來宗教融合之例〉，《中國文哲研究集刊》，
　　40（臺北，2012），頁83-127。
9　王昌偉，〈關學編與明清陝西士大夫的集體記憶〉，收入何國忠主編，
　　《文化記憶與華人社會》（吉隆坡：馬來亞大學中國研究所，2008），頁
　　167-178。

上，探討入清以後，關中學者如何回應前朝前輩所建構的「關學」，以及晚明思想脈絡下被界定的學術傳統如何在清代被同一地區的學者接受、修正或改造，而這些對關學的不同詮釋又能說明清兩代思想史的什麼問題。

過去學者談到明清兩代學術的時候，一般傾向於把經世之學與考據學的興起視爲知識界對理學的否定，並認爲到盛清時期，理學基本上已失去了生命力，其地位也已被考據學所取代。這個自晚清以來就占主導地位的觀點，致使學術界在過去一百年來對清代理學的重視不夠。雖然有錢穆（1895-1990）因爲不滿意章太炎（1869-1936）與梁啓超（1873-1929）輕視清代理學，而不無爭議地把清代三百年的學術史寫成一部理學史，[10]專門討論清代理學的著作仍然是鳳毛麟角。

不過這樣的情況近年來情況已有所改變。2007年出版的《清代理學史》一書共三大冊，極其詳盡地介紹了有清一代理學的發展狀況。[11]此書的作者認爲，清代的理學的衰微主要是體現在缺乏理論上的創新，而在實際的社會生活中，理學則通過科舉考試，繼續在士人社群中發揮作用，并深刻影響他們的社會和文化活動，即使是在漢學大行其道的盛清時期，理學的社會影響也從來沒有間斷過。因此，本書的第二冊就特別用了一章來討論理學與社會文化的關係。其中，作者更以徽州作爲個案，探討理學與區域社會的關係，從「民間的朱子崇拜、宗法觀念的盛行、對婦女的束縛、儒與商的結合」等幾方面論

---

10 關於錢穆如何在《中國近三百年學術史》等著作中特意襃揚理學而貶低考據學，見姜虹，〈錢穆清代理學觀論述〉，《首都師範大學學報》（社會科學版），2（北京，2013），頁20-26。

11 龔書鐸主編，史革新、李帆、張昭君等著，《清代理學史》（廣州：廣東教育出版社，2007）。

證理學的鄉土化和社會化，也兼論及徽州理學的獨特性的問題。[12]雖然由於篇幅所限，本書對理學與區域的關係的討論還不夠深入，也沒有完全擺脫過往以「進步／落後」的二元框架來分析理學的社會作用的成見，但此書的貢獻不可抹殺，也與近年來某些針對區域性理學學派的研究，共同為我們提供了研究清代理學的新視角。[13]

本文也是一次從區域入手，探討社會文化和理學義理之間的互動的嘗試。以往大多數以諸如「閩學」、「關學」、「徽學」、「湖湘學派」等等為題的研究，都把地域性的理學學派視為一不證自明的界定範疇，重點則放在分析學派成員的學術和思想。這一類的研究傾向於比較草率把來自同一地區的思想家都視為同一固定「學派」的成員，而忽略所謂的「學派」，其實是一經過各種思想與學術競爭的場域。[14]而且，在這樣的討論框架之下，地域除了提供一個便於研究者勾勒理學家的社會網絡的範圍之外，并沒有其他更為實質的意義，該地域的社會文化也因此變得可有可無，讀者一般也難以從中理解理學家的義理內涵與他們所處的特定社會文化環境之間的關係。

有鑑於此，本文將通過對生活於康熙、乾隆之際的關中理學家王心敬（1656-1738）對關學學統的重新建構，論證王心敬所處的社會環境，以及他個人對如何才算是正學的理解，如何具體影響他對關學

---

12 龔書鐸主編，史革新、李帆、張昭君等著，《清代理學史》，中卷，第6章。
13 傅小凡、卓尅華主編，《閩南理學的源流與發展》（福州：福建人民出版社，2007）。放寧，〈理學地域化傳衍過程中的異變：論清代嚴州地區理學的復興〉，《江蘇廣播電視大學學報》，23（江蘇，2012），頁64-68。
14 近期學界已更為重視「學派」作為競爭場域的現象。代表作可參閱劉勇，〈中晚明理學學說的互動與地域性理學傳統的系譜化進程〉，《新史學》，6：2（臺北，2010），頁1-60。

的塑造。[15]本文因此會採取思想史的進路，從思想家的時代、所處的地域環境、面對的思想文化傳統，以及其義理之學的內涵入手，一窺他重構一個地方學派的歷史與思想動因。

二、從王心敬的〈家訓〉看清初的關中社會

王心敬，字爾緝，號豐川，陝西鄠縣人。王氏為當地甲族，自明中葉身列「前七子」的著名文人王九思編修了第一部族譜，雖經歷了各種天災人禍，包括明清鼎革的混亂局面，王心敬到了康乾時期仍能在一定程度上維持宗族的格局，人數幾五百人，讓王心敬能夠為族譜進行第四次的編修。[16]儘管如此，王心敬的日常作業基本上還是以家為單位。根據王心敬在為告誡其家中子弟所寫的〈家訓〉中的自述，他十歲喪父，七年之後，其伯父亦復見背，遺下兩個年幼的弟弟，以及一個「愚痴」的僕人。禍不單行的是，在他伯父去世那一年，三藩起兵，於是他「以從未更事之孱軀，上應供軍百需，下有饑寒債負」，家計窘迫，隨時有覆墜的可能。幸好有老母「明晰大體，主持家政」，不但把諸事處理得井井有條，還為王心敬提供了一個能安心

15　目前學界對王心敬的研究還在起步階段。以王心敬為主要研究對象的專著，只有幾部近幾年完成的碩士論文。單篇論文也寥寥可數，且主要集中在探討其易學。見張東鴻，〈王心敬《豐川易說》研究〉（高雄：高雄師範大學經學研究所碩士論文，2010），第1章〈緒論〉，頁1-13。未被列入張文的學位論文包括王振，〈王心敬《豐川易說》思想新探〉（山東：山東大學系所名稱碩士論文，2013）。

16　王心敬，《豐川全集》，續編卷18，〈族譜世系後跋〉、〈四修族譜後序〉，收入《四庫全書存目叢書》（濟南：齊魯書社；臺南：莊嚴文化事業有限公司，1997），集部別集類，第278冊，頁784。一直到今天，王氏仍然維持著宗族的凝聚力，他們最近一次的修譜（第12修）在1996年。見榮恩主編，《王氏族譜》（西安：鄠縣文管會，1996）。

讀書的環境：

> 每午夜擎燈，伯母、老母東西對績，余於其前就燈親書，
> 往往雞鳴未已。次年余補邑庠弟子，又次年，食餼。農事
> 漸理，仲弟亦長。七、八年間，遂得立腳不傾，稍成人
> 家……今老母年且逾七望八，余亦年五十而往。兩弟四子
> 三姪三孫，以及子婦孫女僕婢孕息者五十多人。且幸梟獍
> 未生，長舌弗作，老母家教整肅，每以張、陳、陸、鄭十
> 世同居爲訓。終余之身，當無盪析之虞。[17]

　　這段敍述透露出幾個重要的訊息。首先，與我們從其家中有一僕
人，以及王心敬無須照顧營生，可專心讀書的情況可見，即使在經濟
最爲拮据的時候，王家也有能力供其優秀子弟讀書。另外，王心敬的
父親和伯父到了成家以後顯然沒有分家，所以才會有伯父見背之後，
王心敬需要扛起家庭生活經濟重擔的情況，也才會有伯母、老母夜晚
共同督促他讀書的場景。此一傳統也由王心敬這一輩繼承下來，才會
發展至全家五十多人而仍無盪析之虞的盛況。因此，王家的組織形式
屬於我們所謂的「擴展家庭」（extended family）。

　　王家主要的經濟來源是甚麼？根據所謂「每午夜擎燈，伯母、老
母東西對績，余於其前就燈親書，往往雞鳴未已」的敍述，以及周元
鼎（生卒年不詳）在刊印王心敬所續的《關學編》時增補的豐川傳記
所敍，心敬後來放棄舉業從學李顒（1627-1705）時，「一切需用皆母
紡績質產所供」，[18]似乎家庭式的紡織作業是其家重要的經濟活動之

17　王心敬，《豐川全集》，正編卷26，〈豐川家訓自敍〉，頁594。
18　馮從吾撰、王心敬續修、周元鼎增修，《關學編》，卷6，〈豐川王先
　　生〉，收入《續修四庫全書》（上海：上海古籍出版社，1995），集部別
　　集類，第515冊，頁241。

一。另外，從王心敬補邑庠弟子、食餼，以及家中「農事漸理」的
七、八年間即「稍成人家」的情況可知，從耕、讀所得之收入，才是
最主要的經濟命脈。因此，在〈家訓〉中，王心敬對家族的經濟活動
做了如下的規定：

> 教子弟者，最上教之讀書出身。行志達道。如不能取科
> 第，則教之耕讀相資爲上。不得已而有事以資農耕之不
> 足，則使之教學作幕，亦無不可，但作幕非大有主見，人
> 易於失其所守，尚不如教學之無弊。如更不能教學作幕，
> 則醫藥種樹畜牧亦尚切實可爲。但醫非明理，易至殺人，
> 終不如畜牧種樹，不至無實欺世。至若居市貿易，則最易
> 喪人誠慤之心。古人雖四民並列，然終非傳家教子良法，
> 切不可教之使爲。[19]

明清時期的關中巨富，主要都是從事追求利滾利的商業與放貸活
動的家族。[20]但這一類追求財富的方式，卻與王心敬所憧憬的理學理
想人格格格不入，因此不獲得他的認同。對王心敬而言，最理想的，
莫過於培養家中子弟通過讀書入仕，把所學到的聖人之道付諸實踐。
但在科舉考試競爭異常激烈的情況下，考取功名不易，如應試不成，
則應教子弟邊從事農耕邊讀書。如若還有經濟上的困難，則可考慮教
書、充當幕僚，或者學醫，或從事種植、畜牧業。王心敬對這類非一
般「士君子」所屬意的營生方式不鄙視，究其原因，實與當時關中的
經濟生態不無關係。一些研究該區域的經濟史學家指出，中國共產黨
二十世紀中葉試圖在關中進行土地改革時，就發現明清以來「關中無

19　王心敬，《豐川全集》，正編卷27，〈家訓中〉，頁604。
20　田培棟，《明清時代陝西社會經濟史》（北京：首都師範大學出版社，
　　2000），頁128-130。

地主」。此一結論雖過於絕對，但仍然點出了關中農業生產模式的特色。基本上，明清以來，「關中幾乎是個自耕農的社會，地權極爲分散，地主不是沒有，但確實很少。」一般擁有土地者的經營模式不是租佃而是雇工，許多本身也會參與勞作。[21]因此，受限於經濟條件，關中的地主階層如不投入其他更易獲利的營生方式如經商或放貸，其財富必然有限。

　　根據王心敬對其家族的敘述，王家顯然也是屬於這類雖算富戶，但卻不十分殷實的地主家庭。這在一定的程度上也影響了他對理學的實踐問題的思考。例如在禮制的問題上，王心敬爲其家族做了如下的規定：

> 禮無所不在，何獨於四禮而謹諸？謂四禮生人之最切近也。禮貴得中，即吾夫子亦曰：奢則不孫，儉則固矣，又何容偏取於儉而尚焉？謂儉之尚近於本，而抑且中材下士可企而及也。然維昔吾夫子不又有曰：禮與其奢也，寧儉。又曰：與其不孫也，寧固耶？夫吾夫子豈不知禮之貴中哉？正以儀文繁縟非並禮之本始，失之即且有病其繁而畏難不行者，故寧儉寧固之嘆，吾夫子一言之不已，而至再再言之不已而直至於三。嗚呼！味斯言也，吾夫子殆隱有溯本之深思，挽時之隱意存焉。余家世業耕讀之家也，崇質尚樸，莫儉爲宜，而敢妄希當世大雅之林，用避固陋之誚哉？故暇日就前代傳來家禮纂本，更爲刪其繁縟而題曰《四禮寧儉》，蓋區區愚見，首取其於文不繁爲近本，

21　秦暉、蘇文，《田園詩與狂想曲：關中模式與前近代社會的再認識》（北京：中央編譯出版社，1996），頁44-68，引自頁53。

次更取其簡而易遵爲可行。若博雅君子有覩余編而執固之
一義譏余笑余者，余不敢恤也。[22]

　　針對家族中冠、昏、喪、祭四禮應該如何實行的問題，雖然基本
原則是「得中」，但如果必須在奢與儉之間做一抉擇，王心敬則傾向
寧儉勿奢。究其原因有兩方面，一是王心敬認爲孔子制定禮制的精
神，原本就不在於繁文縟節，然而另一個更爲根本的原因，恐怕是因
爲作爲一耕讀之家，經濟能力有限，如果儀式過於繁複，實行起來會
有困難，最終家族成員將畏難而不行，反而失去在家族生活中失去實
踐禮的機會。因此，雖然王心敬在這個問題上有其文化理想方面的考
量，但我們也不可忽略現實的局限對其學說的影響。也正因爲如此，
王心敬特別留心於農田水利荒政等事業，因爲這與其家族生計息息相
關。然而，對王心敬而言，這不僅是富民一家一戶之事，還是國本堅
固與否的問題。在主張地方官應勸導富民在荒年時參與救災工作的同
時，他特別提醒地方官必須公平對待富民：

故願司牧者平日去矯激之見，無輕摧富而右貧，借口於抑
強扶弱。荒年中又須愼持其平，無輕假公而濟威，借口於
不畏高明，不怕豪強，而輕加挫抑也。要知國家謂百姓爲
國本者，是蓋謂幾箇富民平日安土衛國之獨久，急公輸賦
之獨先。有兵則輓粟運芻之終賴，遇荒亦賦車供馬之莫
辭。總之，時無豐凶而國之所倚賴者，悉此輩也。嗚呼！
凡此富民，眞國家之命脈哉！可無特留意耶？[23]

富戶是國家賴以生存的命脈，故地方官必須維護其基本利益，不

22　王心敬，《豐川續集》，卷3，〈四禮寧儉編〉，頁106-107。
23　王心敬，《豐川雜著》，〈荒政考〉，收入嚴一萍選輯，《關中叢書》（臺
　　北：藝文印書館，1970），第3集，頁5a。

能隨意以各種藉口進行壓制，導致富戶無以爲繼。反過來說，富戶也
必須爲國家分擔管理社會和保衛領土的責任。家國一道是王心敬堅信
不疑的，因此，他特別在〈家訓〉中強調子弟在家之日學習經世知識
的重要性：

> 凡經世理物之事，須於伏處之日逐一講過。將來登第後，
> 庶不至全無知覺，觸處茫然。[24]
> 兵事亦不可不知。仕則有地方之責，不仕亦須知之以教子
> 弟。縱不能身歷行陣，目見親習，亦須從書傳中設身處地
> 體勘一番，從經歷名將前請教印證一番。[25]
> 農田水利，不惟中材以下所宜講究，即高才上智亦正不可
> 不知。蓋老農老圃固非士君子所可甘，奈何學爲人上而通
> 不知稼穡之艱，小民之依？[26]

　　無論將來有無仕宦的機會，子弟「伏處」之時都須掌握諸如農田
水利、兵法之類經世理物的知識。當然，最理想的情況是一旦登第，
這些知識就能派上用場。王心敬對登第的肯定，似乎與他的出處發生
矛盾。王心敬雖蟄居西北，但聲名遠揚，可是朝中權貴一再舉薦，他
仍然追隨其師李顒的步伐，選擇終身不仕。關於王心敬爲何「三徵不
起」，我們可以有不同的推測，[27]但必須注意的是，王心敬并沒有從體
制上或意識形態上反對清廷。因此，王心敬對於舉業，特別是詞章之
學并不排斥，甚至可以說非常留意。他只是希望子弟不要僅止於滿足

24　王心敬，《豐川全集》，正編卷27，〈家訓上〉，頁599。
25　王心敬，《豐川全集》，正編卷27，〈家訓上〉，頁599。
26　王心敬，《豐川全集》，正編卷27，〈家訓上〉，頁600。
27　劉黨庫，〈王心敬理學思想初探〉〉（陝西：陝西師範大學系所名稱碩士
　　論文，2009），第1章〈王心敬其人的 析〉，頁9-13。

當一個詞章之士：

> 文章經國之具，明道之資，豈可不工？但不可使人以詞章
> 之士目我，即我亦不可甘心僅作詞章之士。至於制義一
> 道，深言之，與六經史傳相表裏。淺言之，乃士子進身之
> 筌蹄，尤不可忘其本原，僅從得魚得兔處著眼，又不可以
> 已得魚兔而輒自滿足也。[28]

在王心敬看來，國家設科取士是有一高遠的理想的，只是今人對
此都視若無睹。一旦認清本原與方向，投身科舉之學非但是應該的，
還是必要的。可是現實卻是，能認清本原與方向的人少之又少，這可
從有關王心敬的一段小故事得知：

> 乾隆元年，蒲城某入京廷試，大學士鄂爾泰問豐川安否，
> 其人茫然無以應。鄂笑曰：「士何俗耶？天下莫不知豐
> 川，爾為其鄉人，顧不知耶？」[29]

王心敬以理學名家，聲明遠播，先後受陳詵（1643-1722）、張伯
行（1651-1725）等著名的學者邀請至湖廣、姑蘇講學，但同樣來自
關中地區的新進進士卻不知他為何許人。因此，當王心敬告誡家中子
弟不可甘心僅作詞章之士，在學習舉業也不可忘其本原時，他顯然是
有感於一般士子只專注舉業而不留心理學。另外，當周元鼎在嘉慶年
間為增補以後的《關學編》寫後序時感嘆，「今之學者岐理學與舉業
為二，勢不得不專舉業而遺理學，自豐川先生後，吾關中之學其絕響
矣」[30]，顯然也是深刻掌握了問題的癥結。

28　劉鼒庫，〈王心敬理學思想初探〉，頁599。
29　張驥，《關學宗傳》，卷39，〈王豐川先生〉，收入《儒藏》（成都：四川
　　大學出版社，2008），史部，第164冊，頁541。
30　馮從吾撰、王心敬續修、周元鼎增修，《關學編》，卷6，〈後序〉，頁242。

　　關中士子在舉業以外無暇顧及其他，不但使得理學幾成絕響，甚至制舉原本之高遠理想也被遺忘。王心敬把這種種的問題，歸咎於關中讀書之風氣不盛：

> 南人無論貧富貴賤，無生子不教讀書者，此意甚好。蓋人性本善，一經讀書，無論氣質好者，可望成就。即中材能識得三二分義理，亦是保身保家之藉資。我北人見識鄙陋淺俗，但一貧窮便不令子弟讀書從師。甚且閭鄉百十家無一蒙師，至使富足之家，男丁數十口，並無識丁之人。此風最是可笑可惜也。日後子孫但非癡聾瘖啞，當七八歲後必須令之從師讀書，以下些義理種子。[31]

　　雖然王心敬此處所論爲涵養氣質以及種植義理種子等理學方面的關懷，但在客觀上也反映了北方（包括關中）社會的困境。儘管王心敬認爲關中讀書風氣不盛是南人北人心態的不同所致，但更重要的原因恐怕是關中缺乏允許家族子弟在優良的環境下安心讀書的經濟環境。勿論貧窮之家，即便是一些富足之家，也不願意投資在文化教育上。許多家庭連聘請好的老師，購置好的書籍都覺得昂貴：

> 子弟但氣質清明者，須教之就正人，學正學。勿愛惜小費，勿希圖近功。蓋不惜費，則延師置書自然有薰陶長養之益……每見今人爲子弟延師買書，則吝惜如拔頭毛，至使好氣質子弟亦汩沒於俗師寡陋之下。噫！愚甚矣！[32]

　　對照前段引言關於南人北人的議論，這裡所討論的「今人」，指的顯然也是關中社會的狀況。在經濟能力有限的情況下，一般人教育

31　王心敬，《豐川全集》，卷27，〈家訓中〉，頁603。
32　王心敬，《豐川全集》，卷27，〈家訓中〉，頁603。

子弟，首要考慮自然是把資源投資在舉業上，希冀子弟能中舉入仕，這就是所謂的「希圖近功」。在科舉之外，一般家庭不會特別花錢為子弟聘請能教導正學的老師，或購置與科舉無關的書籍。在這樣的社會條件下，要傳播理學，自然困難重重。我們也可以據此推斷，一切與科舉無關的學術要在關中生根發展，都決非易事，而理學至少獲得朝廷的正式認可，與科舉考試的關係密切，一般士子不管是否以理學作為安身立命的學說，為了應付考試，對理學的典籍和基本命題都不會陌生。也許正因為如此，雖然如前所述，周元鼎在嘉慶年間增補《關學編》時感歎關中理學幾成絕響，他仍然能夠勾勒出一個比較清晰的理學社群的活動狀況。

　　有清一代關中理學的命脈不曾斷絕，還得歸功於李顒在清初所打下的基礎。因此，要了解王心敬如何建構關學，我們必須從他的學術淵源入手，討論李顒對他的影響。

三、從「體用全學」到「全體大用，真體實功」

　　李顒，號二曲，被譽為「海內三大儒」。[33]其父可從在李自成起兵時投軍，死於國難。明亡以後，儘管清廷多次徵召其赴闕，李顒卻選擇終身不仕。忠於前朝或者是其中一個原因，但李顒從未親口證實，而總是以母老、患疾、學無所成為由推辭。但最主要的原因，恐怕是要為世道人心樹立一典範：

　　　　今既以顒為隱逸矣，若以隱而叨榮，則美官要職，可以隱

33　全祖望，〈二曲先生窆石文〉，收入全祖望，《全祖望集彙校集註》（上海：上海古籍出版社，2000），頁233-238。名列三大儒的還有黃宗羲（1610-1695）與孫奇逢（1585-1675）。

> 而坐致也，開天下以飾僞之端，必將外假高尚之名，內濟
> 梯榮之實，人人爭以終南作捷徑矣。顒雖不肖，實不忍以
> 身作俑，使風俗由顒而壞……今若一旦變操，人必以平日
> 講學爲立名之地、媒利之階，轉相嗤鄙，灰其向善之念，
> 顒亦何由藉以默讚今上之化育耶？[34]

在這個方面，李顒顯然繼承了主流理學的社會與文化理念，試圖在廟堂與政統之外，樹立一獨立的道德權威。但在李顒看來，此一道德權威未必與國家的權威相抵觸，反而是相輔相成，可以「藉以默讚今上之化育」的。李顒的這一觀點，深刻影響了其首席弟子王心敬。王心敬終身不仕，卻始終認爲家國一道，在家也可幫朝廷分憂，顯然就是延續其師的思路。

另外，和王心敬一樣，李顒也是由其母撫養長大的。李母也反對李顒習舉業，卻要求他師法古人，讀書明理。十五六歲時，已博覽典籍，有奇童之稱。十九、二十歲之時，讀理學諸書，欽慕周程張朱言行，其後亦涉獵二氏之書，而在三十歲左右，開始究心經濟、兵法等學問。三十一歲左右，因病而發現「默坐澄心」的重要性，自是讀書重視與心相互印證，以濂洛關閩與河會姚涇論學要語爲主，摒棄雜學。[35]

在求學過程中，李顒也曾對《十三經註疏》等典籍進行考訂工作，不拘成說，似乎對考據訓詁之學也有興趣。實際上，如顧炎武（1613-1682）撰寫《日知錄》的學術路徑，是他所不取的：

34　劉宗泗，〈盩厔李徵君二曲先生墓表〉，收入李顒，《二曲集》（北京：中華書局，1996），頁607。

35　許鶴齡，《李二曲「體用全學」之研究》（臺北：文史哲出版社，2004），頁52-63。

友人有以「日知」爲學者，每日凡有見聞，必隨手札記，
考據頗稱精詳。余嘗謂之「日知」者，無不知也，當務之
爲急。堯舜之知而不徧物，急先務也。若舍卻自己身心切
務，不先求知，而惟致察於名物訓詁之末，豈所謂急先務
乎？假令考盡古今名物，辨盡古今疑誤，究於自己身心有
何干涉？誠欲「日知」，須日知乎内外本末之分，先内而
後外，由本以及末，則得矣。[36]

李顒堅持，爲學當先掌握先務，而名物訓詁如果與身心無涉，那
就是末技。那何謂先務？對此，李顒有以下的論述：

明體而不適於用，便是腐儒；適用而不本於明體，便是霸
儒。既不明體，又不適用，徒汩沒於辭章記頌之末，便是
俗儒；皆非所以語於《大學》也。[37]

李顒認爲，相對於腐儒、霸儒、俗儒，眞正的儒者必須能把《大
學》的道理付諸實踐，唯有徹底貫徹《大學》修齊治平的綱領條目，
才算是明體適用的通儒。但在其爲「明體」、「適用」所開出的一系
列書籍中，可知所謂的「體」，是以陸王與程朱的心性之學與涵養工
夫爲内容的。至於「用」，則包括了帝學（《大學衍義》類書籍）、史
學（《文獻通考》、《資治通鑑》、《名臣奏議》類書籍）以及各種經
濟類書籍。由此可見，李顒心目中的「眞儒」、「全儒」，實爲一能通
過參透並實踐心性之學而「合天地生育之德」，並通過掌握經濟知識
而「經綸萬物」的人物。[38]

36　李顒，《四書反身錄》，收入李顒，《二曲集》，頁508。
37　李顒，《四書反身錄》，頁401。
38　許鶴齡，《李二曲「體用全學」之研究》，頁71-132、260-272。

　　如本文開頭所言，一些學者如陳俊民認為，從張載在關中講學開始，關學踐履篤實的性格就形成了，也被元明的學者所持續發揚，而李顒的學術，不過是繼承了這個學派的基本精神而已，而且其中也蘊含了對理學的批判。[39] 其實，從上面的分析可知，李顒的學術從義理的層面講，是對程朱陸王之學的發揮，而從實用的方面講，則來源甚廣，與張載的思想并無明顯的聯繫。另外，李顒對制度的留意，也與元明時期的關中理學學者主要還是在義理的層面闡明學說的取徑大不相同。換言之，李顒在清初所開創的，實際上是一新的學術路徑。

　　作為李顒最著名的弟子，王心敬的學術體系基本延續其師的思路。他所謂的「全體大用，真體實工」，實際上即是對李顒「體用全學」的進一步闡發。他接受程朱與陸王的心性之學的正統性，認為這些理學前輩的學說向世人揭示了聖人之學的內涵，并闡明了善的本質以及為善何以可能的真理。當然，不管是程朱還是陸王，他們的學說都有不完善之處，但問題並不在於學說是否正確，而在於人的氣稟的複雜性，導致某一套學說只能針對某一群人：

　　　大抵朱、陸之學同尊孔孟，而氣稟之高明沉潛不同，故其初之從事未免各從其性之所以近以入。沉潛者所好在篤實，高明者所好在簡易。朱子之學術雖尊孔孟，而其稟賦之篤實與曾子、子夏近，故其生平所學原本於曾子三省與子夏教不躐等之旨。陸子之學術雖亦尊孔孟，而其稟賦之高明與孟子等近，故其生平所學原本於孟子之立大體，求放心，而其立教則有似子游重本輕末。之所謂學焉，各得其性之所近，而即以此各授其徒，亦如親炙孔門者，造就

---

[39]　陳俊民，《張載哲學思想及關學學派》，頁 24-28。

各自成家。[40]

在王心敬看來，程朱與陸王兩大學派的爭議是儒門中極其重要的事，是需要同道特別關注的。但解決的方式不是各守門戶之見，或者是很表面地妄談調和糾紛。另外，就余英時所指出，晚明以來一個解決爭端的途徑是通過訓詁的方式，證明哪一派的意見才比較符合經義的原旨。[41] 但王心敬卻不採取這樣的方式，因為在他看來，訓詁運用得當雖可闡明經旨，然而由於詮釋雜陳，不易辨真偽，再加上當時的學者一般拘泥於語言章句之間，以此當學問，矜為名高，導致「以語言打發二帝三王」的現象出現。[42]

要擺正先儒學說之偏，調停門戶之糾紛，唯一的方法，就是從實踐出發，徹底貫徹「全體大用，真體實工」的理想，而不在於從言語上進行辯論。具體而言，作為「用」、「工」的實踐工夫可分為兩個相互依存的層次。一是個人的立身處世，一是經世致用的成就。康乾之際是朱學占上風的時代，王心敬受張伯行等朱學學者之邀到姑蘇等地講學，經常得面對朱學學者的詰難，挑戰他把程朱之學與陸王之學並列的觀點：

> 時言學者爭以闢陸王為尊朱，先生一不阿附，直陳其所見，力與之辨。先生之子功請曰：「學者諱言陸王，心不沒其長可矣，或以諱言之，以息紛紛之爭。」先生蹵然

40　王心敬，《豐川全集》，續編卷3，〈姑蘇紀略〉，頁633。

41　Ying-shih Yu, "Some preliminary Observations on the Rise of Ch'ing Confucian Intellectualism," *Tsing-hua Journal of Chinese Studies*, 11（1975）, pp. 105-146. 亦參閱余英時，〈清代思想的一個新解釋〉，收入余英時，《歷史與思想》（臺北：聯經出版公司，1995），頁121-156。

42　王心敬，《豐川全集》，卷1，〈語錄一〉，頁330-331；卷9，〈侍側紀聞上〉，頁402。亦可參閱劉黨庫，〈王心敬理學思想初探〉，頁14-19。

曰：「小子言何鄙也。道者萬事之公也。余知言論事四十
年來，頗費心力。違平日素心取悅世儒，心何安乎？」又
曰：「象山義門風規，荊門政績；陽明討寇之略，推功之
仁，使在聖門，恐尚列之德行，不止在政事文學之科。即
無善無惡四字，推以無意無必無極太極之旨，亦未可非
也。」[43]

　　王心敬爲陸王所進行的辯護，是從兩個層面展開的。一是在學術
的層面，辨明其學說大旨與聖人之學（無意無必）或朱子之學（無極
太極）並不相悖。更爲重要的，則是他們在立身與事功方面的成就凸
顯了聖人之教的眞諦，這已經足以讓他們列身聖門的道德之科。換言
之，我們可根據一個人在「工」與「用」兩方面的實踐（包括立身處
世與經世致用兩方面），就斷定他是否爲聖人之徒。王心敬正是秉持
著對「全體大用，眞體實工」的這般理解，續寫馮從吾的《關學
編》。

四、馮從吾的《關學編》及王心敬對關學的認知

　　馮從吾的《關學編》主要部分共分四卷，收錄了北宋至明代著名
陝西學者的傳記，可說是關學這一地方思想學派的譜系。卷一爲以張
載及其門人爲主的北宋學者，卷二爲金元學者，卷三、四則爲明代學
者。前置首卷一卷，收錄四名孔門弟子的傳記。從整個編排看，很顯
然，馮從吾是把北宋作爲關學的正式起點，先秦的部分只是「序
曲」。那關學的內容又是什麼？馮從吾在自序中說：

43　馮從吾撰、王心敬續修、周元鼎增修，《關學編》，卷6，〈豐川王先
　　生〉，頁241。

我關中自古稱理學之邦，文、武、周公不可尚已，有宋橫
渠張先生崛起鄠邑，倡明斯學，鼻比勇撤，聖道中天。先
生之言曰：「爲天地立心，爲生民立命，爲往聖繼絕學，爲
萬世開太平。」可謂自道矣。當時執經滿座，多所興起，
如藍田、武功、三水，名爲尤著。至于勝國，是乾坤何等
時也，而奉元諸儒尤力爲撐持，塤吹篪和，濟濟離離，橫
渠遺風將絕複繼。天之未喪斯文也，豈偶然也哉？[44]

此序開頭雖稱關中自古爲理學之邦，但馮從吾卻把關學創派的功
績歸於張載，並認爲即使是在元代動蕩不安的歲月裏，因爲陝西
（按：陝西在元代屬奉元路）學者的撐持，張載的遺風仍然細水長
流，「將絕複繼」。在馮從吾的建構下，似乎由宋至明，張載作爲關
學的開山祖師的身份，是所有陝西學者所公認的。其實，如果我們仔
細閱讀金元時期陝西學者如楊奐、蕭、同恕等人的文集，就會發現他
們對建立一個地方學派完全不感興趣。他們認同的對象是程朱，張載
對他們而言，只是程朱學派的一分子，張載作爲陝西人的身份，對他
們並沒有特殊的意義。[45]因此，當馮從吾把張載從程朱的影子中獨立
出來奉爲關學的祖師，他實際上是在爲地方文化進行一次新的界定，
以此塑造一個他認爲陝西士人應該共同擁有的文化記憶。

當然，馮從吾在編這一份代表關學的「官方」文件時，必然要有

44　馮從吾等，《關學編（附續編）》（北京：中華書局，1987），〈自序〉，
　　頁1。此現代排印版，除原編外，還收入清代的幾部續編，使用方便。
　　但其中有些段落的斷句有問題。

45　Chang Woei Ong, *Men of Letters within the Passes: Guanzhong Literati in
　　Chinese History, 907-1911* (Cambridge MA: Harvard University Asia Center,
　　2008), pp. 76-131.

所選擇。哪一類的學者可算是關學中人，哪一些不算？這就牽涉到關
學在馮從吾心目中到底是什麼的問題。首先我們發現，漢唐儒者全被
馮從吾排斥在外，顯示他並不重視這些儒者所擅長的經學，不管是注
重名物訓詁的古文經學還是注重微言大義的今文經學。

　　另外，在「凡例」中，馮從吾特別強調「是編專爲理學輯，故歷
代名臣不敢泛入。」[46] 在這個原則下，馮從吾把歷代一些事功顯著的名
臣排除在外，如北宋邊功卓著的大臣遊師雄（1037-1097），以及明中
葉極負盛譽的王恕（1416-1508）。可是遊師雄是張載的學生，而王恕
在《明儒學案》中則被黃宗羲許爲「關學之別派」的「三原學派」的
創始人，[47] 可見，如果馮從吾要把他們包括在關學的範圍內，也是說
得過去的，但馮從吾卻選擇不收錄。清代就有一些陝西學者認爲這些
名臣是應該被包括在內的，如李元春（1769-1854）在續寫《關學編》
時，就把遊師雄收入編中，並在序中說：

　　如遊師雄，受業橫渠，載之《宋史》，學術幾爲事功掩，
　　然事功孰不自學術來？此疑少墟所遺也。[48]

　　李元春認爲，遊師雄的事功雖掩蓋了其學術方面的成就，但他的
事功卻是以學術作爲基礎的，因此懷疑馮從吾是一時疏忽而遺漏了遊
師雄。馮從吾是否眞爲一時疏忽，難以斷定，但他把關學嚴格定義爲
關中的理學，是毫無疑問的，也正因爲如此，關中一些舉足輕重的文
學之士，如於明中葉執文壇牛耳，被後人列入「前七子」的李夢陽
（1472-1529）、康海（1475-1540）、王九思（1468-1551）等人，《關

46　馮從吾等，《關學編（附續編）》，「凡例」。
47　黃宗羲《明儒學案》（臺北：明文書局，1991），卷9，〈三原學案〉，頁
　　188-190。
48　馮從吾等，《關學編（附續編）》，頁67。

學編》中也無法占有一席位置。

　　當然，即使是以理學界定關學，馮從吾仍然有好幾種選擇。首先，張載本身的哲學體系就相當獨特，完全可以被塑造爲對程朱之學的挑戰。明中葉個別的陝西學者就特別強調張載有別於程朱，甚至凌駕於程朱之上的地方，如韓邦奇（1479-1555），就聲稱張載論氣的見識和氣魄，古往今來的儒者無人能及。[49]但這不是馮從吾的取徑。我們只要翻閱馮從吾的文集，就會知道他其實對張載的學說並不在意。他念茲在茲的，就是如何處理王學對程朱學派的挑戰的問題。因此，在他的建構下，關學成了調和程朱與陸王兩派的紛爭的基礎。在《關學編》中留名的學者，就包括恪守程朱規矩，對王陽明非常不滿的馬理（1473-1555），同時也包括王陽明的關中弟子南大吉（1485-1541）。在爲他最佩服的前輩呂柟（1479-1542）作傳時，馮從吾還特別強調呂柟曾經拜訪過王學左派的中堅人物王艮（1483-1541）。這些學者雖然認同的學術派別是不同的，甚至針鋒相對的，但他們共同的陝西人身份，爲馮從吾把他們全都納入一個學派提供了最具說服力的基礎。

　　王心敬在續寫《關學編》時，基本秉持馮從吾的精神，在處理程朱與陸王兩派的分歧時採取兼容並蓄的原則，但卻也對原編進行了兩個重要的改動。首先，王心敬取消了「卷首」的編排方式，直接從「卷一」開始，與馮從吾把張載列於卷一，并把孔門四子列於卷首的做法不同。其次，王心敬新增了許多原編所不收錄的人物。在王心敬的版本中，卷一收錄的是與關中有關係的「聖人」，包括伏羲、泰

49　韓邦奇，《苑洛集》，卷18，〈見聞隨考錄壹〉，收入《文淵閣四庫全書》（臺北：臺灣商務印書館，1983），集部別集類，第1269冊，頁25a-26a。

伯、仲雍、文王、武王、周公。卷二收錄在原編卷首出現的孔門四
賢，並新增漢儒董仲舒（179-104 B.C.）、楊震（54-124）二人。[50]卷
三至卷五基本上是對馮從吾原編的照錄。卷六則收錄了馮從吾來不及
收錄的明末人物（包括馮從吾本人）以及李顒及其弟子。

　　王心敬版本中的編列方式與增加的人物能說明甚麼問題？首先，
卷一直接從伏羲等古聖人開始，要說明的是，關學不僅僅是指宋代以
來關中的理學而已。從伏羲畫八卦開始，天地間的真理就已經在關中
植根並傳播開來。其中關於泰伯與仲雍的討論值得注意。泰伯與仲雍
為周人祖先古公亶父之長子與次子。古公亶父見三子季歷之子昌（即
後來的文王）有聖德，就打算傳位於季歷。泰伯仲雍聞之，遂相攜逃
諸荊蠻，讓季歷順利繼承王位。季歷卒，昌繼位，周遂大興。按照王
心敬的說法，孔子以前，無人知泰伯仲雍之德，至孔子（551-479
B.C.）乃讚嘆泰伯讓天下之至德。[51]

　　然而史書中對泰伯仲雍記錄甚少，後人也無從考究他們的學術，
何以泰伯仲雍能名列關學的殿堂，畢竟顧名思義，《關學編》所著錄
的應該是在學術上有卓越成就的關中人物。王心敬特別對此做出解
釋：

> 吾夫子推泰伯為至德，據其行事論之耳，未及其心學也。
> 然即其如是之行而追想其心之所存注，亦良苦矣。心良苦
> 而其中體認之必精，踐履之必力，以求自遂其心理之安，
> 可以言盡耶？……然讓歷而歷之得卒嗣古公者，亦唯仲雍

50　周元鼎刊印的《關學編》在這一卷中還收錄了由王心敬的同門王承烈
　　（康熙四十八〔1709〕年進士）所附錄的東漢學者摯恂。
51　馮從吾撰、王心敬續修、周元鼎增修，《關學編》，卷1，〈泰伯仲雍〉，
　　頁181。

> 與泰伯同此心行之故，而吾夫子則獨舉泰伯者，舉泰伯以
> 例仲，其仰體父心以讓弟同。其至德自同耳。而周之家
> 學，於文武周公父子之前，遂丕昭於至德之兄弟矣。盛
> 哉！[52]

　　由於仲雍的行為與泰伯相同，可見其心也與泰伯同，因此，孔子盛讚泰伯，也等於盛讚仲雍。從泰伯仲庸的行為，我們可想見其用心之良苦，而從其能以大局著想，仰體父心，就說明其「心學」之精。縱使泰伯仲雍沒有留下隻言片語，後人仍然可以由其踐履之力推斷其學術之純正。

　　另一值得注意的人物是明末的王徵。當然，這是在撰寫原編時，馮從吾來不及著錄的。但即使王徵生於馮從吾之前，我們也很難斷定馮是否會為其立傳，因為王徵的信仰極具爭議性。[53]清末關中學者劉光蕡（1843-1903）在為《關學編》的續編寫序時就因為王徵信奉天主教而不知應否把他載入關學的譜系。[54]王心敬當初把王徵選入編中也不是沒有猶豫的：

> 先生名徵，字良甫，既第後，自號葵心，晚乃自號了
> 一……當是時也，明之季葉，盜賊、饑荒，海以內連綿不
> 絕。先生自未第時即蒿目而憂，講經時濟變之畧，於凡兵
> 陣、城守、積貯、製器之宜，無不究極其要……是時，海

52　馮從吾撰、王心敬續修、周元鼎增修，《關學編》，卷1，〈泰伯仲雍〉，頁181-2。
53　關於王徵的天主教信仰，可參閱黃一農，《兩頭蛇：明末清初的第一代天主教徒》（上海：上海古籍出版社，2006），頁130-174。
54　劉光蕡，《煙霞草堂文集》，卷2，〈重刻關學編後續〉，（蘇州：出版社不詳，1918），頁15b-16a。

內盜賊益眾，而荒旱益甚，先生明見時事，知將益棘，於
是築室於園，嚴事天之課。立心則必以盡性至命爲歸，
曰：「學不至此，則不可以對天」。講學則皆拯溺救焚之
務，曰：「學不至此，不得體天」……既而逆闖攻關，先
生自矢以死報國……從此遂絕粒不食。家人泣進七箸不
御，進藥餌不御，閱七日捐館舍……先生三十年勤事天之
學，刻刻念念，以畏天愛人爲心，至是復以忠憤盡節。君
子雖不語怪，要必有不死者存。遠擬夷齊，近媲文謝，夫
何議焉？[55]

王心敬對王徵的經世致用之學大書特書，[56]更把他與伯夷、叔
齊、文天祥、謝枋得等以死盡節的忠臣相提並論，然而最後的問句卻
透露出時人對王徵不是沒有議論的。王心敬雖沒有明言王徵爲人所議
者爲何，但從「君子雖不語怪，要必有不死者存」這句話中判斷，問
題應該就在於其「事天之學」，在當時某些人看來，這無異於倡導怪
力亂神。而這樣的人物如何可列身關學的殿堂？

可是王心敬明顯有爲傳主平反的意圖。關鍵就在於王心敬對先賢
學術的肯定，主要是以實踐的眞切爲標準。所以儘管王徵的「事天之
學」表面上與怪力亂神相似，但他的處事及殉國卻在在說明，他已經
把聖人之教完全內化，成爲他生命的一部份。王心敬甚至因此爲王徵

55　馮從吾撰、王心敬續修、周元鼎增修，《關學編》，卷6，〈端節王先
　　生〉，頁231-233。續修四庫全書本所根據的原刻本有錯簡，此處因爲對
　　照中華書局1987年版抄錄。

56　王徵對民用及軍用的機械之學深感興趣，著有《新製諸器圖說》與《遠
　　西奇器圖說》等機械工程學的著作。李約瑟把他稱爲中國歷史上的第一
　　位現代工程師。見 Joseph Needham, *Science and Civilization in China*
　　(Cambridge: Cambridge University Press, 1965) Vol. 4, part II, p. 171ni.

的宗教信仰進行辯說。引文中的「有不死者存」接著「君子雖不語怪」而來，說明王心敬很清楚這原指宗教上靈魂不滅之說，但他卻把這句話重新解釋爲忠烈精神從夷齊到文謝到傳主之長存不死。從這個意義上說，在經過王心敬的詮釋之後，關學的精神首重道德實踐，學術的正否則可根據學者的人格與事功加以判斷。也正是基於這樣的認識，王心敬在爲董仲舒立傳時，大篇幅描寫他在藩國任職時對國王的直諫以及在武帝時推明孔氏之功。[57]至於楊震，王心敬更是對他在面對受賄的考驗時所發出的「四知」論大書特書，強調他的「問心無愧」正是《大學》、《中庸》、《孟子》的相關學說的具體實踐。[58]

　　王心敬正是如此以「全體大用，真體實工」爲理論基礎重構關學的傳統，可是他的方式卻不爲後來的關中學者所接受。在十九世紀以後湧現的各種版本的續編中，主筆者如李元春（1769-1854）、賀瑞麟（1824-1893）、柏景偉（1830-1891）等基本上還是按照馮從吾以張載爲關學之始的編排方式，並把王心敬新增的聖人與漢儒刪除。[59]可見在這些晚清學者的心目中，關學的正宗應仍是以能闡發理學的義理的學者爲主，理學以外的關中人物，即使品格高尚，事功卓越，也不能就因此把他們的學術與理學混爲一談。

　　儘管如此，有一種關懷是從馮從吾到晚清學者這二百多年間都不曾間斷的，那就是理學內部的門戶之爭。雖然這些學者所持的立場不

57　馮從吾撰、王心敬續修、周元鼎增修，《關學編》，卷2，〈漢儒，流寓一人（新增）〉，頁187-188。董仲舒祖籍非關中，王心敬得特別強調他雖流寓關中，但「老關中，卒關中，葬關中」，因此完全有資格被列入《關學編》。

58　馮從吾撰、王心敬續修、周元鼎增修，《關學編》，卷2，〈四知楊先生（新增）〉，頁188。

59　馮從吾等，《關學編（附續編）》，頁68-69。

一，但如何處理程朱與陸王兩派的爭議，卻始終是他們編寫關學的譜
系時所必須正視的問題。從學術的角度而言，理學的中心議題始終主
導著有清一代關學譜系的書寫，顯示建構關學的話語權一直都掌握在
理學學者的手中，理學在關中的地位，始終沒有被後來由畢沅（1730-
1797）在撫陝期間企圖大力推廣的考據學所取代。[60]

五、結論

　　王心敬在康乾之際續寫的《關學編》，實際上是明中葉以來關中
士人群體地方意識刺激下的產物。[61]那麼，王心敬的努力，能說明明
清之際思想史的什麼問題？首先，這個現象不是關中所獨有，類似的
肇興於明末，并在清代獲得繼承的建構地方學術譜系的嘗試在其他地
方也可見到。[62]這說明，理學在清代並沒有因爲漢學的興盛而消失，
而是以另一種方式在社會上傳播。這意味著早期學界關於明清思想史
的一種主流的直線型論述—即考據學「取代」了理學—需要被修正。
其實，早在前面引述過的，發表於三十多年前的關於清代思想的經典
論文中，余英時已經指出，考據學的興起實是理學內部智識主義傾向
的產物。程朱與陸王兩派的學者爲了論證本身學說的合理性，紛紛回
歸經典文本，以實例證明本身的學說與聖人之言是相符的。這最終

60　關於畢沅在關中推廣考據學以及受到的阻力，見 Chang Woei, Ong, *Men of Letters within the Passes: Guanzhong Literati in Chinese History, 907-1911*, pp. 188-194.

61　Chang Woei, Ong, *Men of Letters within the Passes: Guanzhong Literati in Chinese History, 907-1911*, pp. 132-184.

62　Thomas A. Wilson, *Genealogy of the Way: The Construction and Uses of the Confucian Tradition in Late Imperial China*（Stanford: Stanford University Press, 1995）, p. 309n130.

導致了以名物訓詁爲求眞手段的樸學的產生。從這個意義上說，與其把考據學視爲理學的反動，不如說考據學是理學內部發展的邏輯性結果。余英時把此一演變稱爲「內在理路」（inner logic）。[63]

余英時的觀察讓我們透過不同學術立場表面的涇渭分明而認識到思想史內部更深層的變動，爲清代的學術史研究樹立了新的典範。不過「內在理路」的說法卻有値得商榷之處。首先，余英時強調，「內在理路」說只處理學術本身的發展，但卻不否定外在因素對學術發展的影響，這固然顯示余英時並非沒有注意到思想變動的複雜性，但無論有沒有把外部原因考慮進來，「內在理路」的取徑，似乎是假定考據學的產生，是程朱與陸王兩派競爭的自然結果。然而，從關學的例子可知，理學內部的爭議其實可以往另外的，反樸學的基本預設的方向發展。從李顒到王心敬到爾後以理學爲學術依歸的關中學者，主要都是從具體的實踐（包括立身處世與經世致用兩方面）出發去回應程朱與陸王兩派分歧的這個重大課題。

正因爲如此，爲余英時所略過不提的外部因素就顯得格外重要。正如艾爾曼（Benjamin Elman）的研究所顯示，考據學的興起更貼切地說，是一個江南，而非全國的現象。實際上，考據學後來在官方的推動下傳入其他區域的時候，經常都會面對相當的阻力，而其在江南的萌芽與扎根，實有賴於此一區域得天獨厚的經濟條件所孕育出的文化氛圍。富商對學術、書院、刻書業、藏書樓的資助，提供了進行考據工作所必備的物質條件。[64]

63　Ying-shih Yu, "Some preliminary Observations on the Rise of Ch'ing Confucian Intellectualism," pp. 105-146. 亦參閱余英時，〈清代思想的一個新解釋〉，頁 121-156。

64　Benjamin A. Elman, *From Philosophy to Philology: Intellectual and Social*

關學的例子證實了艾爾曼的觀察的準確性。通過對王心敬的經歷
及其〈家訓〉的探討，可知明清時期的關中並不具備江南那樣的孕育
考據學的土壤。清代關中學者以理學的義理與工夫配合經世之學的實
踐而建構出來的關學，比起考據學顯然更易於獲得生活在關中的特殊
環境中的士人所接受。

不過，清初的關學與晚明的關學卻有著不同的性格。清初關學的
經世面向是馮從吾在建構關學傳統時所不關注的，但由李顒所開啓的
關中經世之學也走上與江南迥異的道路。以《皇明經世文編》的編者
群爲代表的晚明江南經世學者，有感於國家所面臨的危難以及對士人
空談心性，對經世濟民之事漠不關心的反感，特別強調經世作爲一種
獨立學問的合法性和重要性。與一般的認知相反，這批經世學者的中
堅分子，包括陳子龍（1608-1647）、徐孚遠（1599-1665）、宋徵璧
（1602-1675）等，并不全盤否定理學，如陳子龍并不否認理學對提高
個人道德修養的重要性。[65] 他們只不過是希望能帶動一種新的學術風
氣，把士人的目光轉向國家施政層面的各種技術性的學問。魚宏亮對
這一套學術的特徵有很好的說明：

> 這種知識譜系的特徵是以王朝的行政事務爲中心，以解決
> 統治事務中的具體問題爲內容，以專制體系中稱職的官僚
> 爲培養目標而逐漸形成一套龐雜的知識體系。這套知識體
> 系的傳承很少依靠理論上的說明和哲學上的總結，它更多
> 依靠的是官員在處理實際事務中所形成的經驗通過奏疏、

Aspects of Change in Late Imperial China (Cambridge MA: Council on East Asian Studies, 1984), pp. 7-13.

65 陳子龍，《安雅堂集》（臺北：偉文圖書出版有限公司，1977），卷18，〈答戴石房〉，頁1228-1231。

文集、史傳中的事蹟等形式傳承下來，在某些時代會出現
大量的總結性的著作和上升到理論的說明，但是實用性、
操作性、參考性仍然是這種知識譜系的首要追求。[66]

顯而易見，這一類型的經世之學，與王心敬在建構關學傳統時所強調的「全體大用，真體實工」下的經世之學大相徑庭。這說明兩個問題。第一，當李顒在清初以大儒的身份崛起於關中，他與明末的關中大儒並沒有任何的師承關係。不過，馮從吾通過《關學編》所建構的，以調和程朱陸王之學（而非張載之學）為主要關懷的關學傳統，卻深刻影響了清代關中學者的學術選擇。南宋以來，以掌握行政事務為知識體系的中心的經世思想與以闡述道德的宇宙論、人性論和工夫論的理學經常處於競爭的狀態。[67]但當李顒與王心敬等清初儒者在世變之後把目光轉向經世致用的學問時，他們同時也把經馮從吾梳理的關學傳統也繼承了下來，形成一套以經世之學調停理學內部爭議的，符合關中的社會、經濟和文化環境的知識體系。我們從清代關學的發展軌跡所看到的，是一個影響全國的思想議題（程朱與陸王之爭）如何被在地化的過程。

第二，過去學界在論及明清之際的思想變遷時，傾向於以經世之學在十七世紀的興起和考據學在十八世紀的興盛作為理學已被取代的證據。實際上，理學被取代的現象，主要是發生在江南。在關中，理

66　魚宏亮，《知識與救世：明清之際經世之學研究》（北京：北京大學出版社，2008），頁77。

67　關於南宋時期理學與經世思想如何在科舉考試的場域中競爭的過程，可參閱 Hilde De Weerdt, *Competition over Content: Negotiating Standards for the Civil Service Examinations in Imperial China* (*1127-1279*) (Cambridge MA: Harvard University Asia Center, 2006).

學不僅沒被取代，反而開創出與江南性格不同的經世之學，甚至把考據學排除在外。這提醒我們，所謂的「取代」，不過是由江南的特殊性所促成的，而非一全國性的現象。儘管江南知識界挾著雄厚的經濟和文化實力，在學術思想的傳播上占據領先的位置，也迫使其他地區的士人必須回應他們所提出的思想與文化課題，但顯然，江南的知識份子並無法完全主導思潮在全國範圍內的走向。因此，要更好地把握清代思想史，我們必須從空間上，留意整體與局部之間錯綜複雜的關係。唯有如此，我們才能正視江南在歷史上的獨特性，在進行分析時，才能避免以江南代表全國的偏差。

Wang Xinjing's Sequel to the *Cases of Guanzhong Scholars* and the Construction of the Guanxue Tradition in the Kangxi and Qianlong Eras:
The Regionalization of Scholarship in the Qing Dynasty

Chang Woei Ong

Abstract

Through a case study of the thought of Wang Xinjing (1656-1738), a Daoxue Neo-Confucian scholar active in the Shaanxi region (traditionally known as Guanzhong), this paper attempts to explore that regionalization of Daoxue in late imperial China. It argues that contrary to conventional wisdom, Daoxue had not been completely marginalized by the kaoju (evidential scholarship) movement during the course of the Qing dynasty. In fact, the rise of kaoju scholarship was basically a Jiangnan phenomenon. In many other parts of China, the kaoju premise and claims were often met with skepticism. Such was the case in Shaanxi, where Daoxue scholars had begun to consciously construct a regional school of thought called Guanxue (the Learning of Guanzhong) since the late Ming period. In the late seventeenth and early eighteenth centuries, Wang Xinjing continued the trend of constructing Guanxue within the social, cultural and intellectual context of early Qing Guanzhong. It was at once a product of his philosophical orientation as well as a response towards the changing historical circumstances of his time.

Keywords: Wang Xinjing; Guanxue; Qing scholarship; The Complete Learning of Essence and Application

徵引文獻

方逢辰，《蛟峰集》，收入《文淵閣四庫全書》，集部別集類，第1187冊，臺北：臺灣商務印書館，1983。

王心敬，《豐川全集》，收入《四庫全書存目叢書》，集部別集類，第278冊，濟南：齊魯書社；臺南：莊嚴文化事業有限公司，1997。

_____，《豐川雜著》，收入嚴一萍選輯，《關中叢書》，第3輯，臺北：藝文印書館，1970。

_____，《豐川續集》，收入《四庫全書存目叢書》，集部別集類，第279冊，濟南：齊魯書社；臺南：莊嚴文化事業有限公司，1997。

王昌偉，〈關學編與明清陝西士大夫的集體記憶〉，收入何國忠主編，《文化記憶與華人社會》，吉隆坡：馬來亞大學中國研究所，2008，頁167-178。

王振，〈王心敬《豐川易說》思想新探〉，山東：山東大學系所名稱碩士論文，2013。

田培棟，《明清時代陝西社會經濟史》，北京：首都師範大學出版社，2000。

全祖望，《全祖望集彙校集注》，上海：上海古籍出版社，2000。

余英時，《歷史與思想》，臺北：聯經出版公司，1995。

呂妙芬，〈明清之際的關學與張載思想的復興：地域與跨地域因素的省思〉，收入劉笑敢主編，《中國哲學與中國文化》，第7輯，《明清儒學研究》，南寧：廣西師範大學出版社，2010，頁25-58。

_____，〈楊屾《知本提綱》研究——十八世紀儒學與外來宗教融合之例〉，《中國文哲研究集刊》，40（臺北，2012），頁83-127。

李顒，《二曲集》，北京：中華書局，1996。

放寧，〈理學地域化傳衍過程中的異變：論清代嚴州地區理學的復興〉，《江蘇廣播電視大學學報》，23（江蘇，2012），頁64-68。

林樂昌，〈論「關學」概念的結構特徵與方法意義〉，《中國哲學史》，1（北京，2013），頁59-65。

姜虹，〈錢穆清代理學觀論述〉，《首都師範大學學報》（社會科學版），2（北京，2013），頁20-26。

胡炳文，《雲峰集》，收入《文淵閣四庫全書》，集部別集類，第1199冊，臺北：臺灣商務印書館，1983。

秦暉、蘇文，《田園詩與狂想曲：關中模式與前近代社會的再認識》，北京：中央編譯出版社，1996。

袁桷，《延祐四明志》，收入《文淵閣四庫全書》，史部地理類，第491冊，
　　臺北：臺灣商務印書館，1983。

張東鴻，〈王心敬《豐川易說》研究〉，高雄：高雄師範大學經學研究所碩士
　　論文，2010。

張驥，《關學宗傳》，收入《儒藏》，史部，第164冊，成都：四川大學出版
　　社，2008。

許鶴齡，《李二曲「體用全學」之研究》，臺北：文史哲出版社，2004。

陳子龍，《安雅堂集》，臺北：偉文圖書出版有限公司，1977。

陳俊民，《三教融合與中西會通：中國哲學及其方法論探微》，西安：陝西師
　　範大學出版社，2002。

_____，《張載哲學思想及關學學派》，北京：人民出版社，1986。

陳思編，陳世隆補，《兩宋名賢小集》，收入《文淵閣四庫全書》，集部總集
　　類，第1364冊，臺北：臺灣商務印書館，1983。

魚宏亮，《知識與救世：明清之際經世之學研究》，北京：北京大學出版社，
　　2008。

傅小凡、卓尅華主編，《閩南理學的源流與發展》，福州：福建人民出版社，
　　2007。

馮從吾等，《關學編（附續編）》，北京：中華書局，1987。

馮從吾撰，王心敬續修，周元鼎增修，《關學編》，收入《續修四庫全書》，
　　集部別集類，第515冊，上海：上海古籍出版社，1995。

黃一農，《兩頭蛇：明末清初的第一代天主教徒（修訂版）》，上海：上海古
　　籍出版社，2006。

黃仲元，《四如集》，收入《文淵閣四庫全書》，集部別集類，第1188冊，臺
　　北：臺灣商務印書館，1983。

黃宗羲，《明儒學案》，臺北：明文書局，1991。

榮恩主編，《王氏族譜》，西安：鄠縣文管會，1996。

劉光蕡，《煙霞草堂文集》，蘇州：出版社不詳，1918，王典章思過齋本。

劉勇，〈中晚明理學學說的互動與地域性理學傳統的系譜化進程〉，《新史
　　學》，6：2（臺北，2010），頁1-60。

劉荀，《明本釋》，收入《文淵閣四庫全書》，子部儒家類，第703冊，臺
　　北：臺灣商務印書館，1983。

劉黨庫，〈王心敬理學思想初探〉，陝西：陝西師範大學系所名稱碩士論文，
　　2009。

韓邦奇，《苑洛集》，收入《文淵閣四庫全書》，集部別集類，第1269冊，臺
　　北：臺灣商務印書館，1983。

龔書鐸主編，史革新、李帆、張昭君等著，《清代理學史》，廣州：廣東教育

出版社，2007。

De Weerdt, Hilde. *Competition over Content: Negotiating Standards for the Civil Service Examinations in Imperial China*（*1127-1279*）. Cambridge MA: Harvard University Asia Center, 2006.

Elman, Benjamin A. *From Philosophy to Philology: Intellectual and Social Aspects of Change in Late Imperial China*. Cambridge MA: Council on East Asian Studies, 1984.

Needham, Joseph. *Science and Civilization in China*. Vol. 4. Cambridge: Cambridge University Press, 1965.

Ong, Chang Woei. *Men of Letters within the Passes: Guanzhong Literati in Chinese History, 907-1911*. Cambridge MA: Harvard University Asia Center, 2008.

Wilson, Thomas A. *Genealogy of the Way: The Construction and Uses of the Confucian Tradition in Late Imperial China*. Stanford: Stanford University Press, 1995.

Yu, Ying-shih. "Some preliminary Observations on the Rise of Ch'ing Confucian Intellectualism," *Tsing-hua Journal of Chinese Studies*, 11（1975）, pp. 105-146.

【論著】

晚明理學「止修」學派之宗旨與師承*

劉勇

香港中文大學歷史系博士，現任廣州中山大學歷史系、中山
大學歷史人類學研究中心副教授。主要研究領域為明代史與
中國近世思想文化史。主要論著有《中晚明士人的講學活動
與學派建構——以李材（1529-1607）為中心的研究》、〈中
晚明時期的講學宗旨、〈大學〉文本與理學學說建構〉、〈中
晚明理學學說的互動與地域性理學傳統的系譜化進程——以
「閩學」為中心〉等。

* 本文的研究工作，受到廣東省高校優秀青年創新人才培養計劃和廣東省
  高等學校優秀青年教師培養計劃的資助。作者感謝兩位匿名審查人的細
  心審閱與指正。

晚明理學「止修」學派之宗旨與師承

摘要

　　本文以晚明理學家李材開創的「止修」學派爲中心，探討理學脈絡中學說「宗旨」在師徒之間的傳承問題。「宗旨」是高度概括的理學概念，是代表某種理學學說和學派的核心觀念。通過觀察「宗旨」在師徒之間的傳承情形，有助於理解理學的師徒倫理與學說傳承的關係、師門學說傳遞與追求自得之學的內在緊張。在具體討論中，本文首先從宋明理學的道統觀念與學說授受方式角度，以具體實例探討理學師徒關係的重要性與複雜性；然後簡述「止修」學派的創立者李材的學說傳播方式；最後著重以李材門人徐即登和涂宗濬爲例，從謹守師傳與嘗試修訂師門宗旨兩個方面，詳細檢討「止修」宗旨在師徒傳承過程中所遭遇的接受、修訂與排拒情形。

關鍵詞：李材、徐即登、涂宗濬、止修、明代思想史

一、前言

　　中晚明時期理學學說和學派建構的一種重要模式是「講學須有宗旨，宗旨源於《大學》」。這個模式主要包括改《大學》、拈宗旨、興講學三個關鍵性步驟，即透過對《大學》文本的重新釐定並作出新詮釋，主要從「三綱領」、「八條目」等重要概念中拈出一個高度概括的、學術口號式的學說「宗旨」，作爲一己理學學說的核心觀念，圍繞這個核心觀念演繹出新的理學體系，然後主要借助當時盛行的講學、講會活動傳播學說。其中，「宗旨」是各種新理學學說的標誌，《大學》則是林林總總的理學宗旨得以成立的主要經典依據，而講學活動爲新理學學說和學派提供了最有效的社會傳播途徑。李材（1529-1607）創立的「止修」宗旨，是《大學》「止於至善」（知止）與「修身爲本」（知本）的合稱，「止」爲內心存養的本體，「修」是自我省察的功夫，即所謂「止爲主意，修爲功夫」。這個學說宗旨的提出，正是李材透過上述建構模式，在朱熹與王陽明的《大學》文本和詮釋之間取長補短的結果，從而獲得經典依據和義理邏輯，進而挑戰兩者的權威，建構自己的理學新說。[1]

　　本文主要以李材及其「止修」宗旨爲例來探討理學的學說傳承與師徒關係問題。在理學的師承關係中，一種新的理學學說如何在其追隨者、信奉者中得到傳承和延續？在學說傳承過程中，師門固有「宗旨」能否與理學對自悟和自得的強調協調一致？當集中體現師門學說的「宗旨」與追隨者的自悟自得產生歧異乃至緊張時，當事人怎樣面對和處理師徒異說的情形？對此，本文主要以李材與門人徐即登

1　詳參劉勇，〈中晚明時期的講學宗旨、〈大學〉文本與理學學說建構〉，《中央研究院歷史語言研究所集刊》，80：3（臺北，2009），頁403-450。

（1537-1628）和涂宗濬（1551?-1621）的互動爲例進行探討。

在具體論述中，本文首先對宋明理學脈絡中的師承和師徒關係加以概述，並以具體實例指出，在理學的道統觀念和講學活動影響下，普遍存在的「轉益多師」現象導致師徒關係的認定顯得既重要，卻又敏感而複雜。本文接著討論「止修」學說的創立者李材在學說傳播方式上的特點，最後著重觀察「止修」門下徐即登和涂宗濬二人分別在立說模式、論學宗旨和講學活動等幾個方面，對師門「宗旨」的演繹和宣揚，探討理學學說在延續和傳承過程中可能遭遇的問題。需要指出的是，理學脈絡中的所謂師承與師徒、門人弟子、師友門生等概念存在著各種複雜和變動的情形，在理學學說愈趨多元和講學活動盛行的中晚明時期尤其如此，本身就是非常值得探討的問題。由於受到文獻遺存的制約，我們對絕大多數的「止修」學受眾和追隨者都難以獲得深入瞭解，故在此主要以資料遺存較爲豐富的涂宗濬、徐即登爲個案，觀察「止修」學在李材門人中的傳承情形。

二、理學脈絡中的師承關係

隨著宋代理學的興起和擴大影響，道統與師承觀念也前所未有地高漲起來。被視爲理學集大成者的朱子在生前就已不遺餘力地建立道統觀念、書寫道統系譜，其門人後學則致力於將他本人推向此一道統的延續。日後隨著朱子學逐步成爲官學，其道統觀念及系譜也得到制度性認可，並受到讀書人的廣泛接受。[2]

2　有關道統的研究，本文主要參考陳榮捷，〈朱熹集新儒學之大成〉，《朱子論集》（臺北：臺灣學生書局，1982），頁1-35；劉子健，〈宋末所謂道統的成立〉，《兩宋史研究彙編》（臺北：聯經出版事業公司，1987），

　　理學的興起在許多方面影響和強化了師徒關係，講學活動對此的衝擊尤堪注意。[3] 從有關近世中國教育史、書院史的研究已可觀察到，北宋以後大量興起的書院、精舍，以及寺廟、道觀、祠宇等場所經常成為理學家宣揚其理念的講壇，這些講學活動對師徒關係、學說授受方式都有重要影響。有所建樹的理學學者通常有較多機會面對為數眾多而情況千差萬別的聽眾和信徒。在傳授方式上，講者與學者之間往往有較長時間的朝夕共處、質疑問難。言行舉止的相互影響，當面問辨或書信往還的討論方式，講者既是經師，也是人師，學者不僅接受知識，也揣摩言行，注重內心體悟。這種情形可從理學家的語錄著作，如《朱子語類》中較易獲得親切的認知。[4] 讀書人是理學家最重要

頁249-282；張亨，〈朱子的志業：建立道統意義之探討〉，《臺大中文學報》，5（臺北，1992），頁31-80；黃進興，〈學術與信仰：論孔廟從祀制與儒家道統意識〉，《優入聖域：權力、信仰與正當性》（臺北：允晨文化公司，1994），頁217-311；Thomas A. Wilson, *Genealogy of the Way: the Construction and Uses of the Confucian Tradition in Late Imperial China* (Stanford, Calif.: Stanford University Press,1995).

3　傳統社會的「天地君親師」觀念，余英時認為是在宋代形成的，也有學者主張將這一觀念溯源至先秦的各種經典，或尋求道教、民間宗教的資源，目前對此尚缺乏較為詳盡可據的研究，但可以肯定的是，在明代中期以後這已經是一個「里巷常談」了，特別是在理學家中。余英時，〈談「天地君親師」的起源〉，《現代儒學論》（River Edge, NJ：八方文化企業公司，1996），頁97-101；徐梓，〈「天地君親師」源流考〉，《北京師範大學學報（社會科學版）》，2006：2（北京，2006），頁99-106。這個觀念所代表的價值系統，很可能跟理學、科舉有密切的關係。

4　賈德訥（Daniel K. Gardner）曾經對語錄體著作對於理學思維的影響有討論，參〈宋代的思維模式與言說方式：關於「語錄」體的幾點思考〉，收入田浩編，《宋代思想史論》（楊立華、吳豔紅等譯，北京：社會科學文獻出版社，2003），頁394-425；Robert Hymes, "Getting the Words Right: Speech, Vernacular Language, and Classical Language in Song Neo-Confucian 'Records of Words'," *Journal of Song-Yuan Studies*（《宋遼金

的宣講對象，主要的共通理念是修己治人，以先覺覺後覺，從而實現
對社會產生影響。

　　道統意識的高漲對師徒關係、學術傳承提出了新的要求。在理學
道統系譜的建立過程中，師承關係往往被視爲最重要和最直接的憑據
之一，儘管師徒授受實際上常常難以爲繼，因而不得不訴諸其他各種
關係，包括以血緣和姻親紐帶、地域聯繫，以及所謂聞風興起、讀書
有得、私淑向風等虛實相間的關係作爲輔助方式。[5]理學群體自身也極
爲注重追溯學術淵源，建構宗派意識、書寫道統系譜，如朱子生前就
透過編纂各種「淵源錄」、「言行錄」、師門語錄等予以進行，其門人
弟子中，此類舉動更加不乏其人。[6]

　　在明代中期陽明學興起並迅速盛行的過程中，門人弟子的角色極
爲關鍵。陽明學之所以能夠快速傳播並形成重大影響，原因是多方面
的。「知行合一」、「致良知」相對於朱子學而言所具有的新穎吸引
力，《古本大學》、《傳習錄》等震撼人心而易於流傳的小冊子，[7]王陽

元》），36（2006），pp.25-55.

5　這些概念的早期淵源，可能跟《孟子·盡心下》的見知、聞知觀念有
　　關。有關明清道統系譜延續的實例，參劉勇，〈中晚明理學學說的互動
　　與地域性理學傳統的系譜化進程——以「閩學」爲中心〉，《新史學》，
　　21：2（2010），頁1-60。

6　田浩，《朱熹的思維世界》（臺北：允晨文化實業股份有限公司，1996）
　　尤其注重討論這情形，頁160-167、177-185、324-328、337-340等；李
　　紀祥，〈《近思錄》之「錄」與《傳習錄》之「錄」〉，《道學與儒林》
　　（臺北：唐山出版社，2004），頁15-66；市來津由彥，《朱熹門人集團形
　　成の研究》（東京：創文社，2002），頁483-512。

7　張藝曦，〈明中晚期古本《大學》與《傳習錄》的流傳及影響〉，《漢學
　　研究》，24：1（臺北，2006），頁235-268；林月惠，《良知學的轉折：
　　聶雙江與羅念庵思想之研究》（臺北：臺灣大學出版中心，2005），頁
　　147-174。

明卓越的事功建樹所具有的說服力，都是重要而實在的因素。在傳播
方式上，地方性的講會活動成為陽明學擴展的關鍵機制，[8]講學活動常
常結合書院、宗族、鄉約、慈善等在地性組織和事務進行。不過，就
陽明學的傳承與傳播來看，重要門人弟子的關鍵性作用仍然無可替
代。無論是「致良知」宗旨的義理闡釋，還是師門書籍的整理刊行，
講學活動的興起，定期講會的舉辦，以及對聽眾和信徒的吸引力而
言，陽明高弟的角色都舉足輕重。因此王陽明在生前的講學活動中，
就十分注意誘導有成就的青年俊彥加入門牆。[9]同樣，萬曆二十年代謫
戍福建的李材及其當地門人，也極力希望能夠「汲引」像何喬遠
（1558-1631）那樣學博識遠的學者信從「止修」學。[10]從陽明高弟的
言行還可觀察到，他們所做的遠不止師門學說的傳播與傳承，諸如陽
明身後的喪事料理、家庭事務安排，以及創建書院、祭祀活動、建立
講會、刊刻書籍、吸納聽眾，乃至於力推王陽明從祀孔廟之事上，他
們都可發揮重要作用。

　　然而理學脈絡中師徒關係的認定卻殊非易事。陳榮捷在梳理朱子
門人的研究中就指出，難以對誰是弟子作出定義。[11]特別是在明代中
期陽明學講學活動盛行以後，講者面對的學者、學者可能接觸的講

8　呂妙芬，《陽明學士人社群：歷史、思想與實踐》（北京：新星出版社，
　　2006重印），頁3、18。
9　成功之例如王畿，參彭國翔，《良知學的展開：王龍溪與中晚明的陽明
　　學》（北京：三聯書店，2005），頁518-519；失敗之例如黃佐，參朱鴻
　　林，〈黃佐與王陽明之會〉，《燕京學報》，新21期（北京，2006），頁
　　69-84。
10　詳參劉勇，〈晚明理學的師承建構與宗旨分歧——以李材與何喬遠的講
　　學交涉為例〉，中國明史學會主辦「第十五屆明史國際學術研討會暨第
　　五屆戚繼光國際學術研討會」（山東蓬萊，2013.8.19）會議論文。
11　陳榮捷，《朱子門人》（臺北：臺灣學生書局，1982），頁9。

者，在數量上都突飛猛漲，使得情形更加複雜。在形式上，叩頭拜師、奉贄求教，及面書求進、明言奉侍、自稱弟子者，容或易於判定；其餘號稱私淑、聞風興起，或輾轉問聞、讀書有得者，均難斷案；而對於那些爲了壯大門牆、互劃宗派或攀龍附鳳之舉，研究者常常也缺乏足夠的反證。[12]更加微妙的是，即使有師徒授受之實，但師徒之間在不同情境下的內心相互認同情形，以及在不同他者眼中的認定情形，則更難把握。[13]

　　在講學活動盛行的情形下，講者之間和受眾之間的互相競爭同樣重要。在講者之間，包括所講之學在義理上的高下淺深，個人聲望與社會資源，以及對受眾和追隨者的號召力，都可構成或隱或現的競爭。就受眾之間而言，在具有多種選擇的情況下，「轉益多師」成爲極其普遍的現象。在此背景下，「師—徒」雙方以及他者如何互相看待，情形更爲繁複糾結，尤其當相互之間在學說宗旨、義理立場或個人行事風格不無芥蒂的背景下，衝突往往無可避免。

　　師徒名分發生衝突的一個已知案例，是江右王門高弟劉邦采（1528舉人）與泰州學者顏鈞（1504-1596）之間圍繞爭取門徒陳源（1509-1587）的複雜糾葛。顏鈞年輕時曾向江右王門諸高弟問學，包

12　李材之父李遂與王陽明之間是否存在師徒關係，就存在種種各説其詞的情形，詳參劉勇，〈明儒李遂的講學活動及其與陽明學之關係〉，載中國社會科學院歷史研究所明史研究室編，《明史研究論叢》，9（北京：紫禁城出版社，2011），頁197-213。
13　如陳白沙的門下，張詡就一度自認爲是白沙的衣缽之傳，但在白沙去世之後，張氏面對新的文字證據，才察覺自己「誤判」。參朱鴻林，〈讀張詡《白沙先生行狀》〉，《明人著作與生平發微》（桂林：廣西師範大學出版社，2005），頁214-219；楊正顯，〈白沙學的定位與成立〉，《思想史》，2（臺北，2014），頁1-51。

括師事劉邦采，結果「無所得」，遂轉而從泰州王門徐樾問學，「得泰州之傳」。此後顏鈞蹤跡所至，隨處掀起講學，並與江右王門諸高弟之間屢有抵牾。嘉靖十九年（1540）鄉試之際，顏鈞以「急救心火」為題在南昌同仁祠開講，吸引了大批追隨者，自稱「得千五百友」，而陳源、羅汝芳（1515-1588）等正是其中「領秀」。稍後，陳源率親友87人，邀請顏鈞前往主講。至嘉靖二十五年（1546），陳源「棄館吳地」，專心一意追隨顏鈞問學。然而，陳源「尊信顏先生甚，久之中自疑，若已盡其學，然學何容易也」。遂轉而問學於劉邦采，受其開悟，「恍然有省，而夙心舊學，倒囊盡棄如蕩長風而濯大波也」，然後「入辭顏先生，請從劉先生居。顏鈞先生以為背己，怒嫚罵之，諸同門爭挽留」，最終導致顏、陳師徒之間徹底決裂。此事生動地反映了當時陽明後學中，江右與泰州兩派之間複雜的人事糾葛與學術衝突。從中更能看出隨著中晚明講學活動的盛行，在「轉益多師」比較普遍的情況下，師徒關係如何受到衝擊：它既形象地說明了當時講學活動的主持者就爭取信從者和追隨者而相互間展開競爭，也表明了講學活動的參與者在面對諸多選擇時，可能遇到的抉擇困境。

此事的記錄者、江西建昌府人鄧元錫（1528-1593），日後也不免與當時最富盛名的講學家同郡羅汝芳在師徒名分上產生緊張。鄧氏同當時的許多江右士子一樣，年輕時慕名前往陽明學重鎮吉安府從學於陽明諸高弟，返回家鄉後也常常參與本地的講學活動，與同郡年長的講學名人羅汝芳也有過從。鄧氏的學術成就主要體現在經史著述方面，晚年因此屢屢受到府縣及兩京官員的薦舉，並成功地憑舉人身份受到朝廷以翰林待詔徵聘的禮遇。至此，羅汝芳遍佈各地的講學門人樂於宣稱鄧氏乃羅氏弟子，服膺並推崇羅氏的學說。然而從鄧氏的文字中，完全無法看到他認可羅氏為師的跡象，相較之下他更願意稱呼

自己的蒙師爲「師」。在撰於羅汝芳去世次年的文字中，鄧氏也公開
表示：「元錫固時時從羅先生游，不盡名其學。」所撰〈祭羅近溪先生文〉更明確指出：「在元錫之所以事先生者，時同所同，時異所
異，以自附於助我。」故乾隆《建昌府志》在全文收錄這篇祭文後指
出：「近溪門下氣焰甚盛，其弟子亦不免有張大師門之意，一時名流
如李寅清（李經綸）、鄧潛谷（鄧元錫）之屬，俱引爲內外門生。」
而乾隆《新城縣志》在鄧氏傳中也指出：「時同郡有羅汝芳，悟聖人
之不思不勉，即孩提之不學不慮，而以從心所欲爲學。元錫頗謂是本
心之學也，而以矩閑欲爲說坊之，時與異如水火。」這種現象甚至還
導致鄧氏後人致力於消除鄧氏與羅汝芳的學術交往痕跡。[14]

李材的講學門人中也不乏此類事例。樂安人游澈亦曾經師從羅汝
芳，後來拜在李材門下時，看來就不免心有難安；而李材對此的看法
也殊堪注意：

> 游澈應貢北發，執贄見先生（李材），禮成即辭，請曰：
> 「澈姑未敢多論，只一人而兩師，有是事否？」先生曰：
> 「賢舊師誰？」曰：「曾師近溪先生。」先生曰：「此亦何
> 妨。未論孔子學無常師，只在《孟子》中，便有個的當底
> 大公案。所謂『聖人，百世之師也，伯夷、柳下惠是
> 也』。假令與孟子並時而生，與孔子必並在師資列矣。至
> 論到學上，卻便不然。一則曰『伯夷隘，柳下惠不恭。隘

14 以上兩段所述，詳參劉勇，〈黃宗羲對泰州學派歷史形象的重構——以《明儒學案·顏鈞傳》的文本檢討爲例〉，《漢學研究》，26：1（臺北，2008），頁165-196；劉勇，〈晚明的薦賢、徵聘與士人的出處考慮——以鄧元錫爲例〉，《中華文史論叢》，2012：3（總第107期）（上海，2012），頁61-89。

與不恭，君子不由也』。一則曰『不同道……乃所願，則
學孔子也』。父安得三？只為繼承香火之故，即本生父母
不改尊稱，而嗣續承傳竟從外屬。其人可師，何獨夷、
惠。更有奮乎百世之上，為世興起者，且從而師事之矣。
賢但驗之後來學所得力者，自於何宗承傳嗣續，則合有商
量者耳。」[15]

　　這個問答場景需要結合李材與羅汝芳這兩位當時著名的講學者之
間的關係來看。李材至遲在嘉靖四十一年（1562）會試前後，就已經
在京參與由羅汝芳組織和主導的講學活動，不久羅氏出守甯國府，李
材受命為撰贈序。其時二人皆為講學聚會上「談甚有致」的明星，但
兩人所談並不相近，而羅氏「時雜詼諧」。[16]嗣後二人皆返鄉家居，李
材講學豐城，羅汝芳講學建昌，「其持論未必盡合」。[17]羅氏在鄰邑樂
安縣的多次講學活動中為自己贏得了大批追隨者，如萬曆元年
（1573）大會同志，當地士子領袖「門人詹事謨、陳致和錄刻」《樂
安會語》。[18]不過，當萬曆三年（1575）李材居家講學之後，對樂安士

15　李材，《見羅先生觀學錄要》，收入《四庫未收書輯刊》6：12（北京：北
　　京出版社，2000影印民國十二年刻本），卷3，頁15-16。

16　羅大紘，《紫原文集》，卷10，〈南太常卿徐貞學先生學行述〉，收入
　　《四庫禁燬書叢刊》（北京：北京出版社，2000影印明末刻本），集部，
　　第140冊，頁84。

17　劉元卿，《劉聘君全集》，卷8，〈南太常寺卿塘南王公行略〉，收入《四
　　庫全書存目叢書》（臺南縣：莊嚴文化公司，1997影印清咸豐二年重刻
　　本），集部，第154冊，頁198-200。

18　參程玉瑛，《晚明被遺忘的思想家：羅汝芳（近溪）詩文事蹟編年》，頁
　　87、139、141。羅汝芳的《羅明德公文集》（已收入方祖猷等點校本
　　《羅汝芳集》[南京：鳳凰出版社，2007]）中保存了極為豐富的與樂安士
　　子交往資料，在總共五卷文字中，就有近三分之一標明與樂安有關。

子也產生了很大吸引力，詹事謨、陳致和都轉而隨其講論「止修」
學，在這些當地士子領袖的帶動下，李材自稱「樂〔安〕人士半從予
遊」。[19]游澈無疑也是在這股「轉向止修學」風氣下拜李材爲師的。[20]

　　引文中游澈小心翼翼的詢問、李材輾轉含蓄的論說，在在體現出
講學活動盛行時學者與講者對「轉益多師」現象的高度敏感。尤其需
要仔細斟酌的是李材的回答：他首先反問游澈「舊師誰？」在得知是
羅汝芳之後，雖然立刻表示「此亦何妨」，但婉轉的論說最終指向
「至論到學上，卻便不然」，並提醒游氏，問題的關鍵在於日後「學
所得力者，自於何宗承傳嗣續」。言下之意，曾經師從過誰並不重
要，重要的是重新拜師之後的爲學宗向。

　　上述事例表明，在道統意識和講學活動的影響下，師承關係是相

19　李材撰、熊尚文編，《見羅李先生觀我堂稿》（臺北：中央研究院傅斯年
　　圖書館影印日本內閣文庫藏明萬曆間愛成堂刊本），卷20，〈詹純甫墓誌
　　銘〉，頁9-11。此文撰於萬曆十一年。陳致和日後成爲李材門下高弟之
　　一（黃宗羲《明儒學案·止修學案》所錄李材彙編門下高弟著作而成的
　　《知本同參》中，就有陳氏撰《崇聞錄》，收入沈善洪、吳光主編，《黃
　　宗羲全集》第7冊〔杭州：浙江古籍出版社，2005〕，卷31，頁806-
　　809）；萬曆二十九年秋，在莆田追隨謫戍福建的李材講學期間，陳致和
　　還爲老師李材的著作序（即《見羅李先生讀孫子》〔日本尊經閣文庫藏
　　明抄本〕，卷首，〈刻見羅李先生讀孫子序〉，無葉碼）；不久後陳氏又在
　　建甯摘編李材多種著作而成《見羅李先生經正錄》（美國國會圖書館藏
　　明萬曆三十一年刊本）一書，在當地刊刻作爲士子讀本。詳參該書卷首
　　陳致和殘序，頁1-5；卷末吳道坤〈刻見羅李先生經正錄跋〉，頁1-3。
20　從時間來看，萬曆八年李材有〈答游汝源書〉，見《見羅李先生觀我堂
　　稿》，卷7，頁4-5。游澈字汝源。此外豐城人李庭止（亦名正己）最初
　　亦從羅汝芳學，後來改從李材學，參鄒元標，《願學集》，收入《景印文
　　淵閣四庫全書》（臺北：商務印書館，1983），第1294冊，卷6上，〈布
　　衣儲山李公墓誌銘〉，頁248-249。

當重要而又十分敏感的問題。[21] 從學說宗旨的角度來看，無論提倡者認為一己宗旨是獨得聖人之傳的自得之見，還是強調其宗旨的歷時性，認為是符合當前思想和社會現實之說，它都無可避免地帶有強烈的排他性，這種排他性不僅試圖顛覆理學前賢的見解，同時也必然針對當代諸儒之說從而凸顯自己的獨到獨尊之處，以增強說服力和凝聚力。李材在依託《大學》文本及詮釋以論成「止修」宗旨時，最基本的前提就是要證明朱子「即物窮理」、王陽明「致良知」皆屬錯會《大學》宗旨，且毫不掩飾地認定「止修」才是獨得孔、曾遺意的聖學宗旨，[22] 並據此與同時代的諸儒展開無窮無盡的論辯與競爭。因此，對李材的上述回答需要作更為策略性的理解。而對於入門不久、信道未堅者來說，面對此種情形時，還能有更好的選擇和回答嗎？

三、「止修」宗旨創立者李材的傳學方式

江西豐城縣湖茫李氏的講學歷史，尤其是李遂（1504-1566）、李材父子的講學歷程，與王陽明和陽明後學密切相關，但李氏父子卻又始終與陽明學處於若即若離的微妙關係。李遂終生都與陽明學講學活

---

21 理學脈絡中師承關係的敏感性，還可從中晚明時期宋端儀撰、薛應旂重輯的《考亭淵源錄》末卷特別載錄「考亭叛徒」趙師雍、傅伯壽、胡紘三人體現出來，清初理學名臣張伯行撰《伊洛淵源續錄》時，書末「叛徒附錄」也仍然保留。分別見《考亭淵源錄》，收入《四庫全書存目叢書》（臺南縣：莊嚴文化公司，1996影印明隆慶三年林潤刻本），史部，第88冊，卷24，頁592；《伊洛淵源續錄》，收入《四庫全書存目叢書》（臺南縣：莊嚴文化公司，1996影印清康熙五十年正誼堂刻本），史部，第125冊，卷末，頁315。

22 這類說話在李材的著述中所在多有，如《正學堂稿》（北京大學圖書館藏民國元年豐城李希泌刻本），卷37，〈南靖縣安福禪院會記〉，頁6-7；卷39，〈答姚惟德〉、〈答劉謀卿書〉，頁12、17。

動緊密相聯，其所交往的學者主要是陽明高弟，本人也常常被視爲陽明的門人，但他並未完全接受陽明「致良知」之學，並在晚年鼓勵其子李材另立異說。李材早年參與陽明學講學活動，並且一度拜在陽明高弟鄒守益（1491-1562）門下，後又訪王畿（1498-1583）、錢德洪（1497-1574）等人問學。不過，李材卻在求學過程中逐漸脫離並質疑陽明的「致良知」宗旨。直到隆慶、萬曆之交在嶺西爲官期間，隨著事功成就的建立，李材開始主導講學活動的舉行，並進而主導講說內容，公開提出旨在取代王陽明「致良知」宗旨的「止修」宗旨。至此，李遂、李材父子從陽明學講學活動的參與者轉變爲講學的主導者，從王陽明「致良知」的接受者與信奉者，轉變爲「致良知」宗旨的批判者與反對者。[23]

由講陽明學到講自創「止修」學的這個關鍵性轉變，只是李材的理學學說成立和學派建構的重要步驟之一。更爲現實的工作，是如何在當時各種理學學說多元並存的格局中獲得一席之地，如何面對陽明後學以及其他理學學者的質疑和辨難，以及如何在激烈競爭中爭取傳播學說、擴大影響。在這些問題上，學說「宗旨」相當關鍵，它就像是一塊招牌、一張名片，在紛繁複雜的理學論說和義理系統中，一己之學得以被清晰地界定出來；同時也是使立說者得以區別於前賢及時人，標識出我之所以爲我的獨特所在。講學活動則是當時極爲盛行的有效傳播途徑，它同時也是一種論說和辯論方式，有助於證成學說宗旨的成立和合法性、認受性。在江西和浙江等理學盛行之地，李材的「止修」新說遭遇各種質疑，質疑的聲音來自各方面。陽明後學陣營

---

23 詳參前揭劉勇，〈明儒李遂的講學活動及其與陽明學之關係〉，頁208-210。

顯然看到了「止修」宗旨對於陽明「致良知」的威脅，因此，從胡直（1517-1585）到郭子章（1542-1618）、鄒元標（1551-1624）師徒，持續對「止修」說發起反擊，意在證明「止修」不合孔、曾原旨。管志道（1536-1608）雖然在反對陽明後學流弊方面與李材取得共識，但在論學宗旨上則完全不能接受「止修」之說。他一方面依據《石經大學》來反駁古本，同時試圖從《易經》中提揭「惕龍」之說。李材對於「止修」宗旨獨得聖人之傳的堅持和「強人從己」的講學方式，甚至使得其最好的朋友許孚遠（1535-1604）、萬廷言（1562進士）也無法接受，他們也訴諸《大學》的文本和詮釋提出批評。同樣是陽明學說的反對者，東林學者曾一度受到「止修」學的積極影響，高攀龍（1562-1626）甚至由此入門從事於理學，但最終在《大學》文本和詮釋、學說宗旨問題上都與「止修」分道揚鑣。[24]

　　儘管面臨諸多競爭與批判，但李材透過講學活動宣傳自創「止修」學的熱情有增無減。在雲南、鄖陽等地任官期間，李材充分運用手中掌握的行政力量，動用當地的物質和人力資源以掀起講學活動，講論的重點無一例外地都是自創的「止修」學。在迫切宣講「止修」宗旨的目的下，不僅府州縣官吏、地方士紳、官學士子成為被調動來參與講學的對象，就連土官、土舍、士兵，以及軍用物資也被要求圍繞講學運作。李材在鄖陽以巡撫身份提倡講學而激起兵變，就是事情的極端表現。雖然如此，這位講學家的熱情並未因此而稍減，北京的詔獄、福建的戍所，依然是其孜孜不倦地講論「止修」之地。尤其是後者，在整個萬曆二十年代謫戍福建期間，李材宣講「止修」學的熱

24　李材「止修」學說與當時諸家的辯難和競爭情形，詳參劉勇，《晚明士人的講學活動與學派建構——以李材（1529-1607）為中心的研究》（香港中文大學歷史學系博士論文，2008），第四章，頁166-220。

忱在師友門生的協助之下化爲到處講學的事實。這些活動顯然不止爲
成臣李材的日常生活增添了樂趣，同時也爲其「止修」學說贏得了大
量士子、鄉紳等追隨者和信奉者。[25]

　　值得注意的是李材在講學活動中的具體傳授方式。萬曆十二年
（1584）前後，李材在雲南姚安府德豐寺的講學活動，不但主張向
「理路未深」的士民介紹「修身爲本」的下手處「就是修行」，還強
調：

> 只合教他將此四字符（指「修身爲本」）帖在心頭，如四
> 角撐住；念在口頭，如阿彌陀佛。庶幾漸近道理，有光風
> 俗，而聚會之氣誼爲不徒然矣。

並爲之詳細解說具體如何透過月會、歲會考成，在家庭倫常、日
常生活中修檢，充分運用講會中朋友聯束來相互勉勵、互相促進
等。[26]

　　在傳學方式上同樣值得注意的是，李材對待自己晚年在福建撰寫
的講學小冊子《大學約言》的態度。此書是其整合自己一生有關《大
學》的論說文字而進行的總結，完全可以視爲其「晚年定論」。從萬
曆元年前後在嶺西公開提揭和宣講《大學》「止修」宗旨以來，至此
已歷二十餘年，李材有關《大學》的文本改訂、義理闡釋、論學書信
和講學言說已經不勝其多，學者各得其一，難免無所適從，不易得其

25　劉勇，〈從李材案看晚明清議的形成及其與講學之關係〉，《國立政治大
　　學歷史學報》，32（臺北，2009），頁41-70。
26　李材，《兵政紀略》，收入劉兆祐主編，《中國史學叢書》（臺北：臺灣學
　　生書局，1986影印明萬曆刻本），三編，二輯，卷48，〈德豐寺會語批
　　答〉，頁2083-2089。日後鄒元標在講學活動中就不具名地批評提「修身
　　爲本」四字「如救命靈符」的「近儒」，當是爲李材而發。見鄒元標，
　　《南皋鄒先生講義合編》，卷下，〈大學〉，頁217。

指歸。適時地推出這個晚年定本，無疑有助於其學說的傳播。對此其子李穎指出：

> 公每謂會友、打坐、看書三者爲學之大方，猶恐學者徒讀
> 稿刻，未得指歸，特揭其宗要，題曰《大學約言》，俾之
> 人挾一冊，曰：「大匠誨人，必以規矩，茲其規矩矣。」[27]

李材對此書的重視超乎尋常，要求遊其門者須訂立課程，「必讀之萬遍千周」：

> 《大學約言》實全經旨趣，初纂之直以省學者蒐括之煩。
> 既刻成，業與定一背誦之課，謂無論長少新舊、已出仕未
> 出仕，但遊吾門者，必讀之萬遍千周。蓋必辭洽而後旨
> 融，旨融而後意端不雜，而諸所揭紛紜疑詫者，不但不以
> 挂於口，亦不以之萌於心矣。[28]

此書也是李材常常大量贈人之作，如一次就送給清江門人郭煒八冊，要求其分置於學宮及與諸士子，反復誦讀，講會講論中也據之宣闡。[29]

爲了配合「止修」宗旨的有效宣講，李材還編纂了《哲範》、《鞭後卮言》、《日鑒篇》等書作爲輔助讀本，期望由此提供一套具備操作性的「修身」工夫。《哲範》是其在詔獄期間「時憶古哲人之善行嘉言，或預幾而知勅，或經創而加懲，有感此心，隨筆記注」而

27　李穎，〈李見羅先生行略〉，收入劉家平等主編，《中華歷史人物別傳集》
　　（北京：線裝書局，2003影印民國初年刻本），第22冊，頁261。

28　李材，《正學堂稿》，卷38，〈答楊惟謙書〉，頁5；並參卷38，頁10、
　　11；卷39，頁18等；及《觀學錄要》卷8，頁19。

29　李材，《正學堂稿》，卷38，〈答郭文蔚書〉，頁9-10；並參卷21，頁2；
　　卷25，頁16；卷39，頁8；卷40，頁9等。

成，分為吉脩、慮善、貞遇、增德諸篇，「時省觀之以自鑒」。該書
因其子李穎建議而公開刊行，作為示範怎樣學習研磨「脩身為本」的
具體「條件」，引導信從者具體如何著手進行修身。[30]《鞭後卮言》亦
與此類似，但主要是採擇「老氏之言」中有助於修身之說的內容，錄
出「以廣德慧之助」。[31]

　　《日鑒篇》則更為具體且更具可操作性，形式上頗近於當時流行
於士人之間的修身日記與功過格的結合體。此書的編輯目的與重點可
從其自序推勘：

> 予淺陋，雖謬有測於知本之宗，揭出止脩，日與友朋共其
> 磨煅。而興衛寡閒，箴警多闕，蹉跎伏匿，鏡省無徵，亦
> 恐徒托話言，罔臻實益，因取詩人「日鑒」之義，式時賢
> 自省之科，稍加釐訂，用比韋弦，庶幾咎可徵於既往，善
> 可考於方來，寸累銖稱，動昭鑒戒，出往游衍，如式欽
> 承。聊以自勗，並付剞劂，與同志者共之，以為考道論德
> 之案。

　　由「式時賢自省之科」可推知，李材的「日鑒」在形式上應當有
取於當時士人中流行的修身日記與功過格。「日鑒」的具體規定和操
作如下：「以德業為綱，敬怠義欲為介」、「無怠欲即以屬之敬義，於
其下微點之，可紀者圈之」、「稍涉怠欲者，於其下亦微點之，大者
則又之，不必斥言其事」。善惡不予具體指明，並非掩惜隱匿，因為
還需要「日考之，月稽之，且歲會之，消長犁然，有人心者，覽之能
無惕乎？」猜測很可能是為了盡可能地將這種方式落實推廣，若要求

30　李材，《正學堂稿》，卷33，〈哲範序〉，頁11-12。
31　李材，《正學堂稿》，卷32，〈鞭後卮言小引〉，頁14-15。

將各自的善惡之行詳細記錄，極可能會帶來推廣的阻力。並且這個方式的主要目的也只是爲了「自考」、「自省」，內心省視並由此自我警惕，從而遷善改過是最直接的追求效應。此外，記錄的內容還包括「首之以天時」：霜雹雷風、雨雪明晦、休咎徵應；「次之以人事」：酬應往還、公私纖鉅、經權常變；「次人事之下」：以敬怠考鏡內心以助進德，以義欲考鏡人事以助脩業。[32]

　　《日鑒篇》的做法有可能沿襲了李材早年的講學老師鄒守益在嘉靖末年爲江西安福惜陰會訂立的改過遷善會約。[33]隆慶、萬曆之際李材在嶺西講學已經開始採用類似方式。萬曆十九年（1591），在北京詔獄中從學於李材的嘉善人夏九鼎（1592年進士）也「一言一動皆密有疏記」。[34]這套方法看來既受到宋明理學中修身日記傳統的影響，也有著晚明善書運動，特別是同時代由袁黃提倡的功過格的影子，「式時賢自省之科」，很可能就是指此而言。[35]其思想根源如同許多理

32　李材，《正學堂稿》，卷34，〈日鑒篇序〉，頁14-17。

33　鄒守益，《鄒守益集》（董平編校整理，南京：鳳凰出版社，2007），卷15，〈惜陰申約〉，頁734；呂妙芬對此有所討論，見呂妙芬，《陽明學士人社群》，頁81。

34　謝旻、陶成等纂修，乾隆《江西通志》，收入《景印文淵閣四庫全書》，第515冊，卷61，頁158；高攀龍則稱其「即從獄中受修身爲本之旨，苦思力踐，晝所爲，夕必書之，即夢寐有非是，大自切責，得毋負李先生」，見《高子遺書》（無錫：1922高汝琳重印光緒二年江蘇書局本），卷11，下，〈江西安福縣知縣台卿夏公行狀畧〉，頁8-9。

35　在萬曆二十年前後袁黃曾致信刑科給事中王如堅，詳細陳述營救李材的策略，以及與閣臣王錫爵等論及李材案。李、袁之間雖無直接的文字往來，但他們的交往圈子也有許多疊合之處，參蕭世勇，〈袁黃（1533-1606）的經世理念及其實踐方式〉（國立臺灣師範大學歷史研究所碩士論文，1994），頁22-39；並參酒井忠夫，《中國善書の研究》（東京：國書刊行會，1977），頁318-355。

學修身日記那樣，主要是孔子的「計歲考功，十年一進級」，以及曾子的「吾日三省吾身」。[36]後者應該跟李材重視《大學》在儒家經典中的絕對地位，及其以孔曾代替孔顏、孔孟的系譜一脈相承。整體而言，它注重道德操守的修持，也對善惡行為予以記錄，但卻主要作為自我警醒從而改過遷善之用，並不提倡功過相抵、善惡相抵的因果報應論；其適用範圍，也主要限於「同志」之中，並不準備針對所有人。這種情形，與當時及稍後廣泛存在的如呂坤（1536-1618）提倡「省心」、「治心」等實踐方法的《省心紀》、周汝登（1547-1629）的《日記錄》等所謂「儒門功過格運動」比較相近。[37]這些方法在探索理學的各種形而上命題之餘，為學者尤其是初學者提供了一個易於把握的、有轍可循的「下手功夫」。[38]具體到李材的「止修」宗旨而言，則

36　李材，《正學堂稿》，卷34，〈日鑒篇序〉，頁14。李材〈答周學博〉中指出「日鑒」做法「能體而行之者鮮矣，頃亦有十數友欲以此立課者，後竟不省所詣云何？」周氏似是建議增加「課罰」條目，李材雖表示「尤見逼真」，但未知是否實行。《正學堂稿》，卷23，頁10。

37　包筠雅（Cynthia Brokaw），《功過格：明清社會的道德秩序》（杜正貞、張林譯，杭州：浙江人民出版社，1999），頁63-165；王汎森，〈明末清初的人譜與省過會〉，《中央研究院歷史語言研究所集刊》，63：3（臺北，1993），頁679-712；王汎森，〈日譜與明末清初思想家——以顏李學派為主的討論〉，收入《明末清初思想十論》（上海：復旦大學出版社，2004），頁117-185。

38　李材「日鑒」的主要目的是為「止修」宗旨提供明確而可以持循的功夫，作為「修身」的具體辦法。就此而言，日後劉宗周著名的《人譜》與此頗為接近，其中既包括正面論說人之所以為人及修持的六種功夫，也有各種記過、訟過、改過的法門，黃宗羲指出「《人譜》一書，專為改過而作，其下手功夫，皆有途轍可循」，陳確也認為「吾輩功夫，只需謹奉先生《人譜》，刻刻檢點，不輕自恕，方有長進；舍此，別無學問之可言矣」，紀過改過主要是為有志於聖學者提供有轍可循的下手功夫。分別見黃宗羲，《黃宗羲全集》，第10冊，〈答惲仲升論子劉子節要書〉，頁216；陳確，《陳確集·文集》（北京：中華書局，1979），卷

重在充實其「修身」說，為之提供有跡可循的、能在日常生活中加以實踐並持續跟進的法門。

　　概言之，李材不僅對自創的「止修」學說高度自信，認定「止修」宗旨是超越陽明和朱子的獨得聖人之旨；而且在宣傳己說方面熱情無限，在傳學方式上帶著近乎宗教式的特色，有時甚至帶有強力推行、強人從己的傾向。[39] 然而，在這樣的為學主張和講學方式主導下，作為「止修」學說創始人和作為老師的李材，留給其門人和追隨者多少可資選擇與發揮的空間呢？

四、謹守師傳：徐即登的講學與督學

　　在追隨李材講學的眾多門人中，同邑士子領袖徐即登在萬曆中後期以力倡講學、著述宏富而著稱。徐氏字獻和、德俊（竣），號匡岳，江西豐城人，萬曆元年舉人，萬曆十一年（1583）與李材的另外兩位高弟涂宗濬、李復陽同舉進士。此後徐氏輾轉於郎署近十年，遷福建提學副使、參政，官至河南按察使，致仕歸鄉講學，弟子益進。[40]

　　2，〈與戴一瞻書〉，頁106。

39　李材強人從己的傳學方式，甚至令其摯友許孚遠、萬廷言皆感無奈，並反復致信勸阻，詳參許孚遠，《大學述支言》、《大學述答問》，俱載《大學彙函》（臺北：中國子學名著集成編印基金會，1978影印明萬曆刊本），頁15-17、372-374；萬廷言，《學易齋集》（臺北：漢學研究中心影印日本尊經閣文庫藏明萬曆刊本），卷2，〈與李孟誠〉，頁9；卷3，〈答李孟誠〉，頁6-8、9。

40　何士錦、陸履敬纂修，康熙《豐城縣誌》（臺北：成文出版社，1989），卷11，〈徐即登傳〉，頁10-11；乾隆《江西通志》，卷69，〈徐即登傳〉，頁418；永瑢總裁、紀昀總纂：《欽定四庫全書總目》（四庫全書研究所整理，北京：中華書局，1997），卷23，徐即登《周禮說》條，頁288。

　　本文主要從徐即登的學說宗旨、立說模式、著述特點和講學活動
諸方面，觀察其對師門「止修」學說的傳承與傳播情形，從中清晰可
見「謹守師傳」的傳承和延續方式。尤其當萬曆二十年代李材戍閩期
間，徐氏先後任福建提學和參政，不僅積極協助李材在福建的講學活
動，更借助職務之便，號召福建士子講習「止修」學，並爲此創建書
院、親自主持講會，以至於老師李材也聲稱「閩士之知我也，半多在
徐獻和督學之後」。[41]

　　徐即登雖與李材同邑，但他最初卻是從陽明再傳弟子徐用檢
（1528-1611）講學而有悟的。徐用檢字克賢，號魯源，金華蘭溪人，
嘉靖四十一年與李材同舉進士，授刑部主事，在京與李材、許孚遠、
魏時亮（1529-1591）、萬廷言等郎署新人講學。[42]徐用檢師事陽明高
弟錢德洪、王畿，然其爲學不提良知，而揭「求仁」、「志學」爲宗
旨。隆慶五年（1571），徐用檢被劾降爲江西糧儲道參議，政治上窘
迫之際，學術上則有所體悟。[43]次年過豐城，當地士子領袖徐即登正
在爲諸生進講《中庸》天命章，徐用檢告誡年輕的徐即登：「此未易
言也。此理不覩不聞，而實莫見莫顯，雖發爲喜怒哀樂者，未嘗發此
中也。天命之性，天下之大本也，名之曰獨，必於此而戒愼恐懼焉，
然後中和位育，一以貫之，而性我復矣。此聖學之原也，未易言
也。」並在學宮向諸生闡發自己的最新體悟，徐即登「若豁如而有契

<hr />

41　李材，《正學堂稿》，卷37，〈祭陳象成文〉，頁14。
42　羅大紘，《紫原文集》，卷10，〈南太常卿徐貞學先生學行述〉，頁83-84。
43　羅大紘，《紫原文集》，卷10，〈南太常卿徐貞學先生學行述〉，頁79-
　　80、84-85；《明儒學案》，卷14，〈徐用檢傳〉，頁345-346。《明穆宗實
　　錄》，卷54，隆慶五年二月丙申，頁1330。至萬曆二年正月壬寅，升本
　　省副使，見《明神宗實錄》，卷21，頁572。

於中，蓋舉平日之意想卜測者，一旦覩其指歸矣。乃約二三同志，拜先生之門而受業焉。先生終日與語，不一而足，而於學聖『求仁』之旨，未嘗不三致意也」。在徐即登的帶動下，當地士子「一時風動，拜弟子受業者百餘人」。執贄拜師之後，徐即登「退而與二三同志訂為會，會日『實修』，又與二三同志錄先生語，語日《錄藁》」。萬曆元年，「鄉試初發科，有志者輒謁糧道聽講，先生公餘與諸門人問答辨論，至夕不倦」。[44] 可以想見，就在此科中舉的徐即登，自然也是參與問答辨論的座中俊彥。

但徐用檢當時所悟的為學之旨「求仁」，並未能解答徐即登自早年讀《論語》以來的疑惑——孔子「曷為以一貫授曾子？」在徐即登看來，「曾子平生學問，則所省在交謀傳習，而所貴在容貌色辭，用是戰兢終其身，似又於仁無當者，而日『曾氏獨得其宗』，此何以解焉？」對於「求仁」與「一貫」之間的矛盾，徐即登「求之而不得，牽合之而不可，反復於此者十餘年」，直到萬曆三年，李材以《大學》修身為本之說，方纔徹底融釋了徐即登胸中宿疑。[45]

44　羅大紘，《紫原文集》，卷10，〈南太常卿徐貞學先生學行述〉，頁80-81、84；徐即登，《來益堂稿》，卷5，〈徐魯源先生劍江錄藁後跋〉，頁4-6。

45　徐即登，《來益堂稿》，卷5，〈李見羅先生論語大意序〉，頁3。徐即登的疑惑前提，是基於對曾子傳道地位的認定，而孔子所傳曾子者為「一貫」（《論語·里仁》「子曰：參乎！吾道一以貫之」），無法與徐用檢所提「求仁」相契。對曾子傳道地位的肯定，從其所撰〈朱子諸書要序序〉來看，是源自朱子〈大學章句序〉「三千之徒，蓋莫不聞其說，而曾氏之傳獨得其宗」；《朱子語類》卷9「邵漢臣問顏淵仲尼不同」條在評論孔門諸子時，亦稱「其他諸子皆無傳，惟曾子獨得其傳」，見朱熹著，黎靖德編，《朱子語類》（臺北：正中書局，1973，頁3735-3736）。劉斯原在收錄徐即登《明宗錄》後的按語亦稱，朱子關於曾子獨得其宗之說「語意引而不發」，初讀不易明瞭，「學者尚未知所傳何事？所得何宗？及匡岳先生以明宗一脈語人，而後知朱子之所謂獨得其宗者，『止

萬曆初李材從廣東任上落職返鄉時，正好取代了徐用檢離任江西留下的講學空間。徐氏於萬曆三年轉官陝西學政途經豐城時，正值同年進士、講學舊友李材從廣東引疾返鄉，遂與李材、萬廷言、魏時亮會講，「各攻所短」。[46]此後，徐用檢離開江西，而李材則長期在豐城及附近地區開展講學，以在嶺西完成的《大學》改本及詮釋爲依據，宣講自己最新證悟的「知本」之學、「止修」之旨，吸引了包括徐即登在內的大批本地士子的追隨。徐即登後來兩次回憶初從李材講學的情形云：

> 至歲乙亥（萬曆三年），見羅李先生得告歸，登日侍教於側，乃就所疑質焉。先生曰：「爾不聞《大學》之教乎？『自天子至於庶人，一是皆以修身爲本』，此求仁之竅也，此一貫之宗也。」登於是豁然悟，躍然起而歎曰：「一哉，聖賢之學乎！語仁、語一貫，而非精也；語交際、語言動，而非粗也。《大學》，其仁之燦然者也；《論語》，其本之渾然者也。三千七十，夫誰不曰求仁，而一貫宗傳，乃於省身之曾［子］爲獨得焉，其意蓋可想已！」[47]

> 老師《大學古義》，自乙亥得受讀之，至「格致無傳，一部全書，所以傳格致也」云云，輒撫掌大快，以爲斯言

修』之學是已。止爲主意，修爲工夫……此皆聖經之所本有，特爲拈出，而非以己意創焉者也」。見《大學古今本通考》，收入《四庫全書存目叢書補編》（濟南：齊魯書社，2001影印明萬曆間刊本），第92冊，卷10，頁698-699。

46 羅大紘，《紫原文集》，卷10，〈南太常卿徐貞學先生學行述〉，頁87。

47 徐即登，《來益堂稿》，卷5，〈李見羅先生論語大意序〉，頁3-4。

也，足斷千古格致之案。彼時予尚未究知本之學，而有快
於此者，以向來在身心上體認故也。[48]

李材的《大學》文本和解釋使徐即登久梗於心中的疑惑一掃而
空，對此徐氏在〈朱子諸書要序序〉中的表述可以互勘：「登早歲志
學，讀文公書至顏氏、曾氏之傳得其宗，則有味乎其言之也，於是尋
繹孔學之宗，究諸弟子所以得不得之故……蓋反復於胸中，以考索之
書籍者且十年，而未能信也。一旦李師揭修身爲本之教，而曰『此孔
學之宗也，求仁之旨也』，登於是乎始豁然悟矣。」[49]以接受李材的開
悟爲契機，徐氏逐漸放棄了徐用檢的「求仁」、「志學」之旨，在十
餘年後爲徐用檢《劍江錄虆》重刻本作跋時，徐即登就在文末特別指
出，重刻之舉僅僅在於「以識聞學之自」。[50]此後，徐即登完全接受了
李材的「止修」之學，不斷透過講說和著述予以宣揚。

徐即登講說師門「止修」宗旨最爲重要的文字，仍然圍繞《大
學》的文本和詮釋展開。徐氏著述規模極爲可觀，《千頃堂書目》著
錄有《易說》九卷、《書說》四帙、《詩說》五帙、《周禮說》十四
卷、《禮記說》二帙、《春秋說》十一卷、《四書正學論答》、《儒宗
要輯》二十九卷、《建文諸臣錄》二帙、《文公全集摘要》八卷、《儒
學明宗錄》二十五卷、《中州問答》、《正學堂稿》二十六卷、《徐匡
岳先生來益堂稿》五卷。[51]乾隆《江西通志》據南昌府志還著錄了

48　徐即登，《儒宗要輯》，卷6，〈大學傳‧論格致無傳〉，此段文末注據
　　「《劍江答問》」，頁7。
49　徐即登，《來益堂稿》，卷5，〈朱子諸書要序序〉，頁6-7。
50　徐即登，《來益堂稿》，卷5，〈徐魯源先生劍江錄虆後跋〉，頁4-6。
51　分別見黃虞稷，《千頃堂書目》（瞿鳳起、潘景鄭整理，上海：上海古籍
　　出版社，2001），卷1-3、10、11、26，頁8、23、30、37、40、66、90、
　　284、307、629。其中《周禮說》十四卷，收入《四庫全書存目叢書》經

《儒範》一種，及「詩文若干卷」。[52]康熙《豐城縣志》則載其「著有
《閩中答問》、《天中答問》若干卷」。[53]這還遠非其著作的全部，從門
人子侄分類摘編其各種著作而成《儒宗要輯》中顯示的資訊可知，徐
氏至少還著有《大學約言述》、《劍江未刻稿》、《三山答問》等。此
外，目前還有徐即登晚年在家鄉與師友門生相互唱和之作《劍江倡和
詩》存世。[54]

　　綜觀這個龐雜的著述名單，儘管經史子集四部皆有，但仍可歸納
出一些特點，其中最為明顯的特色在於大都跟講學活動有關，尤其與
演繹師門宗旨關係緊密。各種論說、問答之作自不必言，顯然是講學
語錄和論學書信之類。《儒學明宗錄》書名的所謂「明宗」，乃取義
於其師李材的名言：「[學]不急辨體，要在明宗。」[55]徐氏在福建興化

部冊82影印浙江圖書館藏明萬曆刻本，僅十二卷；而臺北國家圖書館藏
萬曆間刻十四卷本，前十二卷內容版式一如浙圖本，惟多出後二卷。
《儒宗要輯》亦即《四書儒宗要輯》，似又名《四書正學輯要》，見傅武
光編著，《四書總義著述考（一）》（臺北：國立編譯館，2003），頁60。

52　乾隆《江西通志》，卷69，〈徐即登傳〉，頁418。
53　康熙《豐城縣誌》，卷11，〈徐即登傳〉，頁10-11。
54　徐即登等撰，《劍江倡和詩》，不分卷，一冊，江西省圖書館藏萬曆四十
　　六年（1618）徐即登序刊本。
55　徐即登，《儒宗要輯》，卷首，〈明宗論·宗脈〉，頁6-7，引述《儒學明
　　宗錄·鄞江答萬里鵬》、《正學堂稿·見羅李先生書要序》。按：《儒學明
　　宗錄》未見全本存世，《儒宗要輯》中節錄了部分內容，劉斯原《大學
　　古今本通考》卷10集中收錄了部分篇章，黃宗羲《明儒學案》卷31所收
　　李材編《知本同參》，其中也收錄了徐氏《明宗錄》論學語共7則（頁
　　814-815）；沈鯉《亦玉堂稿》卷6有〈明宗錄序〉可參，收入《景印文
　　淵閣四庫全書》冊1288，頁286-287。李材的「不急辨體，要在明宗」
　　之說，按照劉斯原的解讀：「蓋『良知』辨體，所以解見聞之縛也；『止
　　修』明宗，所以實『良知』之虛也。言者不離於宗，則聽者直達天德，
　　要之宗明而體固已辯矣。說者謂洛閩揭《大學》於《戴記》，豐城提
　　『止修』於《大學》，取之虞淵，行之中天，皆有功聖門不淺。斯亦大道

府推動創建書院作爲李材的講學之所，亦取名爲「明宗書院」，並撰有〈創建明宗書院記〉。[56]其諸經之《說》雖多佚失不存，但也與闡發師說相關。如其中僅存的《周禮說》，自序謂「今予之說，非能有加於訓詁之舊，而惟信其爲周公之書，則據茲經文，斷自己見，而不敢狥諸儒疑似之論」。[57]所謂「斷自己見」，實則是以師門修身、知本之學爲斷案，「蓋其（《周禮》）所爲法者，齊家治國平天下之具，而其所以爲法者，則本諸身以出之也」。[58]該書正文首先講說《周禮大意》，亦以李材之說爲據：「李見羅先生曰：《周禮》是周公致太平之書，當與《五經》並傳。今《周禮》獨廢而不講，是經之缺也；京師不爲周公立廟，是禮之缺也。」[59]徐氏《易說》雖已不存，但大約在萬曆十五年（1587）前後於居喪期間曾致信李材，報告自己在家鄉參與和組織講學的情形，同時表示「門生舊常苦心於《易》，稍有窺測，年來體勘師旨，因而悟學於《易》，輒不自量，欲以《易》明學」，並錄示部分已成手稿呈請李材「批削」。[60]

　　對於闡發師門「止修」宗旨而言，沒有比詮釋《大學》更合適的選擇了。目前存世的徐即登著作中，除《周禮說》、《劍江倡和詩》

爲公之論也。」見《大學古今本通考》，卷10，頁699。

56　徐即登，《儒宗要輯》，卷首，〈明宗論·宗脈〉曾節錄〈明宗書院記〉，頁5。

57　徐即登，《周禮說》，卷首，〈周禮說序〉，《四庫全書存目叢書》，經部，第82冊，頁437。

58　徐即登，《周禮說》，卷首，〈周禮說序〉，頁434、436。

59　徐即登，《周禮說》，卷1，〈周禮大意〉，頁440。

60　徐即登，《來益堂稿》，卷7，〈復李見羅先生三〉，頁5-6。徐氏似有文集《正學堂稿》，書名亦與乃師李材的《正學堂稿》完全相同。此書未見傳本，相關信息見何喬遠，《鏡山全集》（臺北：漢學研究中心影印日本內閣文庫藏明崇禎十四年序刊本），卷39，〈正學堂集序〉，頁31-32。

外，其餘無不以《大學》爲論說中心。在徐氏的所有著作中，最明顯地帶有師承色彩的著作，當屬已經失傳的《大學約言述》。[61] 如前所述，《約言》一書是李材在戍閩講學期間，總結自己多年論學要義而成的晚年定論。徐氏「述」之，其用意自是進一步演繹、發揮師說。在劉斯原所輯《大學古今本通考》卷首總目錄中，緊接在《李見羅先生大學古義》之後的，就是徐即登闡釋《大學》之作《徐匡岳先生大學明宗錄》；其正文所錄實際上包括兩部分：《徐匡岳先生大學全經》和《語錄》。前者是一篇綜論《大學》地位、內容與「止修」宗旨的論說之作；後者共36則，全部圍繞《大學》展開講論。[62] 從這個編排來看，徐氏《明宗錄》當是以《大學》爲基礎，闡述「止修」說的論學之作。[63]

　　這個論學和立說策略同樣見於現存徐氏的重要著作《儒宗要輯》。此書序刊於萬曆三十八年（1610），各卷卷題下俱署「豐城匡岳徐先生答問書」，隨後的校訂門人名單，各卷有所異同。據卷末上饒祝汝元撰〈跋〉，此書由徐即登的福建晉江門人蔡增譽（1598進士）捐俸倡刻，福清門人江朝賓（1604進士）贊成其事。[64] 其時蔡氏爲江西提學副使，江氏適爲豐城知縣，時任豐城教諭祝汝元與同官訓導李仲策、蔡學和等，分任校讎之役。[65] 除卷首〈明宗〉、〈任學〉二

61　徐氏《大學約言述》未見傳本，僅《儒宗要輯》中有所節錄。

62　劉斯原，《大學古今本通考》，卷首、卷10，頁559、693-699。

63　《明儒學案》所錄《明宗錄》論學語7則，第一則即闡述「一切以修身爲本」，其餘第二、三、四、五則皆圍繞「止修」命題展開，頁814-815。

64　二人皆爲萬曆二十二年舉人，時徐即登爲福建督學，由此可知，二人從學於徐氏當在此前後。該書卷首蔡增譽、江朝賓各撰序言，亦可資印證。

65　祝汝元，《儒宗要輯》，卷末，〈儒宗要輯跋〉，頁1-4。祝氏雖然在任樂

論外，此書正文全部圍繞《四書》展開，由門人摘錄徐即登各種已刊未刊文字，或自爲歸類，或列入經文各章之下，間附他人問語，成爲語錄形式的「答問書」。其中卷首至卷六專論《大學》：卷首題爲〈大學總論〉，包括〈明宗論〉、〈任學論〉兩篇；卷一題爲〈大學本旨〉，含〈大學全經〉、〈大學傳〉兩篇；卷二至五的卷名〈大學本旨通〉，篇名分別爲〈大學全經〉一至四；卷六〈大學傳〉，包括〈論明親止至善〉、〈論格致無傳〉、〈論誠意〉、〈論修身齊家〉四篇。卷七以下，各論《中庸》、《論》、《孟》。此書雖是針對全部《四書》而論，但其重心則是以《大學》爲本闡發「止修」學說。書中只有關於《大學》的部分，其卷題才特別命名爲「本旨」，編排上由「總論—本旨—本旨通—傳」的形式層層展開，而其餘《中庸》、《論》、《孟》三書皆無此種安排。所謂「本旨」，即指其師門「止修」宗旨而言。以《大學》爲重心，亦可從其兩位倡議刊刻該書的門人，與負責校讎的祝汝元爲此書所撰三篇序跋文字中明顯看出，諸文無不強調此書以《大學》爲典據，闡發「止於至善」、「修身爲本」的「止修」宗旨。當代的書目提要對此也有準確概括：「是編師承李材《大學》爲六籍宗祖之說，以爲儒者求仁，當以修身爲本，止歸至善，力斥格物致知之謬。」[66]

　　甚至連徐即登的文集《徐匡岳先生來益堂稿》之編排體例和內容，也都能反映出其謹守師傳的情形。此書現存兩種版本：一爲日本尊經閣文庫藏萬曆刻本，四卷；一爲中國社會科學院文學研究所藏萬

　　安訓導時就參與講李材「止修」之學，轉官豐城後也從徐即登講學，但跋文自署「晚生」，而非「門人」。

66　國立編譯館主編，《新集四書批註群書提要附古今四書總目》（臺北：華泰文化公司，2000），上冊，頁85。

曆刻本，八卷，但其中卷四、卷六俱缺。此書最初由徐氏同年講學
友、南昌知縣何選與新建知縣佘夢鯉於萬曆十六年（1588）在江西刊
刻，卷數不詳。[67]萬曆二十年徐即登督學福建，次年重刻此書，由貢
生張書紳等「請梓而傳之」，以爲講學之助。[68]尊經閣文庫所藏四卷
本，似即此本。中國社科院文學所藏本大概刊於萬曆二十四年，其中
所收最晚的文字，是徐氏萬曆二十三年底升任福建左參政分守福寧道
後，[69]在短期內「奉例候代，照舊帶管學道印務」，以及「分藩數月」
的告示。[70]尊經閣本筆者未能寓目，但黃仁生對此本的版式、各卷校
訂門人及所錄內容有較爲詳細的描述，[71]據之可對兩種本子作初步對
應和比較：

67　何選，〈來益堂稿敘〉，熊尚文，〈徐匡岳先生來益堂稿序〉，俱載《來益
　　堂稿》，卷首，頁「又一」、「一」，俱署萬曆十六年四月。
68　見該書卷首，萬曆二十一年中秋晉江黃鳳翔殘序，李開芳〈題匡岳徐先
　　生來益堂稿〉、趙子貞〈重刻來益堂稿序〉，何喬遷《來益堂稿序》等。
　　張書紳著有《四書心旨會宗》等，見張伯行，《道南源委》，收入《四庫
　　全書存目叢書》（臺南縣：莊嚴文化公司，1996影印清康熙四十八年正
　　誼堂刻本），史部，第125冊，卷6，頁108。
69　《明神宗實錄》，卷292，萬曆二十三年十二月乙巳，頁5404。
70　徐即登，《來益堂稿》，卷8，〈告示十八〉、〈告示十九〉，頁47-49。該
　　書卷首萬曆二十三年十二月門人蔡復一序，應該就是爲此本而作。前舉
　　《千頃堂書目》著錄的五卷本，目前尚不知是何版本。
71　黃仁生，《日本現藏稀見元明文集考證與提要》（長沙：嶽麓書社，
　　2004），頁264-266。

《徐匡岳先生來益堂稿》兩種版本對比表[72]

社科院本	尊經閣本	內容概要	校訂門人
卷一	卷一	卷題「講意」，收錄〈大學全經〉及論學書函	門人張書紳校
卷二		卷題「講意」，收錄論學書函	門人黃浩校
卷三		卷題「講意」，收錄論學書函	門人黃浩校
卷四（缺）			
卷五	卷二	序跋、祭文等	門人朱鐘文校
卷六（缺）			
卷七	卷三	卷題「書柬」	門人蔡宗禹校
卷八	卷四	學約、告示等公文	門人黃正誼、張洪烈校

　　從這個簡單的比勘可知，在現存兩種不同版本的《來益堂稿》中，〈大學全經〉這篇重要的立說文字，均處於全書正文的首卷首篇，這個安排與前述其《明宗錄》、《儒宗要輯》等書如出一轍。徐即登的〈大學全經〉，看來有如其師李材的《大學古義》，當被收入其他著作中時，無一例外都是那些著作的核心所在，情形一如講學宗旨在理學學說和講學活動中的位置。

　　但徐即登這篇學說靈魂式的〈大學全經〉，內容上卻並無新奇之處，尤其是在與乃師李材的論說相較之下，它幾乎只是推崇《大學》地位、演繹「止修」宗旨的另一個解說版本。該文首句稱：「《大學》

72　這只是基於黃氏描述的粗略對比，即使在「內容概要」相同各卷中，後出八卷本通常也要多出一些篇章，如卷八所收萬曆二十一年至二十四年文字，當然就不可能出現在尊經閣本中，除非後者也經過增補而書目著錄不確。

一經，蓋孔子平生勘定學脈，以傳授曾子，而開宗立教於後世者
也。」接著論述止至善是明德、親民之本體，以「自天子以至於庶
人，壹是皆以修身爲本」爲「孔子立教之宗也，止至善之法也」，認
定正是「老孔子以一布衣抗立萬世師教」之處。這些論說重點，連同
作者的具體論述理據和邏輯，幾乎完全是承襲其師李材的已有論述，
在《大學》文本方面同樣也沒有任何新的進展。[73]徐氏對《大學》的
重視，不僅在講學、著述中如此，當有學生問及做人時，徐氏也示以
熟讀《大學》，且要求「千周萬遍，其理自見」，理由是「《大學》，
人書也，言人者莫辨乎此」。同時還以李材「吾學規模極大，端緒極
微，根柢極深，法度極密」四句口訣皆「從聖經二百一十五字（指
《大學》經文部分）融化出來」，揭以示諸生。[74]這些做法，與本文所
述李材在雲南、福建的講學方式如出一轍。

　　從萬曆三年接受李材「止修」新說、開釋胸中宿疑始，徐即登此
後終生服膺於此，著述立說皆謹守師傳，圍繞師門宗旨展開，居之不
疑。直到萬曆四十六年（1618），徐氏爲師友門生酬唱之作《劍江倡
和詩》作序，序末由小到大排列三枚印章，分別是「修身爲本」、
「獻和」、「文宗憲使之章」（見圖一）。獻和乃其別字。文宗、憲使分
別指其一生所任最重要的兩個官職，即福建提學副使、河南按察使。
排在首位的「修身爲本」，則正是其服膺四十餘年的師門學說宗旨，
而此時其師李材業已去世十餘年了。

73　劉斯原在論及李材、徐即登師徒的論學宗旨時，亦稱李材「特爲拈出
　　『止修』二字以括《大學》之旨」，而「近者徐匡岳先生複表章而光大
　　之」，見《大學古今本通考》，卷10，頁692。
74　徐即登，《來益堂稿》，卷3，〈答高科二〉，頁16-17。

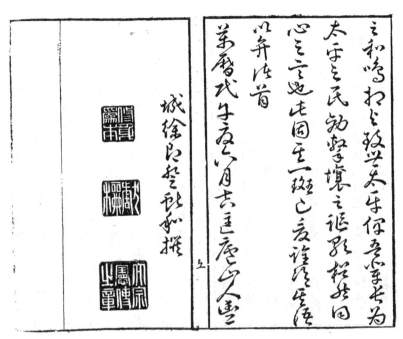

圖一：徐即登《劍江倡和詩序》末「修身為本」印[75]

　　在講學活動方面，無論居鄉在官，徐氏所至之處，一有機會就將所聞於乃師李材之學「到處輒以語人」。詳細情況在此難以縷述，僅從《儒宗要輯》中涉及的眾多地名，就可對其「到處無不語人」的講學情形獲得大體印象。[76]該書各條論學語之後多注明資料出處，其中大部分都是論學書信，從中往往可看出作者論學地點的變換。如該書卷一〈大學全經〉後，僅在連續兩葉中就依次節錄了「劍江答曾其

75　徐即登等，《劍江倡和詩》，卷首，頁5。
76　徐即登，《來益堂稿》，卷7，〈答都閫俞少虛〉，頁65-66。

道」、「天中答胡來貢」、「莆陽答問」、「武夷答王瑛」、「在梁答馬體元」等五份資料，[77]總共涉及徐氏曾分別在豐城、天中書院、莆田、武夷山、大樸等五處地方的講學記錄。在整部《儒宗要輯》中，由此線索可知徐即登曾在江西豐城，河南葵丘、太丘、宛丘、雍丘、大樸、商丘，福建福州、邵武樵川、莆田、清源、劍津等不同地區，以及在芝峰、[78]邸中、署中等不同地點和場所的講學足跡。由於這些論學語經過高度節錄，循例將文本原有的時、地、人事等與論學主旨無關的資訊均予刪削，因此我們只能獲知其曾經在某地講學，但除了十分簡略的論學內容外，對於講學的具體時間、聽眾、場合、氛圍、講論和對話情形等重要資訊，則難望有更深入的了解。[79]

　　徐氏的講學活動，尤以在福建任官時協助謫戍在此的李材開展講學，並以督學身份大力提倡興辦書院、親自主講而著稱。萬曆二十一年（1593），李材在被羈押六年之後終於充軍福建漳州鎮海衛。[80]此時正值徐即登「督學於茲」，又逢李材的進士同年和講學摯友許孚遠任福建巡撫「倡學於上」，「同志師友，一時湊合」，[81]故在萬曆二十年代的福建各地大興講學、講會和書院建設，招徠大批聽眾，致使日後

77　徐即登，《儒宗要輯》，卷1，〈大學本旨・大學全經〉，頁32-33。

78　疑指漳州府龍溪縣的紫芝山，李材曾在此講學，而徐即登曾應當地生員林一鳳等人之請，在山前建龍光書院，匾額即題以紫芝二字，詳見《來益堂稿》，卷8，〈告示〉十三至十七，頁43-47。

79　萬曆三十年春三月，王時槐約萬廷言會於樟鎮，門人何汝定、王梓齡從，「學憲徐匡嶽公亦至，爲會三日而別。會間無多語，其私相印證之言不得聞。別去，先生（王時槐）亟歎思默公之學正當精深。」見《續補王塘南先生恭憶先訓自考錄》頁35，轉引自吳震，《明代知識界講學活動繫年，1522-1602》（北京：學林出版社，2003），頁430。

80　詳參劉勇，〈從李材案看晚明清議的形成及其與講學之關係〉，頁41-70。

81　徐即登，《來益堂稿》，卷7，〈寄熊寧野丈〉，頁43-44。

李材本人也如前所述地聲稱「閩士之知我也，半多在徐獻和督學之後」。徐氏本人還運用職務之便，先後在福州創建正學書院、共學書院，親自主持講學，並試圖藉助自己主管的教育體系將這種講學模式推廣到福建各地。[82]

五、修訂師門宗旨的嘗試：涂宗濬之例

涂宗濬在萬曆後期以疆場事功表現為時人所稱。[83]在萬曆十一年中進士後，涂氏先後四為縣令，萬曆二十年（1592）至二十七年間，又陸續巡按廣西、河南、山西、順天諸處。二十九年（1601）擢大理寺丞，三十四年（1606）升都察院僉都御史，巡撫延綏，三十九年（1611）升宣大山西等處總督，至四十三年（1615）以總督宣大兵部尚書的身份回籍調理，「病痊奏薦起用」。[84]計其前後共在北邊開府近十年，邊功卓著，善處封貢、互市之策。尤其在萬曆三十五年（1607）順義王撦力克、四十年（1612）忠順夫人三娘子（1550-1612）先後去世之際，蒙古政權內部的權力過渡使明蒙關係處於劇烈

82　詳細情形可參其文集《來益堂稿》，由於與本文論旨關係不大，茲從略。

83　南居益在萬曆四十二年序其《續韋齋易義虛裁》時指出：「先生事功，強半著於疆場」，並擬之於陽明之儒，「文成履危而見奇，先生處順而底績」。載涂宗濬，《續韋齋易義虛裁》，收入《四庫全書存目叢書補編》（濟南：齊魯書社，2001影印明萬曆四十二年刻本），第89冊，卷首，頁201；國立中央圖書館編印，《國立中央圖書館善本序跋集錄・經部》（臺北：國立中央圖書館，1992），頁61。並參徐開任編，《明名臣言行錄》，收入《明代傳記叢刊》冊54（臺北：明文書局，1991影印康熙二十年序刊本），卷75，〈尚書涂恭襄公宗濬〉，頁11-19。

84　江召棠、魏元曠等修纂，乾隆《南昌縣誌》（南京：江蘇古籍出版社等，1996影印1960年江西省圖書館鉛印本），卷30，頁1067-1072；《明神宗實錄》，卷540，萬曆四十三年十二月壬子，頁10269。

震盪中，「中外洶洶，謂款事將不可續」。涂氏最終妥善應對危機，[85]
明王朝於萬曆四十一年六月封卜石兔爲順義王，把漢比妓爲忠義夫
人，五路素囊俱各領封，並成功地促成明蒙雙方再次立下封貢、互市
的「規矩條約」。[86]

　　這位叱咤於萬曆後期北方邊務的封疆大吏，同時也是一個以
《易》學名家的學者，更是篤志講學的理學「領袖」。[87]當時的講學名
家馮從吾特別指出：「余惟先生勳勒燕然，望隆台鼎，人人皆以事功
氣節爲先生重，而不知先生之所重者在學問。彼事功氣節，特先生學
問之緒餘，非先生之所重也。」[88]涂氏家鄉江西南昌縣，正是江右陽明
學講學活動的重鎮。但出身貧寒的涂氏雖有志儒學，幼年時卻只能隨
父僦居僧寺，日事雕鏤，「攻木爲神像以自活」。[89]大約在萬曆四十年

85　王士琦，《三雲籌俎考》，卷2詳載這一時期蒙古政權的過渡及其與明朝
　　的關係，作者特別指出：「當是時，夷情幻邊，眾喙惶惑，久淹詔使，
　　廟議責成，章疏累累滿公車，涂公獨任，適當其難，朝夕求所以觸解紛
　　結、辨析危疑，敝舌嘔心，廢箸忘擲，良工之苦，有難以語人者。」收
　　入《續修四庫全書》（上海：上海古籍出版社，1995影印明萬曆刻本），
　　第739冊，頁32-34。涂氏有關此事的奏疏，見陳子龍等選編，《皇明經
　　世文編》（北京：中華書局，1997影印明崇禎間平露堂刊本），卷447-
　　450，〈涂司馬撫延疏草〉，頁4909-4954。
86　《明神宗實錄》，卷500、504、509，萬曆四十年十月庚辰、四十一年正
　　月癸酉、六月甲辰，頁9462-9463、9583-9585、9642-9643；該條約文本
　　見《三雲籌俎考》，卷2，頁36-40。
87　過庭訓，《本朝分省人物考》，收入《明代傳記叢刊》（臺北：明文書
　　局，1991），卷58，頁352。
88　馮從吾，《馮少墟集》，收入《中國西北文獻叢書》（蘭州：蘭州古籍書
　　店，1990影印康熙十二年序刊本），第6輯，卷16，〈百二別言〉，頁
　　288。
89　蔣士銓，《忠雅堂集校箋》（邵海清校，李夢生箋，上海：上海古籍出版
　　社，1993），卷10，〈涂宗濬軼事〉，頁2382。據李箋，作者蔣氏很可能
　　是聞諸友人、涂氏族裔涂逢震。

前後，涂氏向他的講學聽眾回顧自己的爲學經歷云：「余生平以『不自是、不自足』六字時時策勵。方十二時，先君見背，即有志聖人之學，苦無所入；十五讀諸儒性理，二十一學陽明良知，三十一聞李先生止修，四十二在粵中悟性，不敢自是，因舍去；五十時已見光景，亦舍去。蓋生平所歷之境，凡五變矣。」[90]中年以後有悟有見，涂氏何故俱「舍去」？與其所聞李材「止修」之學有何關係？

涂氏最初從讀宋儒書入手，繼之講陽明「致良知」學達十年之久，最後在萬曆初年李材引疾家居講學期間，從其講「止修」學，[91]並由此悟入有得。從涂氏現存著作和語錄來看，自其接受李材止修學後，終其一生的講學活動中，主要以提倡和宣揚師門之學爲主，成爲李材門下少數具有重要影響力的弟子之一。李材晚年在編輯門下高弟著述而成《知本同參》一書時，就收錄了涂宗濬《〔隆砂〕證學記》中的部分內容。

涂氏論學強調經書各有宗旨、主腦，學問的重點在於掌握這些宗旨，並體諸身心。其《陽和語錄》云：「聖人作經，莫不各有宗旨，既得宗旨之後，仍須逐一貼身理會」、[92]「學問先要理會宗旨，宗旨既

90 涂宗濬，《陽和語錄》（江西省圖書館藏明萬曆刻本），卷3，頁11。並參同書卷6：「方先君見背，先慈守節，余年纔十二耳。當時慷慨發憤，雖有志聖人之道，思以立身行道，揚名後世，以顯父母。然株守一經，東西奔走，僅免飢寒，豈妄意有今日哉！」頁20-21。

91 涂氏從學當在李材萬曆三年引疾家居至萬曆十一年復出爲官期間。若從「三十一聞李先生止修，四十二在粵中悟性」來看，涂氏巡按廣西是在萬曆二十年前後，則聞止修說當在萬曆九年。但聞止修說並不必定等於最初從學李材的時間，日後涂氏對待跟從自己求學者就「凡三見而後告以知止之義」，見《隆砂證學記》（臺北：漢學研究中心影印日本內閣文庫藏明萬曆三十二年刊本），卷6，〈別蔡生題辭〉，頁3-6。

92 涂宗濬，《陽和語錄》，卷4，頁13。同書卷1云：「《六經》各有宗旨，

明，便須貼身體勘，體勘得實，隨時必有所見」、[93]「學問宗旨既明，要在反身體勘，對境磨研」。[94]對於師門宗旨，則需謹守不離：「大要全在謹守師說，無離宗旨，庶幾不差。」[95]

在著述體例和形式上，涂氏均模仿乃師李材之為。自序於萬曆二十一年的《隆砂證學記》，乃其最重要的論學之作。此書現存為六卷，首卷全錄《大學》古本，並注明「原出《禮記》，今注疏具存」，為其論學立說最基本的經典依據；次卷題為《大學古義述》，是「述」乃師李材《大學古義》而作，而《古義》則是李材論證「止修」宗旨最重要的經典文本。三卷以下先為《論》、《孟》講義，繼而講學問答，及書信與論學語。這個著述體例，也與李材《見羅李先生觀我堂稿》、《見羅先生書要》、《見羅先生書》諸書如出一轍。

涂氏講學的立說模式亦如其師，以《大學》為典據，重點駁朱子、陽明二家之說，而揭師門「止修」宗旨。其《隆砂證學記》自序云：

> 《大學》古本乃孔門相傳入聖要訣。朱子疑有脫誤，更定補輯，離析舊文，階級大分，頗無義味。陽明王先生復刻

須具隻眼方得其旨。」頁9。卷3：「聖賢垂世立言，各有一個主腦，所以千支萬派，未始出其宗，如《大學》只是聖經一章，盡之矣；聖經又只是『止於至善』一句，盡之矣。《中庸》只是天命一章，盡之矣，究竟只『天命之謂性』一句，盡之矣。推之《論語》，只消『學而時習之』一句，《孟子》只消『亦有仁義而已矣』，《易經》總是〈乾〉〈坤〉二卦，《書經》只是〈堯典〉，《禮記》總是『毋不敬』一句，《詩經》總是『思無邪』一句，《春秋》總是『春王正月』一句。以後看書，先要識他主腦。」頁15。

93　涂宗濬，《隆砂證學記》，卷5，〈與沈生〉，頁21-23。
94　涂宗濬，《隆砂證學記》，卷6，〈與丁時盛諱士望〉，頁21。
95　涂宗濬，《隆砂證學記》，卷5，〈與沈生〉，頁21-23。

古本，聖經復完，然其立教專以「致良知」爲說，亦非經
文本旨。宗濬夙承師訓，沉潛於此蓋已有年，近始忽有所
覺，證之經書微言，無不脗合，信乎聖門有宗傳也。[96]

所謂「夙承師訓」，即指李材所創「止修」宗旨。「近始忽有所
覺」，當指前文所引其自敘四十二歲時「在粵中悟性」一事。

涂氏最重要的立說之作《大學古義述》，也如李材般主張「三綱
領」中至善爲體，而入道功夫則在知止：「《大學》之宗，只是止至
善，入《大學》之道，必先知止，知本乃入止之境，誠正修乃歸止之
功，齊家治國平天下又止善之能事也。以言乎己，則謂明明德；以言
乎人，則謂親民。性之德也，合內外之道也，《大學》之道，其旨蓋
如此。」在這段正面立論之後，涂氏復以問答的形式辨明知止與朱子
格物致知之異同，知止與誠正、本末、終始、讀書窮理等之關係。同
樣也以問答形式討論「《中庸》說理更覺深奧，似與《大學》不同」
的質疑，認爲「聖門只是一個心傳，二之則不是矣。若看得《大學》
透徹，即見《中庸》義理與《大學》一字不差」，指出《中庸》的宗
旨「天命之謂性」即是《大學》「至善」二字，並通過逐條比較兩書
各個重要概念，論述《中庸》所說實皆爲《大學》所涵括。[97]這主

96　涂宗濬，《隆砂證學記》，卷首，頁1。卷首山西左布政劉孟雷、南禮右
　　侍郎范醇、山西提學副使王三才、楚後學袁子讓諸序亦多推崇其「於
　　《大學》宗旨獨得精傳」、「良知兩字，終遜其透，伯安（王陽明）有
　　知，定推益友」，而分守大樑道左參政蕭良幹（1534-1602）序雖然也批
　　評朱子改本「割裂補綴」，但作爲王畿的門人，蕭氏對於陽明就較少批
　　評了：「近世王文成公出，始去分章、復舊本、傍爲之訓釋，《大學》之
　　道，庶幾復明。顧學者狃於習聞，猶或滯於見未徹也。」蕭氏曾刊行
　　《龍溪王先生全集》。
97　俱見涂宗濬，《隆砂證學記》，卷2，〈大學古義述〉，頁1-16。

要是爲了論成《大學》在儒家經典中至高無上的地位，也是乃師李材
舊說之發揮。

　　不過，通讀《大學古義述》卻能發現，儘管作者也提到「知本」
（知修身爲本）這個師門學說中的關鍵概念，但卻明顯未予足夠的重
視，而且對之有所修訂。這個修訂師門宗旨舉動中最具象徵意義之
處，是圍繞《大學》展開的。當初王陽明依據《大學》提揭「致良
知」宗旨，最明確地體現在爲《大學古本》所寫的「原序」和「改
序」的文本變動，以及相應地對兩序寫作時間進行刻意「移花接
木」，尤其是「改序」末句的畫龍點睛之筆：「乃若致知，則存乎心
悟；致知焉，盡矣。」後來李材在依據自定的《大學》改本論成「止
修」宗旨時，則針鋒相對地提出「乃若知本，則存乎心悟；知本焉，
至矣」。[98]至此，涂宗濬則將此句改爲「《大學》之道，止至善焉盡之
矣」。在隨後的問答中，涂氏還特別比較了李材重知止而輕格致誠正
之說，與自己主張的「止的功夫，全在格致誠正」，認爲「若將格致
誠正看得太輕，一味說止，竊恐流於告子之不動心，非《大學》之道
矣」，並要求讀者「要善理會」李材的「止爲主意，修爲功夫」之
說。[99]

　　顯而易見，涂氏試圖對乃師李材「止爲主意，修爲功夫」的
「止」「修」雙揭宗旨有所修訂。這個舉動引起了李材的高度關注，
萬曆二十八年（1600）前後，李材在〈答涂及甫書〉中指出：

　　　　學必以孔子爲宗，《大學》爲案。非悟，則雖日講於《大
　　　　學》，固爲空文；藉令有悟，只一語不契於《大學》，終

98　詳參前揭劉勇，〈中晚明時期的講學宗旨、《大學》文本與理學學說建
　　構〉，頁424、432-438。
99　以上俱見涂宗濬，《隆砂證學記》，卷2，〈大學古義述〉，頁1-16。

爲意見。區區半生體會，誠不專在於書冊上著功，然既透
學一班，則必於《大學》悟增一乘，卒於《大學》之旨靡
有遺明，而吾意亦恰恰合符節，靡有遺憾。故緣此服孔子
爲最深，而緣此知孔子亦自以爲最至。公天慧既爾絕人，
鑽研尤懇，月將日就，緝熙光明，必有豁然能獨得於意言
象數外者。惜地遠無以覿正之耳。然必將二百一十五字按
定作譜，如意可以作方圓而必取衷規矩，手可以搏平直而
必歸則準繩……稿多去，力不能將，《大學約言》、《孝經
疏義》各一冊，略可見一班。謂非自有悟不可，要指其中
半個字不允協於經文，則所未有。淵淵浩浩，只此二百一
十五字，眞有探之無其涯、測之難爲量，而又準平繩直，
毫髮不容於僭差踰越者矣。孤跡浪漫，忽此七年。[100]

信中李材特別強調論學必須以《大學》一書尤其是經文部分的
215字作爲準繩，對於自己的《大學約言》，更宣稱是沒有「半個字
不允協於經文」之作。這個說辭看來仍有相當的模糊性，只從正面強
調論學準繩和己說的重要性與不可改動性，尚未清楚指出涂氏的問題
所在。在隨後讀到涂宗濬寄贈其所著《隆砂證學記》之後，李材復信
指出：

理無兩是，學無二宗，兼搭摻和，如補破衲……二之則不
是也。來簡諸所頌雖極踰涯，然亦何敢過讓。至所著《證
學記》，條貫不妨小參差，大旨自不害。惟以爲必合王、
羅兩家之說，而後蠡管見爲無欠缺也，則非所敢承也。一

100　李材，《正學堂稿》，卷21，〈答涂及甫書〉，頁5-6。此信寫作時間由
　　「忽此七年」推知。

是百是，一差百差，此牽彼搭，如補破衲，眞所謂二之則
不是也。[101]

與前信完全從正面強調不同，此信雖然同樣也揭示「理無兩是，
學無二宗」，但卻明確指出了涂氏的問題所在：其《證學記》書中認
爲老師的止修之學「必合羅、王兩家之說」才算完整。李材對此表示
完全不能接受，自己的止修之學絲毫「無欠缺」，是不可「二之」的
「一是」之說，根本無須「牽搭」、「補衲」於他說。對老師李材的這
項質疑和批評，涂氏在萬曆三十年（1602）前後的信中作出解釋：

> 門生半生問學，廿載仕途……年來有勘於知止兩言，眞孔
> 聖傳心之秘。知本是歸根之地，格致誠正是依止之方……
> 區區揣摩之見，瑣瑣字句之間，又何足置同異之辯於齒牙
> 之間哉！端本澄源、風行草偃，蓋實以身證之，羅、王兩
> 公，蓋因知止、知本二言，頗足相發，姑取證焉，如陽明
> 先生集刊《朱子晚年定論》之意，非謂《大學》意義未
> 明、老師立說未備，而采摭掇拾以爲補湊之書也。蓋因老
> 師之說以求孔、曾之旨，實悟聖人立教，知止兩言不爲
> 少，《六經》、《語》、《孟》不爲多……蓋聞者無不心
> 服，絕無纖介之疑。項因九年已滿，注籍杜門，海內英
> 賢，不招而集，深辟二氏似是之非，直指孔、曾立教之
> 旨……洪生來見，頗悉大旨，歸日當爲老師言之。[102]

---

101 李材，《正學堂稿》，卷30，〈答涂及甫〉，頁13-14。此信爲節錄，「來
　　簡」似已不存。
102 涂宗濬，《隆砂證學記》，卷5，〈奉見羅先生〉，頁8-9。此信的時間從
　　「廿載仕途」、「項因九年已滿」推知，據《明名臣言行錄》卷75：「前後
　　積台資九年，升大理寺丞。」（頁12）涂氏萬曆二十八年五月還在巡按直

　　涂氏此信主旨在於聲明自己在論學要義上與老師步調一致，並非要與老師之說「置同異之辯」，亦非質疑「老師立說未備」。所述具體有兩點：一是申述自己的論學文字和見解，特別是「格致誠正是依止之方」（即前文引其《大學古義述》中所謂「止的功夫，全在格致誠正」）一句對格致誠正功夫的強調，並不足以與師傳「止爲主意，修爲功夫」的「止修」學構成「同異之辯」。二是解釋自己爲何在論學過程中引述和取證羅、王二人之說。從其引證的理由「因知止（止於至善）、知本（修身爲本）二言，頗足相發」來看，這裡的羅、王兩公，應該是指羅洪先（1504-1564）、王艮（1483-1541）而言。信中所說「非謂《大學》意義未明、老師立說未備，而采摭掇拾以爲補湊之書」，當是因涂氏在闡釋《大學》的文字中，尤其是在引申和發揮老師李材沒有「半個字不允協於經文」的《大學約言》過程中，引述牽合羅、王之說，[103] 引起李材的不滿，故而涂氏回信解釋，稱自己的引述僅僅是因其說頗可與李材之說相互發明，無損於師門宗旨乃孔曾眞傳，更非爲針對師門之教而發。

────────────

　　隸御史任上，三十一年三月擢爲大理寺右寺丞，期間一度杜門家居（見《明神宗實錄》，卷346、382，萬曆二十八年四月甲申、三十一年三月乙亥，頁6448-6449、7189）。信末「洪生」，很可能是指龍溪人洪啓源，參《隆砂證學記》，卷6，〈答洪懋仁諱啓源〉，頁13。

103　顧疑當在涂著《大學古義述》中，但今存本並無引述羅洪先、王艮之處，或已經刪除？或者是指其下一通書信末提到的《大學釋義》，但該書似已不存，記此存疑。《隆砂證學記》前四卷是涂氏自己編定，後兩卷爲其門人尤大治續刻，涂氏的這封回信，正是在續刻之列。尤大治《續刻隆砂證學記》（在卷四與卷五之間，無頁碼）亦引及王艮之論以爲取證：「曾氏書具在，綱目犁然，而後儒主敬、主靜、致虛、致良知之學，分門撮指，雖於聖學咸有所窺，而正宗發明者渺矣。王心齋先生曰：《大學》吃緊在止至善，格物卻正是止至善，淵哉微乎！……天啓先生（涂宗濬），聖眞統一……其教每以止修立論。」

　　李材看來在此特別排斥羅洪先、王艮的相似之說，甚至不願門下引述以與己說互相發明；然而值得注意的是，當初在萬曆十年以前，當李材的「止修」學尚處在立說之初時，在其修身爲本之說遭到質疑與批評的情形下，他也曾經訴諸陽明高弟王艮提倡「修身爲本之旨」，並引爲同調。[104]

　　對於涂氏的解釋，李材從莆田致信反復指出「予豈好辨，予不得已」、學「惟其是」，「當仁不讓」之意。並勉勵涂氏，「以公高卓，而又加以沉邃之養，踐更中外，往復參研，其於洙泗之宗，必有覿面孔曾而聆其指授者」，同時寄去「拙刻數種」，請涂氏「必取次讀之，而摘其疵瑕以質」。[105]

　　涂氏在讀畢李材所寄諸書之後，回信表示自己對「止修」說曾經僅有的一點點異見已經「從此一掃而空」，對師門之教也「一唯宗傳是主」：

　　　竊見《大學》歸宗，只有止至善三字；入道眞訣，只有知止兩言。主意、工夫，一齊俱到；定靜安慮，入止漸深；慮而能得，至善到手矣。知本乃歸止之地，格致誠正乃歸止之方，知止兩字，妙義悉已包涵，「物有」以下，條析始爲明悉，非有加也。「止爲主意，修爲功夫」兩言，似覺太分，以此不無疑詫。及讀老師〈與陸仲鶴公祖〉有云：「靈不離虛即是止不離本。」又〈答王玉溪太守書〉有云：「其實只一止字便可了得，何取更著修字？蓋緣經世之學，錯綜於人倫事物之交，牽掣於聲色貨利之取，無

<hr>

104　李材，《觀我堂摘稿》，卷1，〈答鄧元中書〉，頁22。
105　李材，《正學堂稿》，卷17，〈與涂及甫書〉，頁18-20。李材於萬曆二十七年秋從漳州徙居莆田。

奈漏泄者多也。又入門之方固是止，造道之極亦是止，故
不但歸本是止，即從事於格致誠正，其旨意之歸宿者，亦
只是一止而已。」十數年以來之疑團，一旦冰消霧釋，更
無纖芥留滯於胸中矣。但老師說止又說修，正爲說止則近
於玄虛，說修又近於拘執，兩處遮攔，庶免落一邊見解，
其用心良苦矣。二三之障，從此一掃而空之，闇修密證，
闡發敷宣，一唯宗傳是主。「上帝臨爾，毋二爾心」，敢
留餘念哉！諸刻取次讀之，已覺沛然。門生《大學釋
義》，悉依古本，少有不同，不足爲異也。[106]

　　由此信可知涂氏的確曾經在李材「止」、「修」雙揭的「止修」
宗旨中，傾向於強調「知止」的絕對優先性。這個意見最明顯地體現
在其答龍溪人洪啓源信中：

《大學》宗旨，只知止兩字，言知止則主意功夫一起俱
到，物有本末以下至修身爲本，此謂知本，此謂知至，正
發知止之義，經文洞然明白，學者守此，實止實修，即中
人上下，皆可循序而入，乃學者不悟李師立教圓旨，或以
修身爲本，無格致誠正功夫，不知除卻格致誠正，則修之
手勢不知如何用力。[107]

　　大約在萬曆三十年前後，涂氏回復李材之信，明確點出李材曾經
對其論學有「重止略修」的擔憂，「傳之將來，未免落空之弊」。同
時再次表明自己的態度，表示已經領略師門「止修」雙揭之苦心，此
後「謹守法門，更無歧見」：

106　涂宗濬，《隆砂證學記》，卷5，〈奉見羅李老師〉，頁23-24。
107　涂宗濬，《隆砂證學記》，卷6，〈答洪懋仁諱啓源〉，頁13。

許都聞入都，得領老師手書，敬繹其旨，惟恐門生重止略
修，傳之將來，未免落空之弊。誠然誠然。門生看得聖經
以知止爲《大學》之宗，物有本末以下至知本、知至，正
明知止之義。蓋知止爲宗，則主意功夫一齊俱到，已含修
身爲本之義。但兩字雖已含藏，一口竟難道出，必須將事
物本末始終詳細數出，指其歸本之地，教人知所以本之，
然後謂之知至，然後謂之知止，故修身爲本所以了止非二
義也。此門生悟得《大學》全經，只教知止，與老師之
説，似無背違。但爲學者説法，必須止修並提，方始無
弊。門生十年以前曾悟知止眞境，頗因收攝之久，心體忽
然一開，透體汗流，形骸俱化，直與天地萬物上下同流，
渾無彼此之分……自是之後，根本之處似已知所依歸，事
物之來亦已不難剖決，惟是反觀內省，尚有多少習氣急難
銷除……而立説太高，更啓將來卜度之弊，故《大學》聖
經，不可一字抹除，其慮誠深，而老師之力爲堤防，誠爲
直透作經之義，非苟然也。故就身上止，方是平中奇；就
修身爲本教人歸止，方爲中道諦。謹守法門，更無歧見
矣。108

信中所述「十年以前曾悟知止眞境」，是指前引其自述爲學歷程時
提及的「四十二在粵中悟性」。該次悟道體驗對涂氏影響巨大，故在
此辯解書信中還忍不住詳細加以縷述，並且看來他是相當堅持以自身
的此次悟道體驗來印證、取捨老師李材之説的。對該次悟道體驗最爲

---

108 涂宗濬，《隆砂證學記》，卷6，〈奉答李見羅先生〉，頁14-16。此信時
　　間從「門生十年以前曾悟知止眞境」推知。

詳細同時也是最具自信的記載，則見於涂氏致管志道的論學書信中：

> 至壬辰（1592）八月初二日夕，正襟獨坐署中，時可二
> 更。忽然大汗自頂至踵湧出如注，當時形骸盡化，覺與天
> 地萬物合成一片，上無蓋，下無底，四方無邊際，廣大虛
> 空，妙不容言。三更就寢，夢吾宣聖臨顧，發氣滿容，所
> 居堂不類今時居第，有阼階，有西階，吾先師由阼階入，
> 弟恭迎就東楹坐。弟以所悟《大學》知止、知本之義請
> 正，先師喜動眉宇，直指要訣。弟恭受心佩，渾身如在太
> 虛，相對半夜。五更覺來，別是一乾坤也。急起盥漱更
> 衣，焚香拜謝。恐其遺忘，援筆直書夢中所聞，即今《隆
> 砂記》中所解《大學古義》是也。自是歷勘先聖遺言，無
> 不洞然可曉。即後世術數之書，如孔明八陣圖等類，皆能
> 照知其意。又巡歷兩河、三晉及畿輔，無一而非勘學之
> 地，亦無一而非勘學之人。[109]

以此悟道體驗中曾向先師孔子印證過的《大學》知止、知本之義
為基礎，涂氏對師門「止修」宗旨，在義理上始終不免傾向於知
止。[110]但誠如上引致李材信中所說，涂氏在此後「為學者說法」的講
學活動中，的確「謹守法門」，止修並提，以杜立說太高可能導致的
卜度、落空之弊。

---

109 載管志道，《管東溟先生文集》（臺灣中央研究院中國文哲研究所圖書館
藏），〈論學三箚〉，頁23-24；轉引自呂妙芬，〈從杜文煥看晚明儒學與
宗教之交涉〉，中央研究院明清研究推動委員會主辦「明清研究國際學
術研討會」（臺北，2013.12.5-6）會議論文，頁23。

110 此點可從萬曆三十四年馮從吾為涂氏《寓燕課錄》所作序言明顯看出，
見《馮少墟集》，卷13，〈寓燕課錄序〉，頁222-223。

六、結論

　　在宋明理學脈絡中，無論是道統觀念和道統系譜的建構與落實，還是理學學說的延續，都對師徒授受的學說傳承方式有著極高期待。但在講學活動盛行的中晚明時期，「轉益多師」成為普遍現象，加上理學內部各種學說之間的義理論辯，以及現實社會的利益競爭，使得學說的傳承和師徒關係的確立充滿變數。在這種情形下，李材的「止修」宗旨如何在門人之中得以傳承和延續，以及在此過程中師門固有宗旨能否與追求自悟的自得之學協調一致，其間可能會產生哪些變異、衝突和對話的情形，是本文著重以徐即登和涂宗濬為例加以探討的議題。

　　徐即登最初在家鄉豐城領導地方士子的講學活動，隆慶末年跟隨任官江西的徐用檢講學，但後者的學說宗旨未能徹底說服徐即登。萬曆三年李材返鄉之後，以自己依據《大學》悟得的新說「止修」宗旨，使徐即登胸中宿疑一掃而空，從此徐氏完全服膺「止修」學，無論居鄉為官，所至「輒以語人」，透過大量著述和講學活動宣揚「止修」說。在徐氏督學福建時，不僅為流放在此的老師李材提供講學便利，也運用職務之便在福州創建書院，組織講會，並試圖將這種講學模式推及全閩。綜觀徐氏一生的著述和講學，從信奉「止修」師說後就居之不疑，並始終堅持不遺餘力地加以闡揚和講論。無論是其立說依據，還是其宣講方式，乃至於著述編排體例與具體內容，均呈現出謹守師傳的形象。[111]萬曆二十三年（1595）前後，李材在為徐即登的語錄題詞中，回顧了師弟二人的講學因緣：「予倡之，獻和和之，如

---

[111]　鄒元標〈東徐匡岳督學二〉亦云：「得《來益稿》，讀之服丈通道之篤，任道之勇，尊師之誠。」《願學集》，卷2，頁45-46。

出一轍焉，茲來二十年所矣。」[112]正是徐氏謹守師說的最好寫照。

　　涂宗濬同樣曾經在各種理學學說中輾轉徘徊，最後服膺李材的
「止修」學。與李材、徐即登一樣，涂氏履跡所至皆不忘聚眾講學。
其立說方式、講論內容亦與師門之傳大體相合。不過，涂氏卻嘗試以
自己的證悟體驗對師門「止修」宗旨有所修訂，傾向於重「止」而略
「修」，遂引起老師李材不滿，師徒之間為此產生緊張，經過多次對
話之後，涂氏最終仍然堅持以自己的悟道體驗來印證、取捨師門宗
旨，僅表示在教人方面惟師說是從。

　　綜觀徐即登、涂宗濬兩人的著述，其立說方式幾乎都不出李材範
圍，仍然主要以《大學》為最重要的立說經典依據，提揭「止修」宗
旨。王陽明以《古本大學》、《傳習錄》之類的小書宣傳自己的學
說，李材則綜合朱熹和陽明而成就自己的改本與詮釋，並以《大學古
義》、《大學約言》之類的小冊子和講義宣揚「止修」學。徐即登撰
成《大學約言述》、《大學全經》，涂宗濬則撰有《大學古義述》、
《大學釋義》這類旨在演繹師門「止修」說的文字，作為自己的立說
基礎。儘管徐、涂二人的立說方式相同，但在具體內容上，不管是文
本處理，還是義理發揮，都沒有提出突破性的創見，可以說只是師門
「止修」宗旨的別樣版本。涂氏曾經試圖以自己的悟道體驗對師門宗
旨有所修正，在李材「止」、「修」雙揭的論學宗旨中，傾向於強調
「知止」的絕對優先性，但李材批評其說「重止略修」，「傳之將來，
未免落空之弊」。對涂宗濬援據羅洪先、王艮之說，李材也表達不
滿，雖然涂氏聲稱引用的目的是為了論證師門修身為本之說的合理
性。顯而易見，作為「止修」學說的創立者和作為老師的李材，留給

112　李材，《正學堂稿》，卷35，〈題徐獻和莆陽答問〉，頁3。

其門人的發揮空間並不大。由此需要思考的是，學需自悟、學有自得的理學理念，如何與師門學說傳承和學派延續的現實要求之間求得妥善的解決之道？

The Inheritance of the "Purpose" Theory from Master to Apprentice in the School of "Zhi-xiu" Which Created by the Late Ming Neo-Confucian Scholar Li Cai

Alvin Chen

Abstract

This article focuses on the school of "zhi-xiu" created by the Ming Neo-Confucian scholar Li Cai. It explores the inheritance of the theory of "purpose" from master to apprentice in the context of Neo- Confucianism. "Purpose" is a highly philosophical concept and it represents a philosophical doctrine and the core concepts of a school. The observation of the inheritance of "purpose" from master to apprentice may lead to a better understanding of the philosophical relationship between master-apprentice ethics and school inheritance, and also the inner tension between transferring the master's theory and pursuing "self-learning". Specifically, this article first uses concrete examples from the perspectives of philosophical concept and teaching method to discuss the importance and complexity of the master-apprentice relationship in Neo-Confucianism. Second, it briefly describes the communication method of the theory of Li Cai. Lastly, it emphasizes on the cases of Li's disciples Xu Jideng and Tu Zongjun, by examining how the purpose of "zhi-xiu" was accepted, revised, and excluded during the master-apprentice inheritance process from the aspect of strictly keeping the master's teaching as well as the aspect of trying to revise the master's theory.

Keywords: Li Cai; Xu Jideng; Tu Zongjun; zhi-xiu; the Ming Intellectual History

徵引文獻

王士琦，《三雲籌俎考》，收入《續修四庫全書》，第739冊，上海：上海古
　　籍出版社，1995影印明萬曆刻本。

王汎森，〈明末清初的人譜與省過會〉，《中央研究院歷史語言研究所集
　　刊》，63：3（臺北，1993），頁679-712。

王汎森，〈日譜與明末清初思想家——以顏李學派為主的討論〉，收入氏著，
　　《明末清初思想十論》，上海：復旦大學出版社，2004，頁117-185。

包筠雅（Cynthia Brokaw）著，杜正貞、張林譯，《功過格：明清社會的道德
　　秩序》，杭州：浙江人民出版社，1999。

市來津由彥，《朱熹門人集團形成の研究》，東京：創文社，2002。

永瑢總裁、紀昀總纂，四庫全書研究所整理，《欽定四庫全書總目》，北京：
　　中華書局，1997。

田浩，《朱熹的思維世界》，臺北：允晨文化實業股份有限公司，1996。

朱熹著，黎靖德編，《朱子語類》，臺北：正中書局，1973。

朱鴻林，〈黃佐與王陽明之會〉，《燕京學報》，新21期（北京，2006），頁
　　69-84。

朱鴻林，〈讀張詡《白沙先生行狀》〉，收入氏著，《明人著作與生平發微》，
　　桂林：廣西師範大學出版社，2005，頁214-219。

江召棠、魏元曠等修纂，乾隆《南昌縣誌》，南京：江蘇古籍出版社等，
　　1996影印1960年江西省圖書館鉛印本。

呂妙芬，〈從杜文煥看晚明儒學與宗教之交涉〉，中央研究院明清研究推動委
　　員會主辦「明清研究國際學術研討會」（臺北，2013.12.5-6）會議論文。

何士錦、陸履敬纂修，康熙《豐城縣誌》，臺北：成文出版社，1989。

何喬遠，《鏡山全集》，臺北：漢學研究中心影印日本內閣文庫藏明崇禎十四
　　年序刊本。

余英時，〈談「天地君親師」的起源〉，收入氏著，《現代儒學論》，River
　　Edge, NJ：八方文化企業公司，1996，頁97-101。

吳震，《明代知識界講學活動繫年，1522-1602》，北京：學林出版社，2003。

呂妙芬，《陽明學士人社群：歷史、思想與實踐》，北京：新星出版社，2006
　　重印。

宋端儀撰，薛應旂重輯，《考亭淵源錄》，收入《四庫全書存目叢書》，史部
　　第88冊，臺南縣：莊嚴文化公司，1996影印明隆慶三年林潤刻本。

李材，《正學堂稿》，北京大學圖書館藏民國元年豐城李希泌刻本。

李材，《兵政紀略》，收入劉兆祐主編，《中國史學叢書》，三編，二輯，臺北：臺灣學生書局，1986影印明萬曆刻本。

李材，《見羅先生斅學錄要》，收入《四庫未收書輯刊》，6：12，北京：北京出版社，2000影印民國十二年刻本。

李材，《見羅李先生經正錄》，美國國會圖書館藏明萬曆三十一年刊本。

李材，《見羅李先生讀孫子》，日本尊經閣文庫藏明抄本。

李材撰，熊尚文編，《見羅李先生觀我堂稿》，臺北：中央研究院傅斯年圖書館影印日本內閣文庫藏明萬曆間愛成堂刊本。

李紀祥，〈《近思錄》之「錄」與《傳習錄》之「錄」〉，收入氏著，《道學與儒林》，臺北：唐山出版社，2004，頁15-66。

李穎，〈李見羅先生行略〉，收入劉家平等主編，《中華歷史人物別傳集》，第22冊，北京：線裝書局，2003影印民國初年刻本。

沈鯉，《亦玉堂稿》，收入《景印文淵閣四庫全書》，第1288冊，臺北：商務印書館，1983。

林月惠，《良知學的轉折：聶雙江與羅念庵思想之研究》，臺北：臺灣大學出版中心，2005。

徐即登，《徐匡岳先生來益堂稿》，中國社會科學院文學研究所藏明萬曆刻本。

徐即登，《周禮說》，收入《四庫全書存目叢書》，經部第82冊，影印浙江圖書館藏明萬曆間刻十二卷本；臺北國家圖書館藏萬曆間刻十四卷本。

徐即登，《儒宗要輯》，臺北：漢學研究中心影印日本尊經閣文庫藏明萬曆刊本。

徐即登等撰，《劍江倡和詩》，江西省圖書館藏萬曆四十六年序刊本。

徐梓，〈「天地君親師」源流考〉，《北京師範大學學報（社會科學版）》，2006：2（北京，2006），頁99-106。

徐開任編，《明名臣言行錄》，收入《明代傳記叢刊》，第54冊，臺北：明文書局，1991影印康熙二十年序刊本。

涂宗濬，《陽和語錄》，江西省圖書館藏明萬曆刻本。

涂宗濬，《隆砂證學記》，臺北：漢學研究中心影印日本內閣文庫藏明萬曆三十二年刊本。

涂宗濬，《續韋齋易義虛裁》，收入《四庫全書存目叢書補編》，第89冊，濟南：齊魯書社，2001影印明萬曆四十二年刻本。

酒井忠夫，《中國善書の研究》，東京：國書刊行會，1977。

高攀龍，《高子遺書》，無錫：1922高汝琳重印光緒二年江蘇書局本。

國立中央圖書館編印，《國立中央圖書館善本序跋集錄‧經部》，臺北：國立中央圖書館，1992。

國立編譯館主編，《新集四書批註群書提要附古今四書總目》，臺北：華泰文化公司，2000。

張亨，〈朱子的志業：建立道統意義之探討〉，《台大中文學報》，5（臺北，1992），頁 31-80。

張伯行，《道南源委》，收入《四庫全書存目叢書》，史部第 125 冊，臺南縣：莊嚴文化公司，1996 影印清康熙四十八年正誼堂刻本。

張伯行，《伊洛淵源續錄》，收入《四庫全書存目叢書》，史部第 125 冊，臺南縣：莊嚴文化公司，1996 影印清康熙五十年正誼堂刻本。

張藝曦，〈明中晚期古本《大學》與《傳習錄》的流傳及影響〉，《漢學研究》，24：1（臺北，2006），頁 235-268。

許孚遠，《大學述支言》、《大學述答問》，俱收入《大學匯函》，臺北：中國子學名著集成編印基金會，1978 影印明萬曆刊本。

陳子龍等選編，《皇明經世文編》，北京：中華書局，1997 影印明崇禎間平露堂刊本。

陳榮捷，〈朱熹集新儒學之大成〉，收入氏著，《朱學論集》，臺北：臺灣學生書局，1982，頁 1-35。

陳榮捷，《朱子門人》，臺北：臺灣學生書局，1982。

陳確，《陳確集》，北京：中華書局，1979。

傅武光編著，《四書總義著述考（一）》，臺北：國立編譯館，2003。

彭國翔，《良知學的展開：王龍溪與中晚明的陽明學》，北京：三聯書店，2005。

程玉瑛，《晚明被遺忘的思想家：羅汝芳（近溪）詩文事蹟編年》，臺北：廣文書局，1995。

馮從吾，《馮少墟集》，收入《中國西北文獻叢書》，第 6 輯，蘭州：蘭州古籍書店，1990 影印康熙十二年序刊本。

黃仁生，《日本現藏稀見元明文集考證與提要》，長沙：嶽麓書社，2004。

黃宗羲，《明儒學案》，收入沈善洪、吳光主編，《黃宗羲全集》，第 7-8 冊，杭州：浙江古籍出版社，2005。

黃進興，〈學術與信仰：論孔廟從祀制與儒家道統意識〉，收入氏著，《優入聖域：權力、信仰與正當性》，臺北：允晨文化公司，1994，頁 217-311。

黃虞稷，瞿鳳起、潘景鄭整理，《千頃堂書目》，上海：上海古籍出版社，2001。

楊正顯，〈白沙學的定位與成立〉，《思想史》，2（臺北，2014），頁 1-51。

萬廷言，《學易齋集》，臺北：漢學研究中心影印日本尊經閣文庫藏明萬曆刊本。

賈德訥（Daniel K. Gardner），〈宋代的思維模式與言說方式：關於「語錄」體的幾點思考〉，收入田浩編，楊立華、吳豔紅等譯，《宋代思想史論》，北京：社會科學文獻出版社，2003，頁394-425。

過庭訓，《本朝分省人物考》，收入《明代傳記叢刊》，臺北：明文書局，1991。

鄒元標，《願學集》，收入《景印文淵閣四庫全書》，第1294冊。

鄒守益著，董平編校整理，《鄒守益集》，南京：鳳凰出版社，2007。

劉子健，〈宋末所謂道統的成立〉，《兩宋史研究彙編》，臺北：聯經出版事業公司，1987，頁249-282。

劉元卿，《劉聘君全集》，收入《四庫全書存目叢書》，集部第154冊，臺南縣：莊嚴文化公司，1997影印清咸豐二年重刻本。

劉勇，〈中晚明時期的講學宗旨、《大學》文本與理學學說建構〉，《中央研究院歷史語言研究所集刊》，80：3（臺北，2009），頁403-450。

劉勇，〈中晚明理學學說的互動與地域性理學傳統的系譜化進程——以「閩學」為中心〉，《新史學》，21：2（2010），頁1-60。

劉勇，〈明儒李遂的講學活動及其與陽明學之關係〉，載中國社會科學院歷史研究所明史研究室編，《明史研究論叢》，9，北京：紫禁城出版社，2011，頁197-213。

劉勇，〈從李材案看晚明清議的形成及其與講學之關係〉，《國立政治大學歷史學報》，32（臺北，2009），頁41-70。

劉勇，〈晚明士人的講學活動與學派建構——以李材（1529-1607）為中心的研究〉，香港中文大學歷史學系博士論文，2008。

劉勇，〈晚明的薦賢、徵聘與士人的出處考慮——以鄧元錫為例〉，《中華文史論叢》，2012：3（總第107期）（上海，2012），頁61-89。

劉勇，〈晚明理學的師承建構與宗旨分歧——以李材與何喬遠的講學交涉為例〉，中國明史學會主辦「第十五屆明史國際學術研討會暨第五屆戚繼光國際學術研討會」（山東蓬萊，2013.8.19）會議論文。

劉勇，〈黃宗羲對泰州學派歷史形象的重構——以《明儒學案·顏鈞傳》的文本檢討為例〉，《漢學研究》，26：1（臺北，2008），頁165-196。

劉斯原，《大學古今本通考》，《四庫全書存目叢書補編》，第92冊，濟南：齊魯書社，2001影印明萬曆間刊本。

蔣士銓，邵海清校，李夢生箋，《忠雅堂集校箋》，上海：上海古籍出版社，1993。

蕭世勇，〈袁黃（1533-1606）的經世理念及其實踐方式〉，國立臺灣師範大學歷史研究所碩士論文，1994。

謝旻、陶成等纂修，乾隆《江西通志》，收入《景印文淵閣四庫全書》，第

515 冊。

羅大紘，《紫原文集》，收入《四庫禁燬書叢刊》，集部第 140 冊，北京：北京出版社，2000 影印明末刻本。

羅汝芳著，方祖猷等點校，《羅汝芳集》，南京：鳳凰出版社，2007。

Hymes, Robert. "Getting the Words Right: Speech, Vernacular Language, and Classical Language in Song Neo-Confucian 'Records of Words'," *Journal of Song-Yuan Studies*（《宋遼金元》), 36(2006), pp.25-55.

Wilson, Thomas A.. *Genealogy of the Way: the Construction and Uses of the Confucian Tradition in Late Imperial China*. Stanford, Calif.: Stanford University Press,1995.

【論著】

明代陽明畫像的流傳及其作用──
兼及清代的發展 *

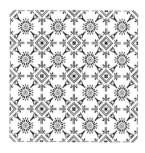

張藝曦

台灣台中人,任職新竹國立交通大學人文社會學系,現居台
北。曾著《孤寂的山城:悠悠百年金瓜石》(2007)、《社
群、家族與陽明學的鄉里實踐:以江西安福、吉水兩縣為
例》(2007)。目前進行的課題是「心學、文學復古與制藝
文社:明末清初江西社集活動」。

---

* 本文寫作期間,承蒙楊儒賓教授慷慨賜贈陽明像圖檔。林勝彩兄幫忙查
對及校訂文稿。兩位匿名審查人給予寶貴意見。謹此致謝。

明代陽明畫像的流傳及其作用——
兼及清代的發展

摘要

　　本文主要處理兩個主題，一是陽明畫像在明代的流行，以及士人對這些畫像的評論，一是人們拜畫像的行為，以及拜畫像所反映的一些現象。由於士人收藏某畫像於齋中，個人或其小群體對畫像予以題詠，或在日常生活間敬祀崇拜，這類個人性的行為常富含特殊意義，所以本文以這類在私人空間中的畫像為主展開討論。時間斷限則集中在心學流行的明中晚期至這清初的這段時間。由於清中期曾有理學的復興，而與畫像對越或崇敬的現象也隨之而興，所以最後一節略及入清以後士人如何看待陽明畫像，以及清中葉的一些變化。

關鍵詞：陽明畫像、孔子像、聖人、王守仁、蔡世新

前言

　　本文主要處理兩個主題，一是陽明（王守仁，1472-1529）畫像在明代的流行，以及士人對這些畫像的評論，一是人們拜畫像的行為，以及拜畫像所反映的一些現象。

　　明中晚期陽明學的流行，講學活動起了很大的作用，但也有其侷限，儘管一些大儒的講學常可吸引數百人甚至數千人的參與，盛況空前，不過人數依然有限。參與講學的人各自回到鄉里及家族後，雖也可以透過在地講學或與人交流而發揮影響力，但陽明學所講究的是對心性的徹悟，這些聽講後的小讀書人所作的二手傳播，畢竟不如大儒親身講授來得有效。也因此，除了講學以外，還須有《傳習錄》等書以助流傳，在陽明學最盛的明中晚期，包括《傳習錄》、古本《大學》，以及大儒語錄或文集的刊刻與流通，使得一些沒有機會親聆大儒謦欬的士人，仍可披覽這類書籍而接觸其學。[1]相對於此，較少人注意到塑畫像作為聖人形象具體化，以及有強化人們對學術認同與歸屬的作用。理學家因對成聖的追求，致力符合聖人形象，使其塑畫像被賦予特別意義，人們不僅在書院或講會中掛立其像，即使在私人的空間中，也有人敬拜理學家畫像，其中以陽明畫像最常見。講學活動的舉行、《傳習錄》等書的流通，加上塑畫像（尤其是陽明畫像），可說是陽明學的三寶。

　　塑畫像的傳統由來已久，如聖賢圖像、孔子聖跡圖都廣為人知，[2]兩宋以來的程朱學者也有塑畫像，如弘治、正德年間的畫家郭詡

1　張藝曦，〈明中晚期古本《大學》與《傳習錄》的流傳及影響〉，《漢學研究》，24：1（臺北，2006），頁235-268。

2　目前的《聖跡圖》最早的版本是正統九年的刊本，見鄭振鐸，〈「聖跡

（1456-1532），便曾受江西豐城程朱學者楊廉（1452-1525）之託，作孔子及二程、朱熹（1130-1200）一聖三賢共四幅像，[3]其中〈文公先生像〉至今仍存。[4]郭詡所擅長不在人物畫像的寫眞，所以他所作的人物形象是比較模糊而不精確的，如他也作周濂溪像以示王守仁，但王守仁所贈詩卻說——「郭生揮寫最超群，夢想形容恐未眞」。[5]但此幅〈文公先生像〉，人物特徵十分明顯，應有所本。國立故宮博物院典藏之宋朱熹〈尺牘〉冊前副頁有「宋徽國朱文公遺像」（圖一），作者不詳，或與郭詡同時代人之作，兩幅畫像頗相似，顯示當時應流行某樣式的朱熹像畫法。

　　所以明中晚期爲陽明學者作像並非創舉罕例。陽明像跟一般聖賢像或理學家像間的差異所在，不在像的畫法或作法有何特殊處，而在於學術本身。陽明學較諸其他時代的儒學，應是精英色彩最淡，最接近基層社會的一支，由於更多觸及基層士人、布衣或庶民百姓，使陽明像發揮更大的作用，甚至帶有宗教化的色彩，例如有人敬祀崇拜陽明畫像，也有因扶乩見王守仁而作像的例子。（後詳）一如《傳習錄》之前雖已有《近思錄》，而《傳習錄》的作用更大且廣；兩宋程朱學者雖有講學活動，但跟陽明學者的講學相比，效果不可同日而語；同樣的，陽明像也因時代及學術性質，而跟過往的聖賢圖像或理學家像

圖」跋〉，收錄於《中國古代版畫叢刊》1（上海：上海古籍出版社，1988），頁 390-392。

3　楊廉，《楊文恪公文集》，收入《續修四庫全書》第 1332 冊（上海：上海古籍出版社，1995），卷26，〈送清狂山人歸泰和序〉，頁8。

4　此幅畫像經過幾次拍賣，所以未能確定其收藏地，請見（明）郭詡，〈文公先生像軸〉，《傳統文化博客資料庫》，http://www.bjdips.com/gwh/result.aspx?ID=GWH-27449（2015/09/08）。

5　王守仁撰，吳光等校，《王陽明全集》（上海：上海古籍出版社，1992），卷14，〈題郭詡濂溪圖〉，1066-1067。

發揮不同的意義。

儒學士人的塑畫像常置於孔廟、學宮等公共空間中供人崇祀，人們可藉敬拜塑畫像宣示其學術依歸，這在私人興建的書院尤其明顯，宋明兩代，程朱學或陽明學門人陸續在各地興建書院，而書院所崇祀的塑畫像，多可具體反映其學術宗主所在，如浙江天眞書院崇祀王守仁，但程朱學者所興建如晚明東林書院，崇祀名單中便無任何跟陽明心學相關的人。[6]

圖一：無款，宋徽國朱文公遺像，國立故宮博物院藏。

塑畫像可讓人直接想像其聖賢形象，效果較諸書籍文字更爲直接，而置於公共空間，接觸的人多，作用也大，但除非是像王艮（1483-1541）留下遊孔廟而有感發的記錄（王艮所見是木主而不是

6　東林書院所崇祀的是木主而非塑畫像，但反映學術宗主的作用是類似的，見斐大中等修，秦緗業等纂，（光緒）《無錫金匱縣志》，收入《中國方志叢書・華中地方・江蘇省》第21號（臺北：成文出版社，1970），卷6，頁16。及至今日，外雙溪錢穆故居仍可見朱熹的塑像，錢先生著作等身，既有《朱子新學案》，也有心學方面的論著，又有《中國近三百年學術史》，但據其書案所置的朱子像，便可知其學術歸屬所在。

像），[7]否則充其量只能統計各地書院的塑畫像的數目多寡。加上這類塑畫像還涉及許多複雜的政治因素，包括禮制（如大禮議中改像爲木主）、祠祀禮儀、官方權力的干涉或滲透，以及地方輿論或期待等，使我們很難確定塑畫像的影響大小。因此本文雖未忽略公共空間的像，但不以此爲主進行討論。此外，書籍上也常見畫像附隨在文集卷首，或是如歷代聖賢畫像之類的版刻畫像，藉由摹寫或刊刻而大量流通，儘管也有人對此類畫像帶有崇敬之情的記載，[8]但直接相關的資料很少，所以本文未把版刻書籍的像列入討論中。

　　相對於此，士人收藏某畫像於齋中，個人或其小群體對畫像予以題詠，或在日常生活間敬祀崇拜，這類個人性的行爲則富含特殊意義，所以本文便以這類在私人空間中的畫像爲主展開討論。時間斷限集中在心學流行的明中晚期至清初的這段時間。由於清中期有理學的復興，而與畫像對越或崇敬的現象也隨之而興，所以最後一節略及入清以後士人如何看待陽明畫像，以及清中葉的一些變化。

　　本文使用的三個詞，稍有區別：理學家包含程朱陸王廣義的理學各學派士人；明中晚期心學家主要指江門心學與陽明心學士人；陽明學者則專指陽明心學的士人。

一、日常生活中的塑畫像

　　畫像的分類存在多種標準，有的按描繪對象而分，如聖賢像；有

7　王元鼎輯，《年譜》，收入《王心齋先生全集》（臺北：廣文書局，1979），卷1，頁2，「丁卯武宗正德二年二十五歲」條。

8　如吳訥在補注熊節（1199年進士）的《性理群書》時，便將原編的宋儒畫像的部份刪除不載，因其認爲把聖賢畫有如真人臨在，而人與其宴處一室，並不適宜。

的按情節內容而分，如雅集圖；有的按表現形式分爲頭像、半身像、整身像、單人像、群像等。單國強把畫像分作幾類：歷史人物像、帝王像、官僚縉紳像、文人名士像、庶民像、女性像、畫家自畫像，[9]若加上塑像，種類可能更多，難以在一篇文章中全部涉及。本文主題是心學家的像，所以此處談人們在日常生活中較容易接觸到的、跟儒學士人有關的地方先賢像及孔子像。

地方先賢像常見於當地的鄉賢祠或先賢的專祠等，一般是爲當地的知名人物作的塑畫像，以供地方士民百姓瞻仰崇祀，如江西永新陽明學者劉朝璽去世後百姓爭相肖像祭祀：

> 劉朝璽，（永新）炎村石泉里人，世爲禾川仕族。……公且爲德于鄉，如議南兌半折，及社倉諸事，沒，使里人爭肖像祀公。[10]

也有個別士人收藏先賢像，如江西泰和王思（1481-1524），他是明初大學士王直（1379-1462）的曾孫，仰慕吉安當地先賢文天祥（1236-1283），所以不僅訪求文天祥遺像，而且在求得遺像後，出入奉像偕行。[11]

孔子像多藏於孔廟或地方學校，如北宋李公麟（1049-1106）的《宣聖及七十二賢贊》，儘管原作已失傳，但宋高宗按此圖及贊語刻

9　單國強，〈肖像畫類型芻議〉，《故宮博物院院刊》，1990年4期（北京，1990），頁11-23。

10　鄒元標，《鄒子存眞集》（國家圖書館藏內閣文庫影印明天啓二年序刊本），卷7，〈大中大夫雲南參政致仕前兵科給事中侍經筵官念南劉公銘〉，頁82-84。

11　鄒守益，《東廓鄒先生文集》，收入《四庫全書存目叢書》集部第65冊（臺南：莊嚴文化事業公司，1997），卷1，〈改齋文集序〉，頁47-48。

成石碑，立於杭州太學旁，至今仍保存在杭州的孔廟中。[12] 在理學流行的年代，書院講學或講會舉行前，常有拜孔子像的儀式，如王守仁的大弟子鄒守益（1491-1562）在祁門的講會，會約便規定拜孔子像：

> 復定邑中之會，春秋在範山書屋，夏冬在全交館，相與拜
> 聖像，宣聖諭，勸善規過，以篤實輝光，共明斯學。[13]

聖像即孔子像。清初謝文洊（1615-1681）講學時亦然，他把孔子畫像懸諸堂前率弟子參拜，而在無孔子像時，則書孔子名於紙幀上以代替，據載：

> （康熙元年）夏五月，張令（按：南豐縣令張黼鑑）歸，
> 奉家傳元人所繪孔聖像，拜納程山曰：「此像唯先生得拜
> 之，黼鑑不敢私也。」先生拜受，懸諸尊洛堂前，設紙
> 帳，朔望及會講日，率弟子啓帳焚香四拜，乃登講席。先
> 是亦拜書紙幀耳。[14]

南豐知縣張黼鑑贈像的理由是：「此像唯先生得拜之」，顯示像還跟學術宗主或道統有關。（後詳）此像在謝文洊臨終前傳予門人曾日都，後懸於程山學舍。[15] 張黼鑑所贈像來自家傳，可知孔子像除了置於公共空間，也在人手間流傳，如艾南英（1583-1646）家亦世藏孔子畫像。[16]

12　趙榆，〈孫悅漢及其收藏的宣聖及七十二賢贊圖卷〉，《收藏家》，2002
　　年1期（北京，2002），頁49-51。

13　鄒守益，《東廓鄒先生文集》，卷7，〈書祁門同志會約〉，頁21。

14　謝鳴謙輯，《程山謝明學先生年譜》，附於謝文洊，《謝程山集》，收入
　　《四庫全書存目叢書》集部第209冊，「康熙元年條」，頁12。

15　包發鷺修，趙惟仁等纂，《民國南豐縣志》，收入《中國地方志集成‧江
　　西府縣志輯》58（南京：江蘇古籍出版社，1996），卷3，〈古蹟〉，頁40。

16　艾南英，《天傭子集》，收入《四庫禁燬書叢刊補編》第72冊（北京：北

　　最常見的父母或祖先的塑畫像，有的擺在家族祠堂供族人敬拜，有的則在家中神龕供奉。前者如明初靖難之變死節的廬陵曾鳳韶（1374-1402）、曾子禎二人，在嘉靖年間政治忌諱漸淡後，曾氏子弟以士紳曾孔化為代表，積極尋訪二人畫像，據說所訪得兩幅畫像凜凜猶生，曾孔化一見之下，馬上哭拜在地，並提請地方官員創建二忠祠以祭拜之。[17]後者如有人把父母畫像編作一冊，隨身攜帶；程朱學者尹襄（1484-1526）的朋友柯信便有一本永感冊，冊中有其父母遺像，柯信出入攜以自隨，「庶幾吾親之在目而不敢忘」。[18]此外，民間常常流行一類故事，即孝子追思早逝的父母，而繪出父母畫像，又或者是人子未能得見父或母，但因夢而知其父或母之面貌形象，所繪畫像維妙維肖。如三吳陸氏的例子：

> 陸翁起三吳世家，少以博學雄文蜚英庠校，居常痛父蚤世，追思不已，至援筆繪像，儼若生存，人以為孝誠所感。[19]

這類故事往往因敘述簡略而頗富戲劇化。涂伯昌（？-1650）的〈孤子夢記〉則詳載其曲折的過程，因頗有趣，節錄於下：

> 有幼失父者，夜夢其親，旦走告耆老曰：「夜夢吾父，吾父鬚眉若是，衣冠若是。」曰：「是非汝父也，汝父鬚眉若是，衣冠若是。」歸而假寐，復夢其親，與耆老之言無

京出版社，2005），卷10，〈家藏孔夫子像贊幷序〉，頁1-2。

17　王慎中，《玩芳堂摘稿》，收入《四庫全書存目叢書》集部第88冊，卷2，〈曾氏二忠祠記〉，頁9-10。

18　尹襄，《巽峰集》，收入《四庫全書存目叢書》集部第67冊，卷9，〈永感冊序〉，頁12。

19　曾同亨，《泉湖山房稿》（國家圖書館藏內閣文庫影印明刊本），卷20，〈封都察院右僉都御史南溪陸公偕配陳恭人合葬墓表〉，頁23。

異。告耆老曰：「吾昨又夢吾父，與耆老言同。非耆老
言，吾幾不識父也。」耆老曰：「予言試汝也。汝前所夢
者真也，汝後所夢者夢也。汝前所夢無因也，汝後所夢因
吾也。」失父者涕泗交顧，皇皇不敢自信。……聞鄉之
人，有畫父像者，展拜而形神俱爽，恍然見父也。氣稍
定，神稍清，熟視之，先所夢者真也，後所夢者夢也。由
是數夢其親，與先之夢無異。[20]

　　記中指出，孤子幼失其父，夢其親而走告當地耆老，形容夢中所
見父親面貌與穿著，但耆老不僅故意否定，還另作一番形容，孤子受
耆老的言語暗示，於是復夢其父，跟耆老所形容一致。待知耆老誑己
後，孤子皇皇不能自信，所幸有人曾畫其父像，孤子見此像後，才終
於肯定最初所夢的父親形象無誤。[21]

　　無論是學校、書院、鄉賢祠或父母祖宗的塑像畫，儒學士人都曾
爭議是否應設像，及細節到「像」是否像或不像的問題。塑畫像流行
於日常生活之中，相關討論自然不少，加上有時又涉及政治事件（如
大禮議）而更形複雜，因此不應以二分法簡單區別贊成或反對設像兩
邊。但程頤（1033-1107）反對設像的言論對時人及後世頗具影響

20　涂伯昌，《涂子一杯水》，收入《四庫全書存目叢書》集部第193冊，卷
　　4，〈孤子夢記〉，頁54。
21　人子常會持這類父祖畫像請人題像贊。湯來賀曾爲王仲鳴作像贊，題
　　曰：「聞君夙昔，孝友和平。覯茲遺像，儼兮若生。子姓拜瞻，翼翼兢
　　兢。致愨則著，視于無形。惟述追乎厥德，斯丕振乎家聲。」見湯來
　　賀，《內省齋文集》，收入《四庫全書存目叢書》集部第199冊，卷28，
　　〈王仲鳴像贊〉，頁11。著眼在子孫睹父祖遺像，不僅瞻拜，還能追惟
　　德，丕振家聲。在此像贊末，謝文洊作評曰：「爲人子孫題祖父像贊，
　　當以此種爲式。」

力，應可代表當時的主流意見。據載程頤在跟學生討論祭禮時，強調禮以義起，所以富豪及士人願行祭禮者，可置影堂以祭，但不可用畫像，他的理由是：

> 若用影祭，須無一毫差可方，若多一莖鬚，便是他人。[22]

儘管程頤未必禁絕塑畫像，但對塑畫像能否代表父母持保留的態度。相對於此，明中晚期不少陽明學者常把重點放在人子的孝心，畫像作為孝心具體投射的對象，如鄒德涵（1538-1581）說：「思親者肖其像而祀之，非祀夫像也，因像以志思耳矣。」[23]雖然沒有直接反對程頤之說，但所強調點已有不同。

　　上述的像，包括塑像、木像，以及畫像。塑像多半不常移動而固定在公共空間，而木像與畫像則可隨身攜帶，或置於私人處所。所以以下的討論將偏重在畫像與木像，尤其是以流傳最廣的陽明畫像為主進行討論。

二、理學家的聖人形象

　　士人文集或筆記資料中不乏關於個人畫像的記載，相關記載的數量與頻率隨著時代越後而增加，這應跟明中晚期常見士人與畫家交遊的現象有關，其中不乏理學之士與知名畫家往來的例子。如郭詡為林

22　程顥、程頤撰，潘富恩導讀，《二程遺書》（上海：上海古籍出版社，2000），卷22上，〈伊川雜錄〉，頁341。明初宋濂也沿襲此說，表示——「人為物靈，其變態千萬，一毫不類，則他人矣。」宋濂，《宋學士文集》（臺北：臺灣商務印書館，1965，《萬有文庫》本），卷37，〈贈傳神陳德顏序〉，頁644。

23　鄒德溥，《鄒泗山先生文集》（傅斯年圖書館藏安成紹恩堂刊本清刊本），卷2，〈畏聖錄序〉，頁7。

俊（1452-1527）畫像，林俊許爲妙品，便推薦給邵寶（1460-1527）
爲其作像。[24]隨著肖像畫的技法持續有創新，到十七世紀即晚明左
右，畫家對面部的描繪有突破性的發展，如活躍於南京、江南一帶的
曾鯨（1568-1650），他透過「渲染數十層」「必分凹凸」的技法，使
所描繪的人物面容更自然，所以許多人都委託他畫像，[25]於是類似與
畫家交遊的例子更不少見。

　　理學家的塑畫像除了像與不像以外，還有道德理想的體現這層含
義，簡言之即聖人形象。作聖是理學家修身的目標，也是其理想人格
的完成，理學家對此事的關懷最深。兩宋程朱學與陽明心學各有其聖
人觀，兩者雖承認聖人可爲，但對成聖的標準卻有不同。兩宋程朱學
的聖人觀的精英色彩較濃，在朱熹的口中筆下，聖人常被描寫成至高
至善、難以企及的境界，一般人必須終其一生追求才有達成目標的可

24　數年後郭詡將成品寄予邵寶，邵寶雖覺不類己貌，然因頗似有道者之
　　容，於是仍寶而藏之且作詩贊。見邵寶，《容春堂集》續集，收入《文
　　淵閣四庫全書》第1258冊（臺北：臺灣商務印書館，1983），卷8，〈贊
　　郭詡所寫小像〉，頁23：「見素先生嘗稱泰和郭詡寫照入妙品，予慕之，
　　未見也，一日見於南昌東湖之上，予揖之數語而退。予去江西之八年，
　　諸生思予，乃屬仁弘想像而筆焉，寄予京師，見者皆曰不類，予愛其有
　　有道之容，未忍棄也，贊而藏之：諸生予懷，郭史予寫，貌豈予如，如
　　古儒者，敬共朝夕，維予夙心，畫哉畫哉，以爲予箴。」
25　鄧麗華，〈從曾鯨肖像畫看晚明文人個人形象的建立〉（臺北：國立臺灣
　　師範大學碩士論文，1991）。曾鯨似曾根據陽明門人的描述而作「陽明
　　先生肖像」，見錢明，《王陽明及其學派論考》（北京：人民出版社，
　　2009），第9章，〈陽明之遺像——形象考〉，頁175。除了這些著名畫像
　　以外，還有大量默默無聞的肖像畫家與民間畫工，他們往往數代畫像寫
　　影，技法純熟，民間人家流傳的祖先畫像幾乎都是出自他們之手。這些
　　民間畫工常用「傳神小稿」，作爲爲人家的子孫追摹祖先或父母畫像
　　時，供其選擇近似形貌用的樣譜，見華人德，〈明清肖像畫略論〉，《藝
　　術家》，218期（臺北，1993），頁236-245。

能，加上兩宋程朱學的格物窮理之說，必須窮盡天下之物之理才能一旦豁然貫通，更增作聖的難度，強化了聖人可望不可即的形象，因此兩宋程朱學者並不輕易許人爲聖。

對程朱學的成聖標準，自陳獻章（1428-1500）已有異議，王守仁則有「滿街人都是聖人」[26]之說，很簡捷直接的表達聖人易爲的觀點，上自賢人君子，下至愚夫愚婦，只須致其良知，便能作聖。尤其是成色分兩說，把原本高高在上的聖人形象，以堯、舜、周、孔這些遠古聖王跟一般的庶民百姓同等並列。即使堯舜周孔也只是致其良知，今人只須致其良知亦能作聖。

聖人易爲說有其時代背景脈絡。陳獻章生前已被尊爲「活孟子」，與亞聖孟子相提並論，[27]顯示程朱學的聖人難爲說已有鬆動的跡象。隨著陽明心學的流行，聖人可爲易爲之說更加普及，如劉元卿（1544-1609）的族人劉本振僅是一般庶民，在復禮書院聽劉元卿說聖人可爲，了解自己也可當聖人，遂踴躍而起，從此折節力學。[28]在此聖人易爲的風氣下，甚至有人自許爲聖，萬曆年間流傳的一則笑話生動的描寫了這股流風：一名狂生先許堯、舜、文王、孔子爲聖人，但待數到孟子，卻遲疑良久不願屈第五指，以爲孟子英氣太露，不免讓人懷疑未能優入聖域，於是——「旁有人拱立曰：宇宙間第五位聖

26　王守仁，《傳習錄》，《王文成公全書》（臺北：臺灣商務印書館，1968，《國學基本叢書》本），第18冊，卷3，〈語錄三・傳習錄下〉，頁26：「王汝止出遊歸，先生問曰，遊何見，對曰，見滿街人都是聖人，先生曰，你看滿街人是聖人，滿街人倒看你是聖人。」

27　胡直，《衡廬精舍藏稿》，收入《文淵閣四庫全書》第1287冊，卷10，〈刻白沙先生文集序〉，頁2。

28　劉孔當撰，劉以城編，《劉喜聞先生集》（東京：高橋情報，1993），卷4，〈石鱗公傳〉，頁20。

人，莫非公乎？遂下第五指，口不敢」。[29]

　　儘管有上述荒誕的故事，顯示當時人不再把聖人視為可為卻難及的境界，但我們仍可推想到，實際上應有許多人仍不自信己能成聖，也因此鄒守益的孫子鄒德涵（1571年進士）在年輕聲名未起時，在復古書院講學中，便因對聖人的見解而引起轟動，據其弟鄒德溥（1583進士）說：

　　　　伯兄起後進行，直任以聖人為必可學，則眾闃目為狂生。[30]

聖人可為是整個宋明理學最基本的概念，參與講學的又都是對理學有興趣的士人，竟因鄒德涵說聖人可為即目為狂生，頗不合理。推測「直任」二字，應即鄒德涵以己可成聖之意。從旁觀眾人目鄒德涵為狂生的反應看，顯示即使在萬曆年間陽明心學流行的高峰時，仍有不少人對自己能否成聖頗為猶豫。這也正可說明一個看似矛盾但又可兩存的現象：人們一方面相信聖人不僅可為而且易為，一方面又尊崇少數儒學士人尤其是心學家，視之為聖人或類似聖人的形象。

　　也因此，在王守仁生前與死後，門下弟子已有尊其為聖的意味，許多陽明學者反覆向世人宣稱，陽明學確是聖學無疑，[31]他們不把陽明學放到宋元以來的理學脈絡來理解，而是以王守仁承接孔聖嫡傳，與孔門弟子顏、曾等人並列，[32]他們雖未明言王守仁是聖人，但其實

29　劉元卿，《劉聘君全集》，收入《四庫全書存目叢書》集部第154冊，卷12，〈第五位聖人〉，頁78。

30　鄒德溥，〈伯兄汝海行狀〉，在鄒德涵，《鄒聚所先生外集》，收入《四庫全書存目叢書》集部第157冊，頁94。

31　黃宗羲撰，沈芝盈點校，《明儒學案》（臺北：里仁書局，1987），〈師說‧鄒守益東廓〉，頁8；卷13，〈浙中王門學案三‧黃久菴先生綰〉，頁280；卷18，〈江右王門學案三‧文恭羅念菴先生洪先〉，頁390、418。

32　呂妙芬，〈顏子之傳：一個為陽明學爭取正統的聲音〉，《漢學研究》，

已相去不遠。如羅大紘（1586年進士）稱王守仁爲百世之師，[33]耿定向（1524-1596）則是仿《史記》〈孔子世家〉的體例而作〈新建侯文成王先生世家〉，把王守仁與孔子、王門與孔門都等量齊觀了。[34]

　　不少陽明後學也被形容爲聖人或類似聖人，如浙江紹興府的范瓘被百姓稱作「范聖人」。[35]如江右陽明學者，他們一方面透過舉行各式講學活動的舉行，向當地士民百姓傳講學術，一方面投身於社會福利事業，爲地方興利除弊，而被當地士民百姓視爲接近聖人般的人物，鄒守益即是顯例，[36]而在劉元卿死後，門人弟子爲建「近聖館」以祭

　　15：1（臺北，1997），頁73-92。在陽明學者所編纂的地方志上，往往可見他們自許超越宋元諸儒而直接承接聖學嫡傳。如萬曆年間王時槐、劉元卿與羅大紘所主編的《吉安府志》，〈理學傳〉便只列陽明學者，而宋元明初的其他理學家則被歸入〈儒學傳〉中。相關研究見張藝曦，〈吉安府價值觀的轉變——以兩本府志爲中心的分析〉，在氏著，《社群、家族與王學的鄉里實踐》（臺北：國立臺灣大學出版委員會，2006），〈附錄二〉，頁403-432。

33　羅大紘，《紫原文集》，收入《四庫禁燬書叢刊》集部第139冊（北京：北京出版社，2000），卷6，〈東撫臺王公〉，頁30。

34　耿定向，《耿天臺先生文集》，收入《四庫全書存目叢書》集部第131冊，卷13，〈新建侯文成王先生世家〉，頁18-49。《四庫全書總目》已指出此點：「（耿）定向之學，歸宿在王守仁。故集中第十三卷以薛瑄諸人爲列傳，而以守仁爲世家。此蓋陰用《史記·孔子世家》之例，不但以守仁封新建伯也。」見永瑢、紀昀等撰，《四庫全書總目》（北京：中華書局，1965），卷178，總頁1601。

35　「（范瓘）少從新建學，卓然以古聖賢自期，晚歲所造益深，……平居無戲言，步趨不越尺寸，里中人無老幼，皆以范聖人呼之。……有司屢表其閭，立石里中，曰：范處士里。」見蕭良幹等修，張元忭等纂，（萬曆）《紹興府志》，收入《中國方志叢書·華中地方·浙江省》第520號（臺北：成文出版社，1983），卷43，〈鄉賢〉，頁32-33。

36　宋儀望，《華陽館文集》，收入《四庫全書存目叢書》集部第116冊，卷11，〈明故中順大夫南京國子監祭酒前太常少卿兼翰林院侍讀學士追贈禮部侍郎諡文莊鄒東廓先生行狀〉，頁24。

祀，推崇之情之高不言可喻。對當地士民而言，鄒守益、劉元卿幾乎
就是當世聖人。

三、明中晚期陽明畫像的製作與流傳

正是在前述脈絡下，陽明像不只是一般的人物像，還有其特殊意
義，因此門人弟子後學除了在公共空間立塑畫像，也製作許多陽明畫
像，這些畫像流傳於人手之間，甚至被當作日常敬拜的對象。因此本
節的討論除了公共空間的像以外，主要以陽明畫像的製作及流傳為
主。由於陽明心學發展之初，江門心學亦與其抗衡，雖迅速中衰，[37]
而聲勢不如陽明心學，但仍有其影響力，所以也兼論江門心學學者的
像。

公共空間的陽明塑畫像常被置於門人弟子所建的書院及舉行講會
處，以王畿（1498-1583）在天眞書院所塑像最著名：

　　（王畿）服心喪三年，建天眞書院于省，肖文成像其中，
　　且以館四方來學者，歲舉春秋仲丁之祭，無問及門私淑，
　　胥以期集，祭畢，分席講堂，呈所見于公取正焉。心喪
　　畢，壬辰始赴廷對。[38]

關於天眞書院的資料不少，我們很容易從其他資料得知此處是塑像而
非畫像。天眞書院是浙江陽明學的重鎮之一，所以許多人會前往此地
講學並拜謁遺像。又如浙東周汝登（1547-1629）則是與友人結會，

37　潘振泰，〈明代江門心學的崛起與式微〉，《新史學》，7：2（臺北，
　　1996），頁1-46。
38　過庭訓，《本朝分省人物考》，收入《續修四庫全書》第534冊，卷51，
　　〈浙江紹興府三〉，〈王畿〉，頁23。

祭告於當地奉祀王守仁的祠廟，此祠廟中便有陽明像：

> 己亥季秋，先生（按：周汝登）同石匱陶公及郡友數十
> 人，共祭告陽明之祠，定為月會之期。[39]

　　也有崇奉木主的例子，[40]如河南尤時熙（1503-1580），屬於北方
王門學派，他早年因讀《傳習錄》而有悟，於是崇奉王守仁神主於書
齋中，士人來學時都須隨其展謁神主：

> 大指率祖文成，而得於體驗者為多。蓋自一見《傳習
> 錄》，寢讀寢入，寢入寢透，齋中設文成位，晨起必焚香
> 拜，來學者，必令展謁，其尊信若此。[41]

此間書齋應跟書屋的性質類似，既是私人讀書處，也是公開講學的場
所。據此引文亦可附見《傳習錄》對當時人的影響。

　　根據錢明考察，目前現存於國內外的陽明畫像、木雕像及銅像，
估計有40種以上。按時代與國別分，則可分為明清遺存塑畫像、日
韓所藏像，及近人塑像三類。遺像的種類有燕居像、朝服像、封爵
像、布衣像及戎裝像。[42]錢明在文中所舉的明清遺存塑畫像，以目前

39　周汝登，《東越證學錄》，收入《四庫全書存目叢書》集部第165冊，卷
　　4，〈越中會語〉，頁5-6。

40　當時拜神主者不乏其人，如東臺縣的吳愛、繆好信，也因慕王艮其人其
　　學，也在家中奉祀其木主。見周右修，蔡復午等纂，（嘉慶）《東臺縣
　　志》，收入《中國地方志集成・江蘇府縣志輯》60（南京：鳳凰出版社，
　　2008），卷24，〈儒林〉，頁6-7。這條資料參考自呂妙芬，〈明清儒學關
　　於個體不朽、死後想像、祭祀原理之論述〉，發表於中央研究院主辦
　　「第四屆國際漢學會議」（臺北，2012），頁22。

41　張元忭，〈河南西川尤先生墓誌銘〉，在尤時熙，《擬學小記》，收入
　　《四庫全書存目叢書》子部第9冊，附錄卷上，頁30。

42　錢明，《王陽明及其學派論考》，第9章，〈陽明之遺像——形象考〉，頁
　　152-189。

現存的為主，多半是塑像、石刻畫像，或是附見於族譜或文集卷首的畫像，明代單幅畫像仍存的不多，所以下文除了幾幅畫像的分析以外，也將輔以文字記錄的內容展開討論。

陽明畫像流傳雖多且廣，但著名畫師則數蔡世新一人。王守仁生前曾找許多畫師為其作像，但因相貌特殊，所以始終沒有能夠讓王守仁點頭的作品，直到王守仁擔任南贛巡撫期間，有人介紹蔡世新給他，蔡當時只是一位無多大聲名的年輕畫師，卻畫出了讓王守仁滿意的像，據載：

> 王文成鎮虔，日以寫貌進者閱數十人，咸不稱意。蓋文成
> 骨法稜峭，畫者皆正而寫之，顴鼻之間最難肖似。世新幼
> 年隨其師進，乃從傍作一側相，立得其真。文成大喜，延
> 之幕府，名以是起。[43]

蔡世新一畫成名。蔡世新所作的陽明畫像不少，在王守仁卒後，門人周汝員（1493-1558）在越中所建的新建伯祠，所用的就是蔡世新版本的像。[44]另據吳慶坻（1848-1924）所述，有一幅王守仁的燕居授書小像是蔡世新所作，小像上有葛曉的跋，跋語說：

> 先生像為蔡世新所傳者極多，惟以多故，隨手輒肖，然至
> 小者亦徑尺。[45]

43　朱謀垔，《畫史會要》，收入《文淵閣四庫全書》第816冊，卷4，頁58。
44　王守仁，《王文成公全書》，卷35，〈附錄四·年譜附錄一〉，「嘉靖十六
　　年丁酉十月門人周汝員建新建伯祠于越」條，頁48：「師沒後，同門相
　　繼來居，依依不忍去。是年汝員與知府湯紹恩拓地建祠于樓前，取南康
　　蔡世新師像，每年春秋二仲月，郡守率有司主行時祀。」此祠應即前
　　述萬曆年間周汝登及其友人共祭告的陽明祠。
45　吳慶坻撰，張文其、劉德麟點校，《蕉廊脞錄》（北京：中華書局，
　　1990），卷7，〈王守仁燕居授書小像〉，頁200-202。

圖二局部

　　葛曉是浙江上虞人，應是晚明曾過手此畫
的收藏家，且與陶望齡（1562-？）有過
往來，[46]其言應可信。

　　蔡世新所繪的陽明像究竟形象若何
呢？目前所存有兩件歸於其名下的作品：
一為上海博物館所藏的白描〈陽明先生小
像〉（圖二），作四分之三側面像，畫中陽
明先生束髮無帽，盤坐在大方巾上，右手
持書靠於腿上，此書似為身側兩函疊置書

46　在陶望齡的《歇菴集》中有與葛曉往來的
　　書信，見陶望齡，《歇菴集》，收入《續
　　修四庫全書》第 1365 冊，〈答葛雲岳〉，
　　卷 12，頁 30。

圖二：傳蔡世新，陽明先生
小像，上海博物館藏。

冊的第一本，腰間所繫繩帶，其尾端結成兩穗，自衣襬間露出。描繪
人物臉部的線條、衣褶與臂肘的呼應關係等處可見並非眞正一流畫家
的手筆，正反應著記載中蔡世新原本並非有名畫家的實況。其用筆尙
屬敬謹，且對人物眼眶上部的輪廓、繩帶於衣袍中的壓疊轉折、書函
中書冊的空缺等細節多有著墨，並非僅憑人物畫一般格套完成的畫
作，或許眞爲蔡世新當日所見陽明先生燕居時的景象。畫幅雖未署
款，但有「蔡世新印」、「少塈父」、「寫以自藏」三方印，應爲傳世
最可靠的蔡世新陽明像。「寫以自藏」印亦頗有趣，似乎代表了此畫
爲蔡世新私藏版本。畫幅玉池有清人許康衢題跋，應亦見此印文，故
稱「蔡少塈氏，虔南畫史，能詩。嘗與陽明先生遊，時相唱和。此幀
爲王文成公寫貌以自珍。古人交誼之深，於此可見。」畫幅左下端另
有「後裔王壽祁敬藏」的題識，可見此畫於蔡世新之後，亦曾爲王陽
明後裔所藏。另一件是《王陽明法書集》所錄，據載藏於中國歷史博
物館（今改名中國國家博物館），爲正面設色本〈王陽明畫像〉（圖
三），據說也是蔡世新所繪，此作人物面容亦有許多細節，例如上唇
上方鬍鬚共分四段，鬚髮亦較豐盛，或許爲王陽明較年輕時之相貌。
惜尙未得見較清楚之圖像，究竟是否眞蹟，尙難考訂。但似乎兩者皆
爲當時普遍獲得接受的王陽明形象。

　　與白描側面像類似的作品較多，也許正如《畫史會要》所記，是
本自蔡世新得到王陽明認可的側面像之作。如上海博物館另藏的一本
佚名〈大儒王陽明先生像〉（圖四），或是普林斯頓大學所藏的佚名
〈王陽明像〉（圖五）、藏處不明的〈天泉坐月圖〉，[47]特別是鄒守益等

47　圖見（傳）曾鯨〈天泉坐月圖〉，Poly Auction 2010/01/23，拍品674號。
　　該作與普林斯頓大學所藏〈王陽明像〉雖背景及家具有異，但陽明先生
　　形象相似，皆著高冠端坐案前，或舉筆欲書，或持卷審閱，或許曾爲陽

圖三：無款，王陽明畫像，中國國家
博物館藏。

圖四局部

圖四：無款，大儒王陽明先生像，上海
博物館藏。

圖五：無款，王陽明像，Princeton University
Art Museum藏。

人編纂的《王陽明先生圖譜》[48]中大
部分的亦均爲此類側面像。作爲王守
仁幾大弟子之一的鄒守益，採用的應
是王陽明認同的圖像。因此，此圖譜
雖是較簡略的刊本，但對於我們了解
陽明學興盛時期流行的王守仁形象，
有極大的助益。《王陽明先生圖譜》
中亦有少部分使用如設色本般的全正

圖五局部

明畫像的一種方便「應用」的模式。如後文提及之蔡懋德之子摹寫的
「侍親問道圖」，亦不無可能以此模式繪製。曾鯨很可能亦描繪過陽明
像，傳稱作品筆者已知兩例，除上述〈天泉坐月圖〉，拍賣另有標爲崇
禎三年（1630）曾鯨款的高冠側面半身像。

48　鄒守益的《王陽明先生圖譜》分別收錄在《北京圖書館藏珍本年譜叢
　　刊》第43冊（北京：北京圖書館出版社，1998），及《四庫未收書輯刊》
　　第四輯第17冊（北京：北京出版社，1997）。

面形象。因此應可推測當時此類正面像亦有獲得弟子認同的版本,或者亦如現存題名所示,亦出自蔡世新之手。

《王陽明先生圖譜》展現了門人弟子頗執著於上述兩種圖像類型。圖譜中自其22歲開始的王守仁面目便與晚年形貌無甚差異(圖六、七)——除了面容消瘦、顴骨突出外,嘴唇上下以及兩頰下緣均蓄鬚。受託爲此圖譜繪製其一生行誼圖像的畫家,無論是否是蔡世新,應都被要求不可妄自想像王守仁的容貌,因此可說自其「成年」之後,都一體應用「已獲認證」的王陽明像。我們若是考慮到《畫史會要》描述王守仁講究己之肖像,曾有數十人爲其寫像,都無法得到王守仁的認可事,則得其認可的蔡世新,應可靠廣大徒眾對陽明像的

圖六:《王陽明先生圖譜》中王守仁15歲像。　圖七:《王陽明先生圖譜》中王守仁28歲像。

需求而擁有相當可靠的市場。相對於此,《聖賢像傳》所收的王陽明
像,其五官與其他聖賢如出一轍,服飾姿態也多雷同。對比此類不重
賦予人物獨特性的像傳,無論是蔡世新或《王陽明先生圖譜》所針對
的群眾,似乎亟欲見到王陽明確切的長相,並因見到其形貌而感到快
慰。茅坤(1512-1601)的這則故事,便可放到這個脈絡下理解:

> 陽明先生沒,而四海之門生故吏,及嘗提兵所過州縣蠻夷
> 之盧,爭像而事之,當是時,陽明先生之像遍天下,而豫
> 章間所傳特甚。予還金陵,一日,考功何君吉陽刺其所爲
> 像者過予,且曰卽豫章間所善像陽明先生而名者也。[49]

善像陽明先生而名者指蔡世新,此段文字的前半段所指的像,可
能是塑像或畫像,但後半段的遍天下之像,既牽涉到流傳,加上此文
是茅坤爲蔡世新所作序,所以應指畫像而言。何吉陽卽何遷(1501-
1574),湛若水(1466-1560)的門人,但頗親近陽明學,他跟茅坤在
南京的相遇,應是嘉靖37年前幾年事,[50]而嘉靖朝正是陽明學從初興
到極盛的時期,所以隨其門人弟子廣佈,畫像流傳也隨之遍天下。蔡
世新憑藉爲王守仁畫像而與陽明學者往來,並得其讚譽引薦而聞名。
在宴席上,茅坤請蔡世新即席揮毫作畫,蔡世新頃刻即就,人皆能識
其所畫是王守仁像。[51]茅坤好陽明學,常以未得見其冠裳容貌爲恨,

49　茅坤,《茅鹿門先生文集》,收入《續修四庫全書》第1344冊,卷11,
　　〈贈畫像者蔡少蟄序〉,頁4。

50　何遷晚年任南京刑部侍郎,在嘉靖37年(1558)任滿後前往北京,故知
　　是此年的前幾年事,見黃宗羲撰,沈芝盈點校,《明儒學案》,卷27,
　　〈南中王門學案三‧文貞徐存齋先生階〉,頁618。

51　「予間攜之,出示所嘗共先生遊者,或覆其半,露其半,卽能按識而呼
　　曰:此某先生也。」見茅坤,《茅鹿門先生文集》,卷11,〈贈畫像者蔡
　　少蟄序〉,頁4。

如今得見其畫像，他說：

> 予嘗慕先生與其門弟子誦說其道，往往以不及從之遊，覩
> 其所爲冠裳容貌爲恨，今廼得依先生之像類甚者，存而禮
> 謁之，幸矣哉。[52]

既是「存而禮謁之」，顯示不是簡單看過像而已，還有崇敬禮謁之意。茅坤同時指出，門人弟子不應只是禮謁畫像，還應遵行陽明之道。畫者苦心孤詣方才得陽明像之神，門人弟子不應連畫者都不如。[53]

前引普林斯頓大學的無款〈王陽明像〉，卷首有王守仁坐於書桌前書寫的白描小像，左方有人立侍一旁，畫幅後接著三則王陽明寫給其甥鄭邦瑞的尺牘，更之後是王陽明門人黃綰（1477-1551）、蕭敬德等人題跋。姜一涵認爲書蹟與圖像分別爲兩個時期所作，書蹟是民國初年收藏家重新裝裱後，延請畫家添繪者。[54]不過起首的白描畫像，並不似出自民初畫家手筆，其風格反而讓人聯想到《王陽明先生圖譜》，兩者均意圖表現王守仁的面容特色，靠椅形式亦均爲高背、頂端後卷的樣式，不無可能出自同一位畫家之手。且全卷各紙（此卷畫幅一紙、陽明書幅三紙、題跋三紙）接合處所鈐騎縫印，除葉恭綽（1881-1968）、王南屏（1924-1985）藏印鮮明完整外，不乏經重新裱

52　茅坤，《茅鹿門先生文集》，卷11，〈贈畫像者蔡少聲序〉，頁4。

53　「像，曲技也，嚮苟非與遊之深，而求之至，習寢食，共几席，朝且夕焉，縷心縷腎，有獨得其神於冠裳容貌之所不及，卽何以能圖寫冠裳容貌如是之工工矣。陽明先生之沒，不知其幾十年矣，抑何以肆焉，而手次之若是也。夫像且爾，況吾黨弟子之誦說其道者，苟不篤志而好之，如爲像者之求先生焉，其能間竊其似乎哉！而況望其又有出於冠裳容貌之外者哉！嗟乎，予感君之獨能，而特耻君之不如焉。」見茅坤，《茅鹿門先生文集》，卷11，〈贈畫像者蔡少聲序〉，頁5。

54　姜一涵，〈普林斯頓大學美術博物館藏王陽明三札卷〉，《明報月刊》，10：1（香港，1975），頁58-65。

裝而有切損的印蹟，顯爲前代藏者之鈐印。畫幅與陽明書幅第一紙的
騎縫印中有「青藜館」一印，經查疑爲明末著名文士周如砥（1550-
1615）藏印，若然，亦可提示該陽明畫像成畫年代必早於周如砥卒
年。鄭邦瑞爲餘姚人，他所寶藏的此卷，應可視爲江南地區流傳之王
陽明像之一例。

　　除了蔡世新以外，也有其他人作王守仁像。江南一帶有文徵明
（1470-1559）的門人陸治（1496-1576）及陳洪綬（1599-1652）作陽
明像，陸治所作像還被蔡懋德（1586-1644）之子所摹寫，其子提學
江西，在吉安時曾夢謁王守仁而叩學，遂在陽明像上加入其父與己之
像，意即己侍父共同問道於王守仁。此圖有八大山人（1626-1705）
題「侍親問道圖」五字。[55] 陳洪綬所作〈陽明先生像〉畫軸（圖八）
藏於哈佛大學福格美術館藏，尚未確定其眞僞，與現存於貴陽扶風山
陽明祠的石刻王陽明畫像（圖九，楊儒賓藏）頗近似，[56] 除臉部不類
外，姿態、衣摺、衣帶之形狀極相似，此應可代表陳洪綬確曾於當時
畫過陽明像。亦爲江南地區流傳王陽明像之一例。陸治並不以畫人物
聞名，他所繪製的陽明像與本人能有幾分相似，頗令人存疑。陳洪綬
則善於以變形方式繪製散發奇古風味的人物，亦非寫實派的畫法。因

55　方濬頤，《夢園書畫錄》，收入《歷代書畫錄輯刊》5（北京：中國圖書館
　　出版社，2007），卷17，〈黃匡民侍親問道圖卷〉，頁31-36。
56　該石刻所本的畫像似已不存，但光緒年間地方人士將此畫像刻在祠之石
　　上，從畫像到石刻的變化，請見劉宗堯纂，（民國）《邊江縣志》，收入
　　《中國方志叢書・華南地方・廣西省》第136號（臺北：成文出版社，
　　1967），頁216-217。此石刻拓本見於張岱編，《陽明先生遺像冊》，收入
　　《中華歷史人物別傳集》第21冊（北京：線裝書局，2003）中。其中鄭
　　珍的跋文詳細考證該像的來源脈絡。清華大學中文所楊儒賓教授有此石
　　刻全幅的拓本圖像，文字的部份與《陽明先生遺像冊》所錄基本一致，
　　而拓本最前端的陽明像，是《陽明先生遺像冊》所沒有的。本文寫作期
　　間承其慷慨賜寄參考。

圖八局部

圖八：傳陳洪綬，陽明先生像，
Fogg Museum 藏。

圖九局部

圖九：無款，石刻陽明像，楊儒賓藏。

此由江南地區畫家描繪的王陽明像，「存眞」或非其要點，創造一個
可被接受的「依託」的形象，供其徒眾追念即可。可能是次於寫實本
的選擇。

此外如黃兆彪，據載：

> 黃兆彪畫王文成公像，瘦而長鬑露齒，後有徐文貞公跋，
> 皆未從祀時語也。[57]

黃兆彪其人生平不詳，但應是畫師。

我們若是注意一些零散的文字資料，也有不少有關陽明畫像流傳
的記載，儘管因資料不夠集中，使我們很難精確分析畫像的來源及流
傳的管道，但至少可知王守仁畫像的流行區域。

王守仁的事功多在江西，加上他晚年學術圓熟以後，所傳弟子也
多半是江西人，所以推測江西當地應有不少王守仁畫像。如徐階
（1503-1583）藉巡按江西時重修南昌仰止祠，肖王守仁像而祠之，所
肖似是畫像。立龍沙會，集學校諸生講學於此。[58] 據載：

> 公（徐階）所稱良知學，本故王文成公守仁，而文成於江
> 西最顯著，自公推行之，且像文成而祀焉，其地遂有生像
> 公以祀者。[59]

除了建祠肖像以外，徐階還從士人家中摹王守仁像，分爲燕居像與朝
衣冠像兩類：

57　袁中道，《珂雪齋遊居柿錄》，收入袁中道撰，錢伯城點校，《珂雪齋集》
　　（上海：上海古籍出版社，2007），下冊，卷2，頁1133。
58　王守仁，《王文成公全書》，卷35，〈附錄四・年譜附錄一〉，「四十三年
　　甲子少師徐階撰先生像記」條，頁64-65。
59　王世貞，〈明特進光祿大夫柱國少師兼太子太師吏部尚書建極殿大學士
　　贈太師謚文貞存齋徐公行狀〉，《弇州山人續稿》，收入《明人文集叢刊》
　　第一期第22種（臺北：文海出版社，1970），卷136，頁7。

陽明先生像一幅，水墨寫。嘉靖己亥予督學江西，就士人
家摹得先生燕居像二，朝衣冠像一，明年庚子夏，以燕居
之一贈呂生，此幅是也。[60]

徐階表示呂生所得的燕居像，人覺極似，而「貌殊不武」：

予嘗見人言此像於先生極似，以今觀之，貌殊不武，然獨
以武功顯，於此見儒者之作用矣。呂生誠有慕乎，尚於其
學求之。[61]

這讓人聯想到《史記‧留侯世家》太史公說張良像「狀貌如婦人好
女」，所以不能以貌取人的典故。徐階說王守仁以武功顯，但此武功
是從其學術發用而來，所以關鍵還在學術而不在武功。學術爲體，武
功爲用，這跟明中期以來的流行觀點是一致的。[62]

　　江西安福張鰲山（1511年進士）也有陽明畫像。張鰲山是進士
出身，在宸濠之變時跟隨王守仁勤王。理學上，他原本師事同鄉李宗
杖，得求放心之說，據方志所載，李宗杖「日行功過錄」，以功過錄
以求放心。[63]此後張鰲山轉師王守仁，王守仁的學術講究自得，張鰲
山頗受啓發，所以在王守仁卒後，繪陽明畫像以自範。鄒守益記述：

60　王守仁，《王文成公全書》，卷35，〈附錄四‧年譜附錄一〉，「四十三年
　　甲子少師徐階撰先生像記」條，頁64。

61　王守仁，《王文成公全書》，卷35，〈附錄四‧年譜附錄一〉，「四十三年
　　甲子少師徐階撰先生像記」條，頁65。

62　錢明比對《年譜》與《世經堂集》中的記文內容，發現稍有不同，《世
　　經堂集》說該像是「贈同年淡泉鄭子」，而非《年譜》所說的「贈呂生
　　舒」。錢明推測有可能是兩幅畫分贈鄭、呂二人。見錢明，《王陽明及其
　　學派論考》，第9章，〈陽明之遺像——形象考〉，頁155-156。

63　姚濬昌等修，周立瀛等纂，（同治）《安福縣志》，收入《中國方志叢
　　書‧華中地方‧江西省》第773號（臺北：成文出版社，1989），卷10，
　　〈名臣〉，頁21。

> 張子鰲山繪陽明先師遺像，及彙書翰爲一卷，夙夜用以自
> 範。某敬題曰：《會稽師訓》。[64]

據「夙夜用以自範」，推測張鰲山可能有敬拜畫像，或與畫像對坐之類的行爲。

王守仁的故鄉浙江一帶也有許多陽明畫像，如明末黃道周（1585-1646）談到，有人從浙江前往福建漳浦任官，便根據從餘姚帶來的陽明畫像作塑像以祠祀之。[65]晚清李慈銘（1830-1894）也指出——「文成公像越中舊家多有傳者」。[66]此外，清初湖北唐建中因遊江南而得畫像，[67]並出示予其友萬承蒼（？-1746），顯示清代江南仍有陽明畫像流傳。

四、陽明畫像的作用

收藏品題

士人常對畫像有所品題，而對理學家畫像的品題或相關文字，常

64　鄒守益著，董平編校整理，《鄒守益集》（南京：鳳凰出版社，2007），卷18，〈題會稽師訓卷〉，頁875。

65　黃道周，《黃石齋先生文集》，收入《續修四庫全書》第1384冊，卷11，〈王文成公碑〉，頁11：「于時主縣治者爲天台王公，諱立準，涖任甫數月，舉百廢，以保甲治諸盜有聲；四明施公莅吾漳八九年矣，……王公既選勝東郊，負郭臨流，爲堂宇甚壯，施公從姚江得文成像，遂貌之。」

66　吳慶坻著，張文其、劉德麟點校，《蕉廊脞錄》，頁200。

67　萬承蒼，《孺廬先生文錄》，在李祖陶，《國朝文錄續編》，收入《續修四庫全書》第1671冊，〈王陽明先生畫像記〉，頁19-21：「唐君赤子遊江南，得王陽明先生畫像，寶而藏之。辛亥冬，相見於京師，出以授余，俾爲記，余每一展視，輒悚然起敬，凝然若有思，如是者三年，未有以復也。……陽明先生畫像，杭州、南安皆有石刻，此幅作辭闕圖，蓋若有隱痛焉。」

涉及品題者對理學的看法或立場。如華亭董傳策（1550年進士）雖非理學家，但心慕陽明學，並與陽明學者往來，[68]所以他在訪陽明祠當晚，夢王守仁與其論學，夢中王守仁以門人弟子空談爲憂，囑託董傳策予以規勸。[69]董傳策應是在此祠中見到陽明像（不確定是塑像或畫像），於是作詩：

> 儒門心脈久多岐，大慧慈湖一派師。拈出良知眞指竅，向
> 來實證得居夷。雄風自昔開山嶽，矓像于今肅羽儀。閱世
> 可禁留應跡，誰尋眞相破群疑。[70]

強調致良知之說是眞指竅，而王守仁謫貶貴州則是致良知的實證地。又如鄒元標（1551-1624），則是談其致良知說：

> 登壇濟濟說良知，不著絲毫更數誰。
> 抛却語言諸伎倆，日星千古自昭垂。
> 羣賢列聖無他語，惟一惟精只此中。
> 臘底雪消山盡處，柴門夜夜領春風。
> 辛苦平生幾問津，遲回歧路倍傷神。
> 于今識得先生面，野草閒花一樣春。
> 吾心宇宙有同然，却道金谿是學禪。
> 不是先生勤指點，誰令吾道日中天。
> 吾鄉先輩盛流傳，疑信相參苦未堅。

68　董傳策親近之叔叔董宜陽亦曾從學於鄒守益，可爲當時松江地區受到王學浪潮拍擊之一例。董宜陽與鄒守益事，可參考邱士華，〈許初竹岡阡表介述〉，《故宮文物月刊》，377期（臺北，2014），頁62-71。

69　董傳策，《邕歈稿》，收入《四庫全書存目叢書》集部第122冊，卷6，〈武夷從陽明祠歸，夜夢訪余論學，殊以空談爲憂，若屬余規之云者，寤而賦此以識二首〉，頁10-11。

70　董傳策，《邕歈稿》，卷2，〈陽明王先生祠像〉，頁4-5。

踏破草鞋無覓處，始知吾道有真詮。

人疑此道大圓通，規矩方圓妙不窮。

效地法天無兩事，圓神方智總吾宗。[71]

鄒元標的學術偏悟的一邊，但對規矩準繩持之甚嚴，他在仁文書院的會約中提出「修悟雙融」之說。[72]因此前引詩的末一段既說此道大圓通，又說規矩方圓妙不窮，末了以「圓神方智總吾宗」作結。

　　品題並不限於陽明學者，如湛若水曾應地方官員之請，為陽明畫像題贊，強調其學術上的發明：

逃釋逃黃，匪狷匪狂；為知之良，文武弛張。目其鳳凰，鐵其肝腸；闇然其章，知柔知剛。萬夫之望，茲非陽明先生之相，而中峯大夫程子之藏。[73]

與陽明學對壘的程朱學者也有留下記錄，如張邦奇（1484-1544），與王守仁同時代人，他譏諷王守仁解格物為正物之說是穿鑿附會，[74]所以題其像說：

屹屹乎楞屬，矯矯乎英異。文事武功，震耀斯世。而其志則凌跨千古，每欲以道而自知也。惜哉乎沒也，未幾而天下以道為諱矣。譬飢渴之飲食，謂夢寐為從义，獨何意歟？吾欲起先生於九原，與之反覆辯議，而不可得也，徒

71　鄒元標，《願學集》，收入《文淵閣四庫全書》第1294冊，卷1，〈題陽明先生像六首〉，頁40-41。

72　鄒元標，《願學集》，卷8，〈仁文會約語〉，頁11-14。

73　湛若水，《湛甘泉先生文集》，收入《四庫全書存目叢書》集部第57冊，卷21，〈廣州程貳守所藏新建伯陽明王先生像贊〉，頁52。

74　張邦奇，《張文定公環碧堂集》，收入《續修四庫全書》第1337冊，卷16，〈陽明先生像贊〉，頁15。

　　爲之瞻遺容而興喟。[75]

此處雖談及王守仁的文事武功，但仍著眼在其學術，張邦奇欲起王守仁於地下與之論辯而不可得，只好對像歎息。

與像對坐

　　除了收藏以外，士人持有這些畫像，往往還有求道與學術上的意義。當時頗流行一些自傳式的遊記或悟道歷程的記載（這讓人很容易聯想起西方的《天路歷程》），這類遊記或悟道歷程，對後學可以起到示範性作用。如鄒守益在王守仁死後，著意編著《王陽明先生圖譜》一書，[76]或錢德洪（1496-1574）等人費心纂述《陽明先生年譜》，都可放在此脈絡下理解。這些大儒在其門人弟子或後學的心中，頗有接近聖人的形象。文字書寫悟道歷程與氣象，而畫像則是這類聖人形象與氣象的直接體現。

　　畫像可能會被看作眞人對待，見畫像時，便彷彿眞人臨在而與其對越，可以收到提醒己心的效果。這類與像對坐的傳統，應與《詩經・周頌・清廟》的「對越在天」（即對越上天之意）有關，如楊儒賓教授所指出，對越其實有上天注視監臨之意，而不是人與上天在平等地位的對看。[77]這也正可解釋當時人懸像對坐的行爲。懸陽明像對坐者，以王瓊（1459-1532）最著名，不少筆記小說都有記載——

　　　晉溪在本兵，時王文成撫贛，每讀其疏，必稱奇才，平生

75　張邦奇，《張文定公環碧堂集》，卷15，〈陽明先生像贊〉，頁15-16。

76　鄒守益編著此書意旨，可參考王宗沐的序，見鄒守益編，《王陽明先生圖譜》，收入《北京圖書館藏珍本年譜叢刊》第43冊，頁1-2。

77　楊儒賓，〈《雅》、《頌》與西周儒家的「對越」精神〉，《中國哲學與文化》第11輯（桂林：廣西師範大學出版社，2014），頁39-67。

> 不見先生面，客有進先生像者，公懸之中堂，焚香對坐，
> 左手抱孫，右手執先生奏讀之，明日入奏事，必盡行其所
> 請。[78]

王瓊是王守仁的上司，他也許只是把畫像視同眞人，而跟王守仁的聖
人形象未必有關。但其行被晚明曹于汴（1592年進士）所效法，他
亦懸馮應京像與其對坐。[79]馮應京（1555-1606）是盱貽人，學於吉水
鄒元標門下，在《明儒學案》被歸類入江右學案。王世貞（1526-
1590）之子曾作詩頌揚王、曹二人事：

> 尚書懸像拜中丞，僕僕生前豈爲名。近見山西曹給事，愛
> 君仿佛似文成。[80]

詩後則註：「王瓊爲大司馬，懸王文成像於署中，日每揖之。安邑曹
給事於汴於慕岡亦然。」

　　也有未曾見過王守仁，但懸像事之的例子，如四川遂寧楊名
（1505-1559）。王守仁謫貶貴陽時，受貴州提學副使席書（1461-
1527）之邀，講學文明書院，並與席書之間有書信往來，楊名與席書
兩家是姻親，所以他幼時便曾讀過王、席二人的通信，此後還與羅洪
先（1504-1564）等陽明學者結社講學。楊名應未見過王守仁，但慕
其學術，於是懸其像如見其人：

> 先是吾外舅元山文襄公督學貴陽，王陽明公以部屬劾劉

78　姚之駰，《元明事類鈔》，收入《文淵閣四庫全書》第884冊，卷16，頁
　　24。
79　曹于汴曾作〈慕岡先生像贊〉，在《仰節堂集》，收入《文淵閣四庫全
　　書》第1293冊，卷9，頁14。
80　錢謙益撰集，許逸民等點校，《列朝詩集》（北京：中華書局，2007），
　　第8冊，丁集第六附見王司勳士麒五首，〈贈馮慕岡二首馮時在詔獄〉，頁
　　4469。

瑾，謫龍場驛。文襄聘居文明書院，相與講定性主靜之
旨，有書札還往，方洲幼覽之，心解。至是與同第羅念菴
洪先、程松溪文德，洎陽明弟子歐陽南埜德、魏水洲良
弼、薛中離侃結社講學，雅契夙心，……懸陽明像于壁，
羹牆如見。[81]

王守仁以下，其門人弟子也有類似的例子，如習於聶豹（1487-1563）門下的聶有善，便懸其師畫像於靜室，對之端坐省身：

聶有善，雙溪人，晚得聶貞襄主靜宗旨，年四十，命圬者
圖其像，上書太極圖說，懸之靜室，終日端坐省身。[82]

敬拜祭祀

除了與畫像對坐，還有敬拜祭祀畫像的行爲。祀像的行爲常見於
家庭或家族中子女祭祀父母，最著名的即丁蘭刻木事親。丁蘭刻木爲
母形，事之如生，「晨昏定省，以盡誠敬」。[83] 祭祀畫像應是取法於此
類孝行故事而來。如葉思忠便有事像如事生之行，據載其父畫像因屋
漏雨受潮，於是他跪伏於像前，直到像乾爲止：

葉思忠，字從本，方基，字本立，俱貴溪諸生，講學於徐
波石、甄寒泉之門，共相砥礪，而以致良知爲主，以庸言
庸行勿自欺爲工夫。思忠執親喪，盧墓側，至服闋，偶屋

81　陳講，〈翰林院編修楊公實卿墓志銘〉，在焦竑編纂，《國朝獻徵錄》
　　（臺北：臺灣學生書局，1965），卷21，頁106-107。
82　王建中等修，劉繹等纂，（同治）《永豐縣志》，收入《中國方志叢書‧
　　華中地方‧江西省》第760號，卷23，〈人物志‧處士〉，頁28。
83　《孝行錄》（東京：合資會社東京國文社，1922），無作者，無頁碼。

漏雨，濡父像，即懸像跪伏竟日，俟乾乃已。[84]

陽明門人弟子也有祀像的行為。如永豐劉溢（1521年進士），他遊於羅洪先之門，祀陽明像於家，所祀是畫像或木像不詳：

> 劉溢，字晃峰，永豐秋江人。……祀王文成像於家，與弟沈同遊吉水羅文恭之門。[85]

太湖李之讓，因學宗良知，於是設陽明像祀之，所祀是畫像或木像亦不詳：

> 李之讓，字太初，歲貢生，為桃源教諭，歲旱，民多饑死，縣令猶督逋賦，之讓泣請不聽，遂棄職歸，益精求性命之旨，……其學宗良知，設王陽明先生像祀之，學者稱太初先生。[86]

理學特別講究心性的領悟，尤其心學強調迷悟只在一念之間，所以一些人面謁大儒，因大儒的一句話大悟，便如從地獄脫身般重生，所以師弟子間的關係可以到十分緊密的程度。王畿、錢德洪二人在王守仁卒後，為其守喪三年，三年喪是父母喪，顯示二人視王守仁為學術上的父母。羅汝芳（1515-1588）事顏鈞（1504-1596）亦然，鄒元標描寫二人的相處情形是——「夫顏橫離口語，學非有加於先生，而終身事之不衰，生之縲絏，周之貲財，事之有禮，此祖父不能必之孝

84　蔣繼洙等修，李樹藩等纂，（同治）《廣信府志》，收入《中國方志叢書・華中地方・江西省》第106號，卷9之3，〈儒林〉，頁43-44。

85　王建中等修，劉繹等纂，（同治）《永豐縣志》，卷23，〈人物志・處士〉，頁28。

86　符兆鵬等修，趙繼元等纂，（同治）《太湖縣志》，收入《中國方志叢書・華中地方・安徽省》第106號（臺北：成文出版社，1985），卷22，〈人物志三・儒林〉，頁1。

子慈孫，而得之先生。」[87] 幾乎跟子女侍奉父母一般無異，小自不敢有違其言，大至終身事奉而無倦色。

羅汝芳卒後，也有門人弟子敬拜其像，這可從李至清（萬曆時人）處得到佐證，據載他因湯顯祖（1550-1616）而專程前往南城拜羅汝芳像，羅汝芳是湯顯祖之師：

> 李至清，號超無，江陰人，初爲諸生，能詩，有奇俠氣，已而爲頭陀，過臨川，湯顯祖奇之。一日，問若士何師何友，更閱天下幾人？答云：吾師明德夫子，而友達觀，其人皆已朽矣。達觀以俠，故不可以竟行於世。天下悠悠，令人轉思明德耳。遂至盱拜羅明德像，後又去頭陀爲將軍，弓劍之餘，時發憤爲韻語，題曰《問劍》，顯祖爲之序。[88]

至於羅汝芳的傳人楊起元（1547-1599）不僅敬拜其師像而已，而且「出入必以其像供養，有事必告而後行」。與此相似的還有周汝登（1547-1629）的故事：

> （周汝登）已見近溪，七日無所啓請，偶問「如何是擇善固執」？近溪曰：「擇了這善而固執之者也。」從此便有悟入。近溪嘗以《法苑珠林》示先生，先生覽一二頁，欲有所言，近溪止之，令且看去。先生竦然若鞭背。故先生供近溪像，節日必祭，事之終身。[89]

87 鄒元標，《願學集》，卷6上，〈明大中大夫雲南參政近溪羅先生墓碑〉，頁51。

88 李人鏡修，梅體萱纂，（同治）《南城縣志》，收入《中國地方志集成‧江西府縣志輯》55-56，卷8之8，〈流寓〉，頁13-14。

89 黃宗羲撰，沈芝盈點校，《明儒學案》，卷36，〈泰州學案五‧尚寶周海

也是供奉羅汝芳像，終身奉祀。[90]黃宗羲（1610-1695）對此評論是：

> 自科舉之學興而師道亡矣，今老師門生之名徧於天下，豈
> 無師哉，由於爲師之易，而弟子之所以事其師者，非復古
> 人之萬一矣，猶可謂之師哉！[91]

則是著眼在師弟關係上，而其理想的師弟關係幾乎等同於父子關係。
顧憲成（1550-1612）的評論頗有意思：

> 羅近溪以顏山農爲聖人，楊復所以羅近溪爲聖人。[92]

顯示這類學術上父母的角色跟聖人形象有關。

　　當時與陽明心學抗衡的江門心學，也有陳獻章像或湛若水像的製
作與流傳。湛若水常建書院以奉祀其師，而湛若水的弟子仿而效之，
所以二人像都被置於書院等公共空間。如龐嵩（1534年舉人），廣東
南海人，他早年習於王守仁門下，晚年歸鄉從湛若水遊，聞隨處體認
天理之說，感歎幾虛此生，[93]而龐嵩所至之處皆建書院以奉其師：

> 易菴在南海之弼唐，弼唐者，龐振卿先生所居之鄉也，
> ……他所至，則爲一書院以奉甘泉，而甘泉平生所至，亦

門先生汝登〉，頁854。

90　方祖猷曾檢查周汝登的《東越證學錄》以及其他相關記載，主張周汝登
　　應算是王畿的門人，受羅汝芳的影響相對較小。因此這段記載很可能是
　　後人在抄錄中把楊起元傳誤移到周汝登傳中。方祖猷，《王畿評傳》（南
　　京：南京大學出版社，2001），頁425-426。

91　黃宗羲，《南雷文定三集》，收入《清代詩文集彙編》第33冊（上海：上
　　海古籍出版社，2010），卷2，〈廣師說〉，頁44。

92　黃宗羲撰，沈芝盈點校，《明儒學案》，卷34，〈泰州學案三・侍郎楊復
　　所先生起元〉，頁806。

93　瑞麟等修，史澄等纂，（光緒）《廣州府志》，收入《中國方志叢書・華
　　南地方・廣東省》第1號（臺北：成文出版社，1966），卷116，〈列傳
　　五〉，頁28-31。

　　輒爲書院以奉白沙，二先生者，皆可謂能尊其師者也。[94]
此處所言的奉白沙、甘泉，除了興建書院以外，應也包括崇祀其像，
所崇祀的可能是畫像或塑像，所以龐嵩有〈瞻甘泉遺像詩〉曰：「精
華日月在顱首，兩耳之旁南北斗。」[95]門人後學如史桂芳（1518-1598）
也有像而受人尊崇，據載江西萬年縣的蔡毅中，年少受教於史桂芳，
史桂芳學宗陳獻章。日後蔡毅中因事過其所居地時，「亟訪師第宅，
瞻拜遺像；立傳賦詩，以敘懇誠」。[96]

　　懸像於私室者，則有廣東區準高懸白沙像的例子：

　　　　區準高，字德園，……穎悟博學，年十五補入邑庠，十七
　　　　食餼，試輒高等，一時名噪諸生，……生平有器識，善議
　　　　論，黜浮華，務爲有用之學，齋頭常懸陳白沙小影，嚴師
　　　　事之。及病，猶賦詩見志，專以無欲爲邵病奇方，其潛心
　　　　理學，雖死不懈如此。[97]

　　至於把陳獻章像當作父母像一般敬拜祭祀，則以賀欽（1437-
1510）的故事最爲人所熟知。賀欽是浙江定海人，他與陳獻章相識於
北京，聞其學後拜師稱弟子，在辭官歸鄉後，賀欽便懸師像於別室，
出告反面——

　　　　賀欽時爲給事中，聞白沙論學，歎曰：至性不顯，寶藏猶
　　　　靈。世卽我用，而我奚以爲用。謁白沙執弟子禮，卽日抗

94　屈大均，《翁山文外》，收入《清代詩文集彙編》第119冊，卷2，〈過易
　　菴贈龐祖如序〉，頁203。
95　瑞麟等修，史澄等纂，（光緒）《廣州府志》，卷161，〈雜錄二〉，頁8。
96　項珂、劉馥桂等修，（同治）《萬年縣志》，收入《中國方志叢書・華中
　　地方・江西省》第258號，卷9，〈藝文志總論〉，頁21。
97　陶兆麟修，蔡逢思纂，（光緒）《高明縣志》，收入《中國方志叢書・華
　　南地方・廣東省》第186號，卷13，〈列傳二〉，頁41。

疏，解官還家，肖白沙像懸于別室，出告反面。[98]

賀欽的行為已不單純是祭祀先賢或崇禮師尊而已，而是把陳獻章當作
父母一般看待。另有資料記載，賀欽曾率家中子弟敬拜畫像。[99]南海
陳庸（1474年舉人）也有拜像之舉，載於《雒閩源流錄》：

> 陳庸，字秉常，廣東南海人，力行好古，舉成化甲午，聞
> 江門之學往師事之，白沙深取其德量，……病革，沐浴更
> 衣，設白沙像，焚香再拜而逝。[100]

此處僅記陳庸卒前設陳獻章像，焚香再拜而逝，但推測平日應已有此
像，否則卒前從何處得來？既有此像，平日可能也有焚香祭祀之舉。
即使江門心學已衰的萬曆年間，仍有安福陽明學者劉元卿的族人劉燾
（1538年進士），他與陽明學者講學，又嚮慕陳獻章之學，於是前往
陳獻章的故鄉，三造其廬，並仿作其遺像，持像歸家崇祀：

> 劉燾，層巖人，性端重樸，雅慕白沙之學，三造其廬，歸
> 仿其遺像祀之，與劉元卿暨諸弟講學。[101]

　這類供養祭祀其師畫像的作法，讓人很容易聯想到禪宗的祖師
像。[102]相關研究指出，儒家的圖像常受到佛、道教圖像傳統的影響，

---

98 孫奇逢，《理學宗傳》，收入《孔子文化大全》（濟南：山東友誼書社，1989），卷20，〈陳白沙公獻章〉，頁27-28。

99 陳仁錫，《無夢園初集》，收入《續修四庫全書》第1382冊，馬集4，〈重刻醫閭賀先生稿序〉，頁66。

100 張夏，《雒閩源流錄》，收入《四庫全書存目叢書》史部第123冊，卷14，〈陳庸〉，頁10-11。

101 姚濬昌等修，周立瀛等纂，（同治）《安福縣志》，卷11，〈人物志·儒林〉，頁19。

102 有關頂相一辭的理解的變化，可參考長岡龍作編，《講座日本美術史》第4卷《造形の場》（東京：東京大學出版會，2005），第2章「造形と個別の磁場」，頁125-150。

如《孔子聖蹟圖》便是一例。[103] 早在隋唐時代，前往中國求法的日僧常隨身攜帶中國製的高僧畫像回國，儘管各宗派皆有類似作法，不限於禪宗，但禪宗講究不立文字，以心傳心，所以日本禪僧除了攜帶歷史上的祖師像以外，所師從的中國禪師的像更是必攜之物，這是禪僧給予弟子，作爲法脈繼承（印可）的證明。加上禪師的形象常因公案而具體化、複雜化，所以這類畫像也可作爲公案的對象，亦即公案的繪畫表現。[104] 尤其值得注意的是，這類畫像也在祖師忌辰拈香時張掛，[105] 所以也有學者認爲祖師像是作爲儀式用或紀念品的性質而被贈與，後來成爲禮拜對象。[106] 前述楊、周二人學術與禪學在內容上常常只有一間之隔，加上常與僧人往來，所以雖然缺乏直接的證據證明，但未必沒有可能是受到祖師像的影響。

學術宗主所在

畫像還有代表文化傳承或學術宗主的象徵意義，隨其學術傳承或宗主之別，所拜的像便有不同。前引楊廉請郭詡作二程及朱熹像，便

103　Julia K. Murray, "The Temple of Confucius and Pictorial Biographies of the Sage," *The Journal of Asian Studies*, Vol.55, No.2(May 1996), pp.269-300.
104　德永弘道，〈南宋初期の禪宗祖師像について——拙菴德光贊達磨像を中心に〉，《國華》929（東京，1971），頁 7-17；930（東京，1971），頁5-22。也可參考相井手誠之輔，〈頂相における像主の表象——見心來復象の場合〉，《仏教芸術》282（九州，2005），頁13-35；李宜蓁，〈入明使節的肖像：妙智院藏《策彥周良像》之研究〉（臺北：國立臺灣大學藝術史研究所碩士論文，2010）。
105　萱場まゆみ，〈頂相と掛眞——興国寺本法燈国師像からの考察〉，《美術史研究》33（東京，1995），頁93-108。
106　T. Griffith Foulk and Robert H. Sharf, "On the Ritual Use of Ch'an Portraiture in Medieval China," *Cahiers d'Extreme-Asie*, no.7(1993), pp.149-219.

因其以二程、朱熹爲學術宗主，所以楊廉獲像後十分珍視，有意將這幾幅畫像「日日而張之，則日日聖賢在目也；時時而張之，則時時聖賢在目也；豈不足以起後學敬仰之心乎！」[107] 相對於此，陽明學者鄒守益在祁門舉行講會時，祁門屬徽州府，當地的程朱學風頗盛，所以鄒守益選擇拜孔子像，應是爲避免爭議的選擇，但在陽明心學獨盛的江西安福惜陰會中則改拜先師像——

> 家立一會，與家考之，鄉立一會，與鄉考之。凡鄉會之
> 日，設先師像於中庭，焚香而拜，以次列坐。[108]

孔子像是先聖像，此處的先師像應即王守仁像，與會者須先焚香拜祭後方才就坐。

　　學術宗主之別在變局間尤易凸顯。[109] 明清之際，許多人將亡國歸罪於理學，尤其是陽明心學更是眾矢之的，於是有人藉由拜畫像確立及宣示其學術宗主。如陳確（1604-1677），他在詩作中指出：

> 憶昔游山陰，滔滔乘末祀。哲人憂喪亂，不替千秋志。眷
> 言集朋儔，竭蹶三之會。肅肅陽明祠，確時預執事。（原
> 註：癸卯日記：昔歲游山陰，先師時集同人于每月三之
> 日，講學陽明祠，確亦撰杖以從，痛今何可得。）皇天忽

107　楊廉，《楊文恪公文集》，卷26，〈送清狂山人歸泰和序〉，頁8。
108　鄒守益，《東廓鄒先生文集》，卷7，〈惜陰申約〉，頁20。
109　明清之際便有士人因亡國之痛而拜聖賢圖像，聖賢圖像儼然成爲華夷之辨的文化象徵所在。如楊益介便隱於江西西山冰雪堂，列聖賢圖像，作人社，行禮講學陳祭其中，據載：「（楊）益介字友石，明甲申三月之變，椎心頓足，痛不欲生，作採薇之歌，歌畢，放聲而哭於峯下，構冰雪堂，列聖賢圖像，作人社，引集同志之士，行禮講學陳祭其中。」歐陽桂，《西山志》，收入《四庫禁燬書叢刊》史部第72冊，卷5，「上天峯」，頁17。

崩頹，梁木久顛墜。披圖何儼然，瞻拜時隕涕。呈我辨學
書，遑遑不知辠。世士競相非，往復一何巫。古學不可
誣，焉能泯同異。竊見兩先生，好辨亦不置。開懷與諸
儒，牴牾豈有意。千聖同一心，邈哉俟冥契。[110]

此詩作於康熙 2 年（1663），「辨學書」應即陳確作於順治 11 年
（1654）的〈大學辨〉。《大學》一書的爭訟，歷宋元明三代不止，尤
其在王守仁提出《大學》古本後，使各式各樣的《大學》的改本或解
釋層出不窮，即連劉宗周（1578-1645）也曾被豐坊僞作的石經《大
學》所惑，[111]陳確因作〈大學辨〉等篇，受人質疑違離其師劉宗周之
學，於是他祭祀王、劉二人畫像，並作詩自擴懷抱。他雖推翻王、劉
二人之說，但拜謁畫像之舉則表明他不是站在競爭者或反對者的角
色。一如《易經》〈蠱卦〉中的「幹父之蠱」，既是修正，又有繼承
的意思。[112]陳確所拜奠的王、劉二人畫像可能出自江南一帶的畫師之
手。陳確的族人陳之問在寫給黃宗羲的一封信上說：「吳子昇臨陽明
先生像，附使者以往。」[113]《國朝畫識》中著錄徽州畫師吳旭，字子
升，善人物寫照，[114]有可能是同一人，亦即吳旭畫王守仁像，陳之問
託人送去給黃宗羲。因此王、劉二人畫像很可能出自吳旭之手。

110 陳確，《乾初先生遺集》，收入《清代詩文集彙編》第 20 冊，《詩集》，
　　卷 3，〈癸卯正月三日設陽明山陰兩先生像拜之，呈性解二篇，感賦一
　　首〉，頁 3-4。
111 王汎森，〈明代後期的造偽與思想爭論——豐坊與《大學》石經〉，《新
　　史學》，6：4（臺北，1995），頁 1-20。
112 與年譜有關的部份，見《陳乾初先生年譜》，收入《北京圖書館藏珍本
　　年譜叢刊》第 68 冊，卷下，康熙 2 年條，頁 17-18。
113 黃宗羲，《南雷文定前集》，《附錄》，〈陳之問令升來函〉，頁 9。
114 馮金伯，《國朝畫識》，收入《中國歷代畫史匯編》第 4 冊（天津：天津
　　古籍出版社，1997）卷 13，頁 7。

　　秦松岱也是一例。秦松岱是無錫人，因讀《傳習錄》有悟，於是構願學齋，作陽明畫像而奉祀之。無錫是晚明東林書院所在，當地學風傾向程朱學，加上明末以來對陽明心學的批評日益增多，所以秦松岱崇祀陽明畫像的行為，等於是宣示己之學術宗主。此後他參與江、浙一帶的講學活動，師事從陝西南下江南的李顒（1627-1705）。李顒文集中記載此事：

> 燈巖秦子諱松岱，潛心陽明之學，構願學齋，肖像嚴事。
> 志篤力勤，聞先生講學明倫堂，趨赴拱聽，又會講於東
> 林，徘徊不忍去。[115]

秦松岱之兄秦松齡（1637-1714）以文辭著名，《道南淵源錄》中的〈秦燈巖先生傳〉即出自秦松齡的玄孫秦瀛（1743-1821）之手。[116] 秦松岱所奉祀的畫像有可能一直留存下來，所以乾隆年間秦瀛也有題陽明畫像詩。[117]

　　清初施閏章（1618-1683）來江西任官，在青原山舉行會講，鄒元標的弟子李元鼎（？-1653）奉持羅洪先與鄒元標兩人的遺像，率領當地士人前往講學，據載：

> 時守憲愚山施公開講青原，公持鄒忠介、羅文恭兩先生遺

---

115 李顒，《二曲集》，收入《清代詩文集彙編》第105冊，卷10，〈南行述〉，頁10。

116 鄒鍾泉，《道南淵源錄》，收入《四庫未收書輯刊》第9輯7冊，卷12，〈秦燈巖先生傳〉，頁23。

117 秦瀛並非理學中人，所以他的詩中只是簡單誇讚了王守仁的學術與事功：「宗臣遺像鬢毛蒼，公已騎鯨去帝鄉。慷慨誓師傳贛水，艱危得力憶龍場。制科一代勛名在，學術千秋謗欱張。莫道蚍蜉能撼樹，斯文日月耀精芒。」秦瀛，《小峴山人詩文集》，收入《續修四庫全書》第1464冊，詩集卷11，〈題王文成公遺像〉，頁9。

像，率諸生拜階下，使知所宗，言學則首發明良知良
能。[118]

李元鼎，吉水人，天啓2年（1622）進士，入清後官至兵部左侍
郎。李元鼎屬於谷平李氏家族，族祖李中是羅洪先的老師，族父李邦
華（1574-1644）則是鄒元標的弟子。羅洪先與鄒元標先後在吉水的
講學活動，谷平李氏族人都是主要成員。爲了表明當地學術宗主，李
元鼎選擇的方式，是率領當地士人，共同奉持羅、鄒二人遺像參與講
學。

與學術宗主有關的，還有儒釋合流這個長期糾纏陽明心學，造成
兩造間存在既緊張、競爭但又常相交集的現象。如廣東番禺屈大均
（1630-1696）在明清之際的動亂後爲了抗衡釋氏，鼓勵地方士人把理
學家畫像懸於堂室中以爲師表。前有提及龐嵩往來王守仁、湛若水門
下，家中收藏有王、湛及陳獻章畫像，屈大均遂建議龐嵩的曾孫龐祖
如（名嘉蓉）把三人像加上龐嵩的畫像掛出：

> 自庚寅變亂以來，吾廣州所有書院皆燬於兵，獨釋氏之宮
> 日新月盛，使吾儒有異教充塞之悲，斯道寂寥之歎，……
> 祖如家中復有白沙、甘泉、陽明與先生（按：龐祖如之父
> 龐易菴）遺像，吾欲祖如嘗懸於易菴之堂，以爲吾人之師
> 表。[119]

但也有一種情形，是雙方因陽明畫像而有交集，如清初吳謙牧
（1631-1659）在一封信中談到他受託裝裱陽明畫像，請施博尋覓善手：

---

118 張貞生，《庸書》，收入《四庫全書存目叢書》集部第229冊，卷5，〈李
　　少司馬七十序〉，頁16。
119 屈大均，《翁山文外》，卷2，〈過易菴贈龐祖如序〉，頁203-204。

又有一事，乃家仲兄前曾奉懇者，有王文成公遺像，乃龍
山許氏家藏，託爲裝裱，工人不善，致有損壞，欲煩左右
於郡中覓一善手別爲裝過。[120]

吳謙牧兄弟是劉宗周的學生，而施博的學術取向則在儒佛之間，
如他自述：「余孔氏門牆中人，每兼好禪宗家言」，[121]二人因畫像而有
共通的交契。

當心學家所講學的書院——尤其是具象徵意義的書院被改爲佛寺
時，也會觸動一些士人的敏感神經。如羅洪先講學的石蓮洞，因位處
僻遠而少見人跡，但當石蓮洞及正學書院被僧人買去改建爲佛寺時，
便有士人無法接受而試圖阻止，[122]所採取的方式是奉羅洪先木主入屋
中正坐。據清初講學石蓮洞的吳雲追述此事：

予讀書洞中，周子懋則侍，懋則即周柳川先生之裔孫，柳
川即公之賢弟子。自公（按：羅洪先）後中落，僧買正學
書院爲佛寺，懋則之嚴君周中丞忠節公，俟其佛寺既成，
忽自冠帶鼓樂，送公木主，以柳川先生配，入屋中正坐

120　吳謙牧，《吳志仁先生遺稿》（中國國家圖書館藏清鈔本），卷5，〈與施
　　　易修〉，無頁碼。此條資料是王汎森老師所提供。
121　許三禮，《政學合一集》，收入《四庫全書存目叢書》子部第165冊，不
　　　分卷，〈丁己問答〉，頁23。
122　石蓮洞是羅洪先的私人書屋，規模不大，因此在萬曆《吉安府志》的
　　　〈學校志〉中並未將之列入，請見余之禎，王時槐等纂修，（萬曆）《吉
　　　安府志》，收入《中國方志叢書・華中地方・江西省》第768號，卷15，
　　　〈學校志〉，頁9。至於石蓮洞南後來又築正學書院，並由羅洪先本人親
　　　自作記，但其名雖爲「書院」，其實仍未達到一般建制化書院的規模，
　　　因此連胡直也只稱之爲「正學堂」。請見羅洪先，〈正學書院記〉，在周
　　　樹槐等纂修，（道光）《吉水縣志》，收入《中國方志叢書・華中地方・
　　　江西省》第766號，卷31，頁7-9；與胡直，〈念菴先生行狀〉，《衡廬精
　　　舍藏稿》，卷23，頁15。

焉。然後責於僧曰：「爾何敢擅買書院乎？」今公木主猶

坐洞中，神有所依，中丞之力也。[123]

事件還有後續。羅洪先的裔孫不以木主為足，所以尋訪羅洪先中狀元時的畫像，拜於書齋二年，才又回到石蓮洞中敬拜木主，吳雲續道：

公裔孫為中丞壻，得請公狀元在京，自寫及第謝恩像，朝

冠朱衣，象簡黃表，面如滿月，秀目清眉，請至書室，拜

禮二年，仍歸於令孫，而後至洞中拜木主焉。[124]

據此可知奉羅洪先木主以阻僧人應有成效，所以石蓮洞中仍奉此木主。另從敘述內容，畫像因可讓人明白覯見相貌，作用與木主仍稍有別。

　　還有僧人曾對鄒元標的畫像作出評論，據載：

無學，廬陵良家子也，常住西峰寺，……皆以為狂僧也。

工詩善書，見鄒南皋畫像，拈筆題曰：「烈著都門，名噪

天下。世人見之，謂是仗節死義之臣，無學視之，仍是水

田老者。」[125]

鄒元標處在晚明三教合一的風潮下，對二氏並未明顯抵斥，其學偏悟，並跟羅大紘、郭子章（1542-1618）等人共同講學青原山，羅、郭二人的學術都傾向三教合一，所以很容易讓人誤會鄒元標的學術近於禪學。無學的題辭指鄒元標以諫張居正（1525-1582）奪情事聞名天下，但若是除此不論，其實只是一名田邊老者而已。我們若是考慮到

123　吳雲，《天門詩文稿》（江西省圖書館藏清鈔本），不分卷，〈石蓮春〉，
　　　無頁碼。

124　吳雲，《天門詩文稿》，不分卷，〈石蓮春〉，無頁碼。

125　謝旻等修，陶成等纂，（雍正）《江西通志》，收入《中國方志叢書‧華
　　　中地方‧江西省》第782號，卷104，〈仙釋二〉，頁10。

鄒元標作為陽明學者的背景，而題辭只提其諫奪情事，又指其為田邊老者，而完全不及於其悟道與否，則此恐怕跟儒、釋兩家的競爭有關。

五、清代的一些變化

入清以後，陽明學受到不少詬病，一些人或者傾向官方正統的程朱學，或者對理學有所詬病而專志考據，於是對王守仁的態度或所持立場遂有轉變。如以尊程朱學而得意官場的熊賜履（1635-1709）著《閑道錄》，尊朱子而闢陽明，視王守仁為異類。[126]如翁方綱（1733-1818）便從程朱學的角度批判王守仁，他特別作〈姚江學致良知論〉以駁陽明學，說：

> 幸至今日，經學昌明，學者皆知奉朱子為正路之導，其承姚江之說者，固當化去門戶之見，平心虛衷，以適於經傳之訓義，……考證之學仍皆聖賢之學也，良知之學則無此學也。[127]

翁方綱的這段話主要是在綰合理學與考據學的過程中作篩選，而把陽明學篩出了這個圈子外，但並未到深惡痛絕的程度。翁方綱收藏陽明像，曾為此畫像題辭。[128]清代有部份士人流行在每年蘇軾生日時

126　永瑢、紀昀等撰，《四庫全書總目》，卷97，「《閑道錄》三卷」條，頁825。

127　翁方綱，《復初齋文集》，收入《清代詩文集彙編》第382冊，卷7，〈姚江學致良知論上〉，頁5。

128　翁方綱，《復初齋外集》，卷15，〈新建王文成公像，方綱以去年所得公手書春游詩臨於幀，次韻敬題〉，頁1：「北學猶堪一脈尋像摹自交河王氏，靜中真意儼冠簪。瓣香俎豆交河近，倒影星辰越水深。客坐空慚挂私祝，春游誰解續高吟。暫來合眼蒲團上，又恐疏蕪少定心。」交河王氏

集會慶祝，[129]翁方綱同樣也在蘇軾生日當天，將蘇軾像與黃庭堅、顧仲瑛、沈周、毛奇齡、朱彝尊等共六人像一同祭祀。[130]翁方綱的有趣處在於，他本身既是經學家，卻更推尊文人，而讓幾位經學家都配食於蘇軾之側。[131]

　　儘管清人對心學頗有批判，但仍持續有製作陽明畫像的例子。當時甚至有人透過扶乩拜王守仁為師，且因王守仁入夢而作其畫像，據說畫像上王守仁「凜凜然有生氣」──

> 陳春嘘名昶，陽湖人，入籍大興，中式順天鄉試，出為浙江知縣，歷署桐鄉、秀水、餘姚諸縣事，皆有惠政。在餘姚時，有仙壇一所，相傳陽明先生嘗降此壇。春嘘素不信，為駁詰數事，乩中俱能辨雪，乃大服，請受業為弟子。一日早起，忽見陽明先生現形，修髯偉貌，高冠玉立，而面如削瓜，遂下拜，已不見矣。因手摹一像，凜凜然有生氣。余嘗見之，雖老畫師不及也。[132]

　　有可能是王蘭生，他是河北交河人，康熙60年（1721）進士，隨李光地習律呂歷算音韻之學。

129　如畢沅率領屬吏門生禮拜明人陳洪綬所作的蘇軾小像，見錢泳撰，張偉點校，《履園叢話》（北京：中華書局，1979），卷23，〈雜記上〉，頁611，「蘇東坡生日會」條。

130　方濬頤有〈毛西河朱竹垞二先生像小幅〉，應即此祭拜所用像，見《夢園書畫錄》，卷23，頁34-37。

131　翁方綱在所題詩的詩題，明白表露說：「是日齋中供山谷、玉山、陽明、石田及毛、朱二先生像，以配東坡生日之筵。山谷像不敢以配意題也。敬題四軸各一詩」，另一首詩的詩題則是──「黃文節公像雖日懸蘇齋，然以配食之例為詩，則不敢也。載軒編修以摹本來，並奉齋中屬賦」，黃文節即黃庭堅。可知王守仁等人是配食於蘇軾之側。翁方綱，《復初齋外集》，詩卷第15，頁14、15。

132　錢泳撰，張偉點校，《履園叢話》，卷6，〈耆舊〉，「春嘘叔訥兩明府」

這類名人降乩的事件應不罕見，明清不少士人參與降乩活動，所以類似陳春噓因降乩入夢而作陽明畫像，不必是清以後才有。但這類事件在清以後似乎更常見於筆記小說間，似也象徵了陽明畫像與理學、聖人形象的脫鉤。

馴至嘉慶、道光年間，由於時局動亂，一些有識之士思考經世之途，曾燠（1759-1830）對陽明畫像的題辭，應可代表清中葉左右一些憂心時勢的官員的立場與態度——不論其理學，而在乎其事功。曾燠是江西南城人，乾隆46年（1781）進士，編有《江西詩徵》，他對宋明理學並無好感，在一首題陸贄從祀孔廟詩詩末，曾燠坦率明言兩宋理學不如漢唐儒者之見，[133]但他對王守仁卻頗為心儀，曾燠任兩淮鹽政期間，在當地建有題襟館，此館名震大江南北，[134]而館中便收藏有包括王守仁畫像的許多畫像。曾燠兩次為王守仁畫像題辭，在一次的題辭上他說：

> 不畫麒麟閣，誰圖冰雪顏。一官終嶺表，千祀接尼山。性命空談易，經綸實效艱。知兵儒者事，八輔小人患。漢武輕銜楸，周王縱轍環。……去思縣世代，拜像重悲顏。今日烽常警，官軍甲久攘，生申何不再，竊願破天慳。[135]

條，頁167。感謝何淑宜教授提供資料。

133　張維屏編撰，陳永正點校，《國朝詩人徵略二編》（廣州：中山大學出版社，2004），卷41，〈曾燠〉，頁1001，〈陸宣公從祀孔廟詩〉附識：「北宋以前無道學之名，自漢至唐，其間忠臣義士直行己意，轟轟烈烈，多有宋以後講學之儒所不能及者。」

134　方濬頤，《二知軒文存》，收入《清代詩文集彙編》第661冊，卷20，〈儀董軒記〉，頁1-2。

135　曾燠，《賞雨茅屋詩集》，收入《清代詩文集彙編》第456冊，卷5，〈敬題王文成公畫像二十四韻〉，頁4。

這首詩因達二十四韻，所以此處引文有所省略，此詩起首先說「性命空談易，經綸實效艱」，顯示所重在經綸而不在性命，引文中間省略的部份，則是引用古人故事講王守仁的諸多事功，最後以「拜像重悲潸」，來反應今日缺乏經綸人才以平定禍亂。在另一次的題辭中，曾燠仍把重點放在緬懷王守仁的事功上：

> 學在陽明洞裏天，兵銷彭蠡澤中煙。元黃未起東林黨，黑白幾誣北狩年。乍得披圖覘道氣，想從憂國見華顛。重吟紙尾懷歸句，尚爲征蠻緬昔賢。（原註：畫像後附公自書〈雨中歸懷〉一律，有「五月南征想伏波」之句。）[136]

看似是王守仁緬懷先賢，其實又暗喻了曾燠懷想王守仁事功之意。

賀長齡（1785-1848）對王守仁學術與事功的注意，應跟他巡撫貴州的經歷有關。賀長齡出身湖南，是嘉慶、道光年間的經世派大臣與學者，曾主持《皇朝經世文編》的編纂工作，「經世文編」顧名思義即收錄一些跟經世有關的文章，而其體例編排則是以「學術」爲首，收錄許多理學方面的文章，其次依序是治體、吏政、戶政、禮政、兵政、刑政，顯示賀長齡在經世事務上給了理學一個位置，正如李慈銘所言：「其實當漢學極盛之後，實欲救漢學之偏，以折衷於宋學，……而又欲合洛閩之性理、東萊之文獻、永嘉之經制、夾漈之考索諸學爲一。」[137]

賀長齡在道光16年後長達九年的時間擔任貴州巡撫，貴州是王守仁當年被謫地與悟道處，當地扶風山陽明祠有大小兩幅王守仁畫

136　曾燠，《賞雨茅屋詩集》，卷5，〈再題王文成公畫像〉，頁4。

137　李慈銘著，由雲龍輯，《越縵堂讀書記》（上海：上海書店出版社，2000），〈集部‧總集類〉，「皇朝經世文編」條，頁1205-1206。

像，若據鄭珍（1806-1864）所述，此大小兩幅像，大幅即侯服側面
大像，幅高六七尺許，上書封新建侯敕；小像是燕坐小像冊，應類似
前述吳慶坻所見的燕居授書小像，王守仁裔孫所藏，先後經唐鑑
（1778-1861）、賀長齡之手，最後入扶風山陽明祠中。[138]賀長齡及其
友人戴熙（1805-1860）、何紹基（1800-1874）等都曾爲陽明畫像題
辭，把陽明畫像跟理學及經世的傾向被緊密聯繫在一起。[139]

　　相對於曾燠與賀長齡重視事功，也有人從考據學轉向兩宋理學。
如何紹基之父何凌漢（1772-1840），他在提學浙江時，便曾積極尋訪
黃宗羲始編，全祖望續編而成的《宋元學案》，顯示他對兩宋學術的
關注。[140]他還懸掛兩宋理學家的畫像於家中，朝夕瞻仰，據載：

　　　（何凌漢）居恆莊敬刻厲，無欹坐，無疾趨，獨坐必斂容。
　　　急遽時作字，必裁劃正坐而後書。畫鄭君及周子、二程
　　　子、張子、朱子像懸齋壁，昕夕瞻仰。家範嚴肅稱於時。[141]

　　何凌漢的作法凸顯他所傾心的是兩宋理學，所以他選擇掛的是北
宋五子中除邵雍外的其他四人像，另加上朱熹像。文中「鄭君」不確
定是否指鄭玄，若是，則顯示他並未把考據學與理學對立起來。

138　張岱編，《陽明先生遺像冊》，頁277。
139　賀長齡，《耐菴詩文存》，收入《清代詩文集彙編》第550冊，詩存卷
　　　3，〈題陽明先生像有引〉，頁17-18；何紹基，《東洲草堂詩鈔》，收入
　　　《清代詩文集彙編》第604冊，卷10，〈中丞丈人見示陽明先生遺像敬賦
　　　書後〉，頁8；朱鱶，〈題賀中丞藏王文成公畫像〉，見孫雄輯，《道咸同
　　　光四朝詩史》，收入《歷代詩史長編》第18種（臺北：鼎文書局，
　　　1971），甲集卷1，頁54。
140　相關研究見張藝曦，〈史語所藏《宋儒學案》在清中葉的編纂與流傳〉，
　　　《中央研究院歷史語言研究所集刊》，80本3分（臺北，2009），頁451-505。
141　李元度，《國朝先正事略》（臺北：臺灣中華書局，1965），第3冊，卷
　　　24，〈何文安公事略〉，頁21。

　　何凌漢之子何紹基不僅曾隨從賀長齡而為陽明畫像題辭，還在北京主持顧祠祭，即崇祀顧炎武的活動，這個活動頗有挑戰當時的考據學的意思。[142] 由於顧炎武說過「經學即理學」，所以何紹基對考據學與理學的態度及立場，跟何凌漢差異可能不大。他們雖然反對純粹的考據學，但又未必認為考據學與理學是相悖而不能並立的。何凌漢父子的作為，反映當時學風的轉變與理學的復興。此後直到清末仍不斷有陽明畫像的製作與流傳，以詩書畫三絕著稱的溥心畬（1896-1963），便有〈王文成公像〉（圖十）的畫作傳世，人物形態與陳洪綬所作的相近。今寄存於國立故宮博物院。

圖十：溥心畬，王文成公像，國立故宮博物院藏。

142　王汎森，〈清代儒者的全神堂——《國史儒林傳》與道光年間顧祠祭的成立〉，《中央研究院歷史語言研究所集刊》，79本1分（臺北，2008），頁63-93。

小結

　　本文對陽明像的討論涉及兩部份：一是聖人理想的追求與學術宗主，一是士人對像的崇敬或敬拜。講學有時間與空間的限制，而《傳習錄》等書籍的流傳雖可以讓學術的影響力擴大到更廣的地域，但這類書多半是語錄或一些自傳類的文體，對心學家的悟道過程仍偏重從文字描寫。畫像則可以具體體現理學家的形象，這些形象又跟明人對聖人理想的追求重疊在一起。包括陳獻章、王守仁，以及一些心學家都有畫像流傳，而不少士人收藏這些畫像，或與畫像對越，甚至把畫像當作真人或父母一般敬拜。

　　儒學與社會中下層人民的關係始終不強，而陽明學可能是儒學中走得最遠的一支。在許多相關記載中，都指出陽明學者的講學活動吸引一些商人、農夫或百姓的聽講，這批庶民很可能會有人供奉或敬拜王守仁及其門人弟子的畫像，但很可惜沒有這方面的資料留存。本文所討論的對象仍限於士人群體，而尚未對塑畫像與庶民的關係作更多的探討。

　　入清以後，考據學盛起而理學轉衰，作為官方所承認的程朱學仍不乏隨從者，但以陽明學為主的心學則衰退最多，也因此人們對陽明畫像的崇敬之意遠不如明人。但在清中葉理學復興之際，有志理學者除了蒐集理學相關文獻（如《宋元學案》），另一個具象徵意義的行動就是崇祀畫像。何凌漢懸兩宋理學家畫像，及何紹基祀顧炎武，都可看作是新學風將起的先兆，這些像的崇祀或敬拜活動在清中葉以後所起的作用，也許值得我們作更多的觀察。

Worshipping the Sage
The Fabrication and Circulation of Portraits of Wang Yangming in the Ming Dynasty

Yi-xi Zhang

Abstract

Portraits of Wang Yangming were extremely popular and circulated widely in the hands of local literati and ordinary people from the mid-Ming to the early Qing, when Yangming Learning was popular as well. Local people collected and cherished these portraits, or even worshiped them, regarding them as sage portraits or portraits of their own scholarly "parent." Such portraits, along with public lectures and pamphlets such as the *Chuanxi lu*, were regarded as the three main ways to contact local people and to spread Yangming Learning.

Keywords: Wang yangming; sage portrait; *Chuanxi Lu*; Cai Shixin

徵引文獻

（傳）曾鯨，〈天泉坐月圖〉，Poly Auction 2010/01/23，拍品674號。

《孝行錄》，東京：合資會社東京國文社，1922。

尹　襄，《巽峰集》，收入《四庫全書存目叢書》集部第67冊，臺南：莊嚴文化事業公司，1997。

方祖猷，《王畿評傳》，南京：南京大學出版社，2001。

方濬頤，《二知軒文存》，收入《清代詩文集彙編》第661冊，上海：上海古籍出版社，2010。

＿＿＿＿＿，《夢園書畫錄》，收入《歷代書畫錄輯刊》5，北京：中國圖書館出版社，2007。

王元鼎輯，《年譜》，收入《王心齋先生全集》，臺北：廣文書局，1979。

王世貞，《弇州山人續稿》，收入《明人文集叢刊》第一期第22種，臺北：文海出版社，1970。

王守仁，《傳習錄》，《王文成公全書》，臺北：臺灣商務印書館，1968，《國學基本叢書》本。

＿＿＿＿＿撰，吳光等校，《王陽明全集》，上海：上海古籍出版社，1992。

王汎森，〈明代後期的造偽與思想爭論——豐坊與《大學》石經〉，《新史學》，6：4，臺北，1995，頁1-20。

＿＿＿＿＿，〈清代儒者的全神堂——《國史儒林傳》與道光年間顧祠祭的成立〉，《中央研究院歷史語言研究所集刊》，79本1分，臺北，2008，頁63-93。

王建中等修，劉繹等纂，（同治）《永豐縣志》，收入《中國方志叢書‧華中地方‧江西省》第760號，臺北：成文出版社，1989。

王慎中，《玩芳堂摘稿》，收入《四庫全書存目叢書》集部第88冊。

包發鸞修，趙惟仁等纂，《民國南豐縣志》，收入《中國地方志集成‧江西府縣志輯》58，南京：江蘇古籍出版社，1996。

永　瑢、紀昀等撰：《四庫全書總目》，北京：中華書局，1965。

朱謀垔，《畫史會要》，收入《文淵閣四庫全書》第816冊，臺北：臺灣商務印書館，1983。

朱　艧，〈題賀中丞藏王文成公畫像〉，見孫雄輯，《道咸同光四朝詩史》，收入《歷代詩史長編》第18種，臺北：鼎文書局，1971。

艾南英，《天傭子集》，收入《四庫禁燬書叢刊補編》第72冊，北京：北京出版社，2005。

何紹基，《東洲草堂詩鈔》，收入《清代詩文集彙編》第604冊。

余之禎，王時槐等纂修，（萬曆）《吉安府志》，收入《中國方志叢書・華中地方・江西省》第768號。

吳　雲，《天門詩文稿》，江西省圖書館藏清鈔本。

吳慶坻撰，張文其、劉德麟點校，《蕉廊脞錄》，北京：中華書局，1990。

吳謙牧，《吳志仁先生遺稿》，中國國家圖書館藏清鈔本。

吳騫編，《陳乾初先生年譜》，收入《北京圖書館藏珍本年譜叢刊》第68冊，北京：北京圖書館出版社，1998。

呂妙芬，〈明清儒學關於個體不朽、死後想像、祭祀原理之論述〉，發表於中央研究院主辦「第四屆國際漢學會議」，臺北，2012。

＿＿＿＿，〈顏子之傳：一個為陽明爭取正統的聲音〉，《漢學研究》，15：1，臺北，1997，頁73-92。

宋儀望，《華陽館文集》，收入《四庫全書存目叢書》集部第116冊。

宋　濂，《宋學士文集》，臺北：臺灣商務印書館，1965，《萬有文庫》本。

李人鏡修，梅體萱纂，（同治）《南城縣志》，收入《中國地方志集成・江西府縣志輯》55-56。

李元度，《國朝先正事略》，臺北：臺灣中華書局，1965。

李宜蓁，〈入明使節的肖像：妙智院藏《策彥周良像》之研究〉，臺北：國立臺灣大學藝術史研究所碩士論文，2010。

李慈銘著，由雲龍輯，《越縵堂讀書記》，上海：上海書店出版社，2000。

李　顒，《二曲集》，收入《清代詩文集彙編》第105冊。

周右修，蔡復午等纂，（嘉慶）《東臺縣志》，收入《中國地方志集成・江蘇府縣志輯》60，南京：鳳凰出版社，2008。

周汝登，《東越證學錄》，收入《四庫全書存目叢書》集部第165冊。

屈大均，《翁山文外》，收入《清代詩文集彙編》第119冊。

邱士華，〈許初竹岡阡表介述〉，《故宮文物月刊》，377期，臺北，2014，頁62-71。

邵　寶，《容春堂集》續集，收入《文淵閣四庫全書》第1258冊。

長岡龍作編，《講座日本美術史》第4卷《造形の場》，東京：東京大學出版會，2005。

姚之駰，《元明事類鈔》，收入《文淵閣四庫全書》第884冊。

姚濬昌等修，周立瀛等纂，（同治）《安福縣志》，收入《中國方志叢書・華中地方・江西省》第773號。

姜一涵，〈普林斯頓大學美術博物館藏王陽明三札卷〉，《明報月刊》，10：1，香港，1975，頁58-65。

胡　直，《衡廬精舍藏稿》，收入《文淵閣四庫全書》第1287冊。

茅　坤,《茅鹿門先生文集》,收入《續修四庫全書》第1344冊,上海:上海古籍出版社,1995。

孫奇逢,《理學宗傳》,收入《孔子文化大全》,濟南:山東友誼書社,1989。

涂伯昌,《涂子一杯水》,收入《四庫全書存目叢書》集部第193冊。

秦　瀛,《小峴山人詩文集》,收入《續修四庫全書》第1464冊。

翁方綱,《復初齋文集》,收入《清代詩文集彙編》第382冊。

耿定向,《耿天臺先生文集》,收入《四庫全書存目叢書》集部第131冊,卷13。

袁中道,《珂雪齋遊居杮錄》,收入袁中道撰,錢伯城點校,《珂雪齋集》,上海:上海古籍出版社,2007,下冊。

張元忭,〈河南西川尤先生墓誌銘〉,在尤時熙,《擬學小記》,收入《四庫全書存目叢書》子部第9冊。

張邦奇,《張文定公環碧堂集》,收入《續修四庫全書》第1337冊。

張岱編,《陽明先生遺像冊》,收入《中華歷史人物別傳集》第21冊,北京:線裝書局,2003。

張貞生,《庸書》,收入《四庫全書存目叢書》集部第229冊。

張　夏,《雒閩源流錄》,收入《四庫全書存目叢書》史部第123冊。

張維屏編撰,陳永正點校,《國朝詩人徵略二編》,廣州:中山大學出版社,2004。

張藝曦,〈史語所藏《宋儒學案》在清中葉的編纂與流傳〉,《中央研究院歷史語言研究所集刊》,80本3分,臺北,2009,頁451-505。

_____,〈吉安府價值觀的轉變——以兩本府志為中心的分析〉,在氏著,《社群、家族與王學的鄉里實踐》,臺北:國立臺灣大學出版委員會,2006,〈附錄二〉,頁403-432。

_____,〈明中晚期古本《大學》與《傳習錄》的流傳及影響〉,《漢學研究》,24:1,臺北,2006,頁235-268。

曹于汴,《仰節堂集》,收入《文淵閣四庫全書》第1293冊。

符兆鵬等修,趙繼元等纂,(同治)《太湖縣志》,收入《中國方志叢書·華中地方·安徽省》第106號,臺北:成文出版社,1985。

許三禮,《政學合一集》,《四庫全書存目叢書》子部第165冊。

陳仁錫,《無夢園初集》,收入《續修四庫全書》第1382冊。

陳　確,《乾初先生遺集》,收入《清代詩文集彙編》第20冊。

陳　講,〈翰林院編修楊公實卿墓志銘〉,收入焦竑編纂,《國朝獻徵錄》,臺北:臺灣學生書局,1965。

陶兆麟修,蔡逢思纂,(光緒)《高明縣志》,收入《中國方志叢書·華南地方·廣東省》第186號,臺北:成文出版社,1966。

陶望齡，《歇菴集》，收入《續修四庫全書》第1365冊。

黃宗羲，《南雷文定三集》，收入《清代詩文集彙編》第33冊。

_____，《南雷文定前集》，收入《清代詩文集彙編》第33冊。

_____撰，沈芝盈點校，《明儒學案》，臺北：里仁書局，1987。

黃道周，《黃石齋先生文集》，收入《續修四庫全書》第1384冊。

單國強，〈肖像畫類型芻議〉，《故宮博物院院刊》，1990年4期，北京，1990，頁11-23。

斐大中等修，秦緗業等纂，（光緒）《無錫金匱縣志》，收入《中國方志叢書‧華中地方‧江蘇省》第21號，臺北：成文出版社，1970。

曾同亨，《泉湖山房稿》，國家圖書館藏內閣文庫影印明刊本。

曾　燠，《賞雨茅屋詩集》，收入《清代詩文集彙編》第456冊。

湛若水，《湛甘泉先生文集》，收入《四庫全書存目叢書》集部第57冊。

湯來賀，《內省齋文集》，收入《四庫全書存目叢書》集部第199冊。

程顥、程頤撰，潘富恩導讀，《二程遺書》，上海：上海古籍出版社，2000。

華人德，〈明清肖像畫略論〉，《藝術家》，218期，臺北，1993，頁236-245。

賀長齡，《耐菴詩文存》，收入《清代詩文集彙編》第550冊。

項　珂、劉馥桂等修，（同治）《萬年縣志》，收入《中國方志叢書‧華中地方‧江西省》第258號。

馮金伯，《國朝畫識》，收入《中國歷代畫史匯編》第4冊，天津：天津古籍出版社，1997。

楊　廉，《楊文恪公文集》，收入《續修四庫全書》第1332冊。

楊儒賓，〈《雅》、《頌》與西周儒家的「對越」精神〉，《中國哲學與文化》第11輯，桂林：廣西師範大學出版社，2014，頁39-67。

瑞麟等修，史澄等纂，（光緒）《廣州府志》，收入《中國方志叢書‧華南地方‧廣東省》第1號。

萬承蒼，《孺廬先生文錄》，在李祖陶，《國朝文錄續編》，收入《續修四庫全書》第1671冊。

董傳策，《邕歔稿》，收入《四庫全書存目叢書》集部第122冊。

過庭訓，《本朝分省人物考》，收入《續修四庫全書》第534冊。

鄒元標，《鄒子存真集》，國家圖書館藏內閣文庫影印明天啓二年序刊本。

_____，《願學集》，收入《文淵閣四庫全書》第1294冊。

鄒守益，《東廓鄒先生文集》，收入《四庫全書存目叢書》集部第65冊。

_____著，董平編校整理，《鄒守益集》，南京：鳳凰出版社，2007。

_____編，《王陽明先生圖譜》，《北京圖書館藏珍本年譜叢刊》第43冊。

_____編，《王陽明先生圖譜》，《四庫未收書輯刊》第四輯第17冊，北京：北京出版社，1997。

鄒德溥，〈伯兄汝海行狀〉，在鄒德涵，《鄒聚所先生外集》，收入《四庫全書存目叢書》集部第157冊。

＿＿＿＿，《鄒泗山先生文集》，傅斯年圖書館藏安成紹恩堂刊本清刊本。

鄒鍾泉，《道南淵源錄》，收入《四庫未收書輯刊》第9輯7冊。

趙　榆，〈孫悅漢及其收藏的宣聖及七十二賢贊圖卷〉，《收藏家》，2002年1期，北京，2002，頁49-51。

劉元卿，《劉聘君全集》，收入《四庫全書存目叢書》集部第154冊。

劉孔當撰，劉以城編，《劉喜聞先生集》，東京：高橋情報，1993。

劉宗堯纂，(民國)《邊江縣志》，收入《中國方志叢書·華南地方·廣西省》第136號，臺北：成文出版社，1967。

德永弘道，〈南宋初期の禪宗祖師像について——拙菴德光贊達磨像を中心に〉，《國華》929，東京，1971，頁7-17；930，東京，1971，頁5-22。

歐陽桂，《西山志》，收入《四庫禁燬書叢刊》史部第72冊，北京：北京出版社，2000。

潘振泰，〈明代江門心學的崛起與式微〉，《新史學》，7：2，臺北，1996，頁1-46。

蔣繼洙等修，李樹藩等纂，(同治)《廣信府志》，收入《中國方志叢書·華中地方·江西省》第106號。

鄧麗華，〈從曾鯨肖像畫看晚明文人個人形象的建立〉，臺北：國立臺灣師範大學碩士論文，1991。

鄭振鐸，〈「聖蹟圖」跋〉，收錄於《中國古代版畫叢刊》1，上海：上海古籍出版社，1988，頁390-392。

蕭良幹等修，張元忭等纂，(萬曆)《紹興府志》，收入《中國方志叢書·華中地方·浙江省》第520號，臺北：成文出版社，1983。

錢　明，《王陽明及其學派論考》，北京：人民出版社，2009

錢　泳撰，張偉點校，《履園叢話》，北京：中華書局，1979。

錢謙益撰集，許逸民等點校，《列朝詩集》，北京：中華書局，2007。

謝　旻等修，陶成等纂，(雍正)《江西通志》，收入《中國方志叢書·華中地方·江西省》第782號。

謝鳴謙輯，《程山謝明學先生年譜》，附於謝文洊，《謝程山集》，收入《四庫全書存目叢書》集部第209冊。

羅大紘，《紫原文集》，收入《四庫禁燬書叢刊》集部第139冊。

羅洪先，〈正學書院記〉，見周樹槐等纂修，(道光)《吉水縣志》，收入《中國方志叢書·華中地方·江西省》第766號。

井手誠之輔，〈頂相における像主の表象——見心來復象の場合〉，《仏教芸術》282，九州，2005，頁13-35。

萱場まゆみ，〈頂相と掛眞——興国寺本法燈国師像からの考察〉，《美術史研究》33，東京，1995，頁93-108。

Foulk, T. Griffith. and Robert H. Sharf, "On the Ritual Use of Ch'an Portraiture in Medieval China," *Cahiers d'Extreme-Asie*, no.7(1993), pp.149-219.

Murray, Julia K. "The Temple of Confucius and Pictorial Biographies of the Sage," *The Journal of Asian Studies*, Vol.55, No.2, May 1996, pp.269-300.

郭詡，〈文公先生像軸〉，《傳統文化博客資料庫》，http://www.bjdips.com/gwh/result.aspx?ID=GWH-27449（2015/09/08）。

【論著】

Confucian Principles and Representations of a Scandal:

Writing about Zheng Man in the Seventeenth and Eighteenth Centuries

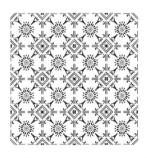

Ying Zhang（張穎）

美國俄亥俄州立大學歷史系

Ying Zhang, Assistant Professor of Chinese History at the Ohio State University. Zhang received her Ph.D. in History and Women's Studies from the University of Michigan. Her research and publications focus on Ming politics, the Ming-Qing transition, and gender in pre-modern China. Her monograph on the image politics of seventeenth-century China is forthcoming with the University of Washington Press.

Confucian Principles and Representations of a Scandal:
Writing about Zheng Man in the Seventeenth and Eighteenth Centuries

Ying Zhang

Abstract

The arrest and execution of the official Zheng Man for ethical violations was a peculiar event in late Ming politics. Modern scholarship often studies it as a personal tragedy symptomatic of government dysfunction. But this paper investigates the case and its representations in a broader, more complicated context. The paper first analyzes some Donglin figures' defense of Zheng in the Chongzhen court. Then it delves into how the case was documented in a few representative early Qing accounts and compares their moral-political messages. Lastly, through a close examination of the roles played by certain Qing literati in disseminating negative images of Zheng Man, it considers the relationship between political identification and the historiography of the Donglin, exposing the complicated ways in which political historical sources were produced. They reflect the diversity and disparities among literati understandings of Confucian moral-political principles and how those principles should be applied in political, social, and intellectual life.

Keywords: Donglin; factionalism; Ming-Qing transition; political historiography; Confucianism

In 1639, an official named Zheng Man 鄭鄤 (1594-1639), who stood accused of beating his mother and other offences, was executed by *lingchi* 凌遲 ("death by a thousand cuts") after years of imprisonment.[1] Zheng Man hailed from Wujin 武進 County, Changzhou Prefecture. His father, Zheng Zhenxian 鄭振先 (*jinshi* 1595), gained fame by criticizing a clique of power abusers in the Grand Secretariat but retired at the height of the factional struggles in the Ming Wanli 萬曆 reign (1573-1620). At some point, both the father and the son were considered members of the Donglin faction, a major player in seventeenth-century political history.[2] Zheng Man himself became a target of factional persecution in the Tianqi 天啓 reign (1621-1627) as a result of his actions again the eunuch faction. In the mid-Chongzhen 崇禎 reign (1628-1644), just as Zheng Man returned to a government post after two terms of mourning for his deceased parents, he was brought up for impeachment on the charge that he had beaten his

---

[1]   I thank the two anonymous reviewers for their valuable comments and suggestions on the draft. I also wish to thank Dr. Miaw-fen Lu for an extremely helpful discussion with me about this case study. I am responsible for any errors and misinterpretations.

[2]   A large amount of research has been done on the Donglin. It mainly falls into three areas of research: the history of the Donglin Academy in the late Ming and the intellectual contributions of the officials associated with this institution; the so-called "Donglin movement" which combines its explorations in Neo-Confucian scholarship and socio-political reforms; and the Donglin as a political faction in the late Ming. Representative works on its political activities include: Dardess, *Blood and History*, 1; Fan Shuzhi, "Donglin shuyuan de shitai fenxi;" Hucker, "The T'ung-lin Movement;" Miller, "Opposition to the Donglin Faction" and "Newly Discovered Source Sheds Light on Late Ming Faction;" Ono, *Ming ji dang she kao*.

mother. The emperor ordered him arrested. Unverifiable accusations of other ethical violations, such as raping a daughter-in-law and violating his father's concubine, soon followed. As circumstantial evidence, these accusations complicated and transformed the case. For instance, vernacular novels were composed by his political enemies and presented to the emperor as "public opinion." The development of Zheng's case was deeply entangled in the factional infighting at the court amid the Chongzhen emperor's struggle with Donglin-identified officials in a series of policy and personnel debates.[3] Zheng's execution put a horrific end to his ordeal, but only enhanced the sensation his case caused among the reading public. In the seventeenth and eighteenth centuries, this case frequently appeared in literati works on the history and politics of the late Ming.

In modern historical scholarship, Zheng Man's death has been studied as a personal tragedy symptomatic of government dysfunction in the late Ming. But this paper investigates this case in a broader, more complicated context. Although we might not be able to accurately reconstruct what happened behind the walls of the Zheng family or of the interrogation room in prison, we will see how the interplay between Confucian principles, politics, and intellectual concerns determined how Zheng Man's case was discussed and represented, especially after his death. We begin with an analysis of some Donglin figures' defense of Zheng Man in the Ming Chongzhen court. Then we will delve into how the Zheng Man

---

3　Ye Jun, "Zheng Man yanjiu;" Zhang, "Politics and Practice of Moral Rectitude." Many of these officials were identified at the time as Donglin associates.

case was documented in certain, representative early Qing accounts and compare their moral-political messages. Lastly, through a close examination of the roles played by certain Qing literati in disseminating negative images of Zheng Man, we will consider the relationship between political identification and the historiography of the Donglin.

These texts from the seventeenth and eighteenth centuries expose the complicated ways in which political historical sources were produced. They also reflect the diversity and disparities among literati understandings of Confucian moral-political principles and how those principles should be applied in political, social, and intellectual life. Such diversity and disparities shed light on the elite's dynamic engagements with the Confucian tradition as the empire was going through its early modern transformation.

The (Im) possibility of Moral Defenses

The Analects includes a famous conversation between Confucius and the Duke of She:

> The Duke of She informed Confucius, "Among us here there are those who may be styled upright in their conduct. If someone's father has stolen a sheep, he will bear witness to the fact." Confucius said, "Among us, in our part of the country, those who are upright are different from this. The father conceals the misconduct of the son, and the son conceals the

misconduct of the father. Uprightness is to be found in this."[4]

This passage has rich meanings. First, it plainly conveys the Confucian emphasis on the foundational morality of the father-son bond. Second, it demonstrates that one's resolve to uphold moral values in all circumstances is itself an important Confucian virtue. Lastly, the significance of "truth" is appreciated not in isolation but rather in connection with fundamental moral concerns.

These ideas had tremendous influence on the behavior of elite men in imperial China. They determined, in the 1630s, what Zheng Man and his defenders would and would not say when they tried to fight the moral charges leveled against Zheng by their factional enemies. Decades after Zheng Man's execution, at his son's request, the early Qing historian and political critic Huang Zongxi 黃宗羲（1610-1695）composed an epitaph for Zheng Man. Huang wrote a very straightforward account of the Zhengs' domestic dispute: Zheng Man was a reputable man in his hometown. His mother was jealous of his father's love for a concubine. She created so much trouble in the household that her husband took the concubine with him on a tour to Buddhist temples. Zheng Man asked a Buddhist nun, whom his mother had befriended, to help settle the conflict between his parents. The nun instructed him to pretend to have received a mysterious message through *jixian* 箕仙, which warned his mother of

---

4　Translation adapted from Ames and Rosemont, Jr., *The Analects of Confucius*, 13.18, with minor changes.

potentially serious consequences of her terrible behavior. Hence, Zheng Man's father was able to restore domestic order. According to Huang Zongxi, somehow this harmless trick devised by the nun was dramatically distorted in the gossip—which later became an official charge—that Zheng Man had used a bamboo stick to discipline his mother.

Well aware of the taboo against exposing the older generation's faults, Huang explains why he feels obliged to detail the confrontation between Zheng Man's parents, which later fostered rumors and provided material for vicious accusations against their son:

> [Zheng Zhenxian's] infatuation with his concubine and his wife's jealousy, that is, mistakes made by the parents, are minor problems. Considering that [Zheng Man] has been subjected to public ridicule and criminal charges, isn't it obvious that we should differentiate the minor problem from the serious one? Only when we clarify what happened in Zheng Man's case could we expose the evil doings of the vicious grand secretary. This is our responsibility.[5]

"The evil grand secretary" in this passage refers to Wen Tiren 溫體仁 (1573-1639), the major anti-Donglin figure in the mid-Chongzhen reign. He had successfully engineered and supported attacks on a few Donglin

---

5   Huang Zongxi, "Zheng Miyang xiansheng mubiao" 鄭峚陽先生墓表, *Nanlei wen ding*: Vol. 3: 2.7b-8b.

figures and the Fu She 復社（Restoration Society）, an empire-wide literary society nicknamed "the Little Donglin" due to their overlapping political concerns and memberships. Huang Zongxi is known to have had his own partisan affinity to the Donglin-Fushe community. But he rightly points out that Zheng Man had to protect his parents' reputation. In fact, Zheng Man had no better options. If he publicized his parents' problems to defend his own innocence he would have violated the principle of filial piety.

　　Filial considerations occupied a significant place in literati lives and careers; many had encountered similarly delicate situations and had to make difficult choices. The son's decision, his contemporaries' reactions, and the consequences of his decision together stand as a good illustration of how elite men practiced Confucianism at the intersection of everyday life and politics in particular historical circumstances. Zhang Pu 張溥（1602-1641）and Zhang Cai 張采（1596-1648）, founders of the Fu She, can be briefly examined here as an interesting contrast. Zhang Pu was the son of an unassertive father and a maid-turned-concubine. His uncle, who had risen to the powerful position of president of the Board of Punishment, tolerated his servants' abusive treatment of Zhang Pu's father, who subsequently died in depression. It became well known that Zhang Pu wrote in his own blood on a wall: "I do not deserve to be called a son if I don't seek revenge against the evil servants!"[6] Meanwhile, the father of his

---

6　Zhang Pu, "Xiankao Xuyu fujun xingzhuang" 先考盧宇府君行狀, *Qiluzhai shiwen he ji*, 571–95. Lu Shiyi, *Fushe ji lue*, 47.

friend Zhang Cai had died from longtime psychological abuse inflicted by a half-brother born of Zhang Cai's grandfather and a favorite concubine.[7] The two Zhangs' shared experience of losing their fathers in unfortunate domestic circumstances and practicing filial devotion toward their widowed mothers was emphasized by Zhang Pu to show the depth of their friendship.[8] These episodes were highly publicized by the Fu She to show their commitment to the Confucian Five Cardinal Relations (*wulun* 五倫). However, a former Fu She member, the official Zhou Zhikui 周之夔 (*jinshi* 1631), who became a public enemy of the Fu She and the Donglin due to his conflict with the two Zhangs, denounced the Zhangs as "disloyal and unfilial" (*bu zhong bu xiao* 不忠不孝).[9] Publicly and privately, he had argued that their very act of portraying themselves as filial sons by exposing family scandals was unfilial.[10] Zhou's criticisms may well not have been his alone or purely politically motivated. In the epitaph for Zhang Pu's father composed by the official Ma Shiqi 馬世奇 (*jinshi* 1631), a Fu She member who also entered the Donglin roster, Ma felt it necessary to justify Zhang Pu's action: "He revealed details [of a domestic abuse] that had tormented his father but which his father himself could not

---

7   Zhang Pu, "Zeng Wenlinlang Zhang taiweng feng ruren Su Taimu he zang muzhiming" 贈文林郎張太翁封孺人蘇太母合塋墓誌銘, *Qiluzhai shiwen he ji*, 417–28.

8   Zhang Pu, "Zeng Wenlinlang Zhang taiweng feng ruren Su Taimu he zang muzhiming," "Zhang bomu yingfeng xu" 張伯母膺封序 and "Zhang Shouxian gao xu" 張受先稿序, *Qiluzhai shiwen he ji*, 899–906 and 963–68.

9   Zhou Zhikui, "Shang Lin Rang'an libu shu" 上林讓菴吏部書, *Qicao erji*, 49.

10 Zhou Zhikui, "Shang Chen Shengreng shiyu shu," *Qicao erji*, 42.

reveal. A brother and a son have different moral responsibilities."[11] The actions by Zheng Man and the two Zhangs, and the reactions they received, illustrate that in the late Ming, a filial performance could be interpreted in drastically different ways for various political, social, and cultural reasons.

Modern readers might ask: Why could Zheng's friend-colleagues not help him clarify the matter and repudiate the rumors?[12] We must again remember the Confucian culture to which the literatus-official adhered. He was supposed to not only "refrain from criticizing people of superior status" (*wei zun zhe hui* 爲尊者諱) but also avoid "talking about other people's private matters" (*tan ren guiwei* 談人閨闈). No serious officials would want to publicly discuss topics such as the beating of a mother or the rape a daughter-in-law by a colleague, even if they knew the allegations were false, because then they would have to openly address the private content

---

11   Ma Shiqi, "Xuyu Zhang gong muzhiming" 盧宇張公墓誌銘, *Danningju wenji*, 236. Some Fu She scholars came to be identified as members of the Donglin faction in the late Ming after they passed the examinations and became officials. Ma Shiqi was included in both Fu She and Donglin lists. See Wu Shanjia, *Fu She xingshi zhuanlue*, 3.16a; Gao Tingzhen et al., *Donglin shuyuan zhi*.

12   Two public statements by the Zheng clan in Wujin, released several months after Zheng Man's execution, strongly and explicitly condemning Zheng Man's brother for the part he played in incriminating Zheng Man and causing his tragedy. "Zheng shi tong zu ji wen" 鄭氏通族祭文 and "Zheng shi tong zu zhu bu di Zheng Yiqian xi" 鄭氏通族誅不弟鄭一謙檄, in *Miyang caotang wenji* (hereafer *MYCTWJ*), 504-07. Zheng Man's uncle also wrote a testimony in support of Zheng. Zheng Zhenyuan, "Bianyuan jie" 辯冤揭, in Tang Xiuye, *Zheng an chuanxin lu yuangao*, no page number.

of these kinds of incidents, in particular someone's sexual conduct. This may explain the reticence of the Donglin official Sun Shenxing 孫慎行 (1565-1636), president of the Board of Rituals and the Zhengs' hometown friend-neighbor who happened to be at home when the alleged crimes occurred. When the Board of Punishments asked Sun to provide first-hand information, Sun responded that he did not socialize much during his temporary retirement and therefore could offer no "local knowledge."[13]

Prominent scholar-officials who actively made efforts to rescue Zheng Man resorted to a similar approach. Instead of discussing the specifics of the scandal, they pointed out to the Chongzhen emperor the danger of letting unverifiable, sensational attacks enter political discussion. In defense of Zheng Man, insisting on the principle of not bringing up domestic matters in policy debates, the official Huang Daozhou 黃道周 (1585-1646) submitted a memorial to illustrate the connection between loyalty and other virtues. He identifies "loyalty" with the moral principle that a righteous man should not defame others, especially regarding personal matters. By doing so, Huang suggested that those who tried to implicate Zheng Man on charges of lacking filial piety and sexual immorality were "disloyal."[14] This argument was echoed by the renowned

---

13   No one could fully substantiate the charges. So the emperor ordered the Board of Punishments to obtain the testimony of a number of Wujin natives. Sun Shenxing did not provide any incriminating evidence. It was well known that Sun were very close to the Zhengs. Zheng Man, *Tianshan zixu nianpu* (hereafter *TSZXNP*), 492.

14   Zhang, "Politics and Practice of Moral Rectitude."

scholar-official Liu Zongzhou 劉宗周（1578-1645), who also tried to defend Zheng Man upon his arrest.

Two years after Zheng's execution, in a memorial to the Chongzhen emperor, Liu Zongzhou again invoked the case to argue that Confucian principles would be jeopardized should the practice of prosecuting officials based on dubious charges of personal immorality be allowed to persist. He suggested that the emperor's intention to punish immorality and promote filial piety to restore political order might have been manipulated by vicious officials. The political responsibility of the emperor, Liu argued, includes the ability to differentiate loyal subjects from evil officials, which required that he have faith in his officials and refrain from punishing them on the basis of groundless accusations.[15]

Huang Daozhou and Liu Zongzhou, both widely admired for scholarly accomplishments, did not simply invoke age-old Confucian principles. They reiterated these principles because Zheng Man's case had reflected new political, social, and cultural problems of the time. As the empire had become increasingly mobile and connected, people craved to hear the latest stories of current events and prominent figures. The printing boom allowed them to quickly pass on "new stories" (*xinwen* 新聞), information flowing outside—and often unverifiable by—official channels.[16] In parallel with the religious and cultural syncretism of the

---

15　Liu Zongzhou, "Yuan ren gongbu zuo shilang Liu gong Zongzhou xi gao pou xin ken qi sheng jian shu" 原任工部左侍郎劉公宗周席稿剖心懇啓聖鑒疏 in Zheng Man, *MYCTWJ*, 503.
16　I translate this seventeenth-century term as "new stories" to differentiate its

time, popular literature, whose readership expanded tremendously in the late Ming, increasingly employed moral rhetoric to justify contesting Confucian norms themselves or simply to create a setting for entertaining stories.[17] In addition to political maneuvers, cynicism and indifference across society also contributed to the irresponsible circulation and appropriation of these stories.

In the mid-Wanli reign, officials began to take notice of the political repercussions of these phenomena. The literati had become aggressive in their self-expression and behavior; their methods of moral-political attack took on new forms, too. As the official Wu Yuancui 伍袁萃 (*jinshi* 1580) observed at the beginning of the seventeenth century,

In recent years, the literati have become malicious and spiteful. Things are especially serious in the Wu 吳 area (Wu Yuancui's home region). Even just trivial grievances against officials and local notables cause them to band together and hurl insults. Their attack methods include making up folk songs, writing Southern plays (*chuanqi* 傳奇), or appropriating phrases from the classics. How strange that the censors and governors quote these things in their memorials! The malicious and spiteful atmosphere has been worsening and seems to be out of control.[18]

---

usage from the modern ones. For discussion about print and politics, see for example Wang Hung-tai, "Shehui de xiangxiang" and "Ming Qing de zixun chuanbo."

17   For analyses of literature and Confucian values of this period, see for example, Sieber, *Theater of Desire*; Epstein, *Competing Discourses*; Huang, *Desire and Fictional Narrative*; and Vitiello, *Libertine's Friend*.

18   Wu Yuancui, *Yi'antang gao: Tu ji* (zazu pian), 31a.

Consequently, Wu continues, these conditions made officials vulnerable:

> Nowadays, officials who comment on politics [risk] being
> punished. They could be either stripped of their official
> positions or impeached. Those who lose their jobs might still be
> able to [win some measure of] fame. But those who are
> slandered suffer grave consequences.[19]

Wu goes on to point out the two most contemptible tendencies in officials' memorials:

> The most ridiculous kind [of memorial] present to His Majesty
> things like public postings. The most condemnable kind inserts
> the content of private letters and conversations into evidence for
> impeachment. In particular, *memorials that collect rumor,
> fantasy, and stories about someone raping a daughter-in-law
> merely pass on frivolous and vulgar theories*; they are absurd
> and filthy. They are definitely inappropriate for memorials.[20]

In light of these interlocking developments in politics, culture, and society, the wide circulation of rumors about Zheng Man's sexual

---

19   Wu Yuancui, *Yi'antang gao: Si ji* (yishi pian), 43a.
20   Wu Yuancui, *Yi'antang gao: Si ji*, 69b-70a. Emphasis by this author.

immorality becomes understandable. Charges like this not only took advantage of the Confucian preoccupation with domestic order but also played on contemporary readers' interest in political news and sensational stories. The flourishing print culture helped sell such stories. The accusations of Zheng's sexual aggression against his daughter-in-law "inspired" at least three biographies, *Minjie waishi* 愍節外史, *Han lienu zhuan* 韓烈女傳, and *You zhuan* 又傳. These texts elaborate on Zheng's alleged affair with his father's beloved concubine and alleged attempt to rape his daughter-in-law, a young woman surnamed Han 韓, the daughter of Zheng Man's good friend and fellow Wujin resident, Han Zhongxun 韓鐘勛 (*jinshi* 1631).[21] The biographies of the Han daughter offer juicy details about Zheng's attempted rape and the claim that she committed suicide to preserve her chastity against her sexual predator. The above quote by Wu Yuancui informs us that accusations against officials for raping a daughter-in-law were not a rare occurrence. It helps explain why vernacular novels were written to elaborate on the sensational charges against Zheng Man, and why the novels could reach the emperor as evidence of his moral corruption. Zheng Man's case—and the ways in which popular literary taste, publishing, and "public opinion" influenced political communication—was not an abnormality.[22] Thus, Confucian moral expectations, the particular socio-cultural conditions of the late

---

21 These biographies are included in Zhang Xia, *Yuqiaohua.*
22 For example, see how the literatus Li Xunzhi considered Xu Xi's memorial to the emperor as representing the public opinion. Li Xunzhi, *Chongzhen chao jishi*, 509.

Ming, and the ways in which Confucian moralism was appropriated all created obstacles for Zheng and his sympathizers.

If an official accused of lacking filial piety could not expose domestic disputes and his parents' flaws for the purpose of self-defense, what could he resort to? As Zheng Man's subsequent actions would show, publicizing one's exemplary performance of Confucian values had become an important method. But again he had to avoid exposing his parents' faults. To fulfill his filial duty and at the same time battle the manipulation and misappropriation of his family affairs by political enemies, Zheng Man while in prison produced printed and hand-copied public letters, postings, memorials, poems, and essays to create an ideal moral image for himself and his parents. Instead of describing exactly what had happened between his father and mother, Zheng strove to defend the family reputation and especially his parents' virtues.

Zheng's chronological autobiography is representative. The act of defending his parents' character and reputation was itself fulfilling the mission of filial piety, but such performance seemed even more urgently needed as his accusers were beefing up circumstantial evidence to "prove" his violation of filial duties.[23] In addition to defending his father's political

---

23　The last date mentioned in Zheng's autobiography is Chongzhen 11/8/20 （1638）, a year before his execution. Between 8/15 and 20, Zheng Man recorded how he and his son were waiting in prison to hear the decision from the Board of Punishments and the emperor's final word on his case. No final decision was made then. Zheng Man tells the reader that he had contemplated compiling the chronological autobiography almost immediately after he was arrested. But illness delayed the project. In the summer and early fall of 1638,

loyalty, Zheng Man represents him as a filial son who was almost austere in terms of worldly matters. He portrays an ideal father and literatus-official as the first steps in establishing a moral and upright family tradition.[24] According to Zheng's autobiography, the family value of filial piety is transmitted patrilineally. It is embedded in the seamless transition of the autobiographical focus from the father's filial piety to the son's.

Ever since he was arrested, through a variety of media, Zheng Man's defense of his parents' spousal harmony had constituted a significant part of the battle to prove his own moral character. In this autobiography, Zheng Man insists that his parents travelled *together* to Buddhist sites. (Interestingly, as we saw earlier, Huang Zongxi claimed that Zheng's father took the beloved concubine on a trip to various Buddhist temples.) The representation of his parents comports well with the contemporary ideal of *yin fu yi qi* 隱夫逸妻 (a couple in reclusion), an interesting historical variation on the cultural practices of *yin* 隱 (eremitism; withdrawal from the mundane world) popular in the late Ming and early Qing. Traditionally the gender of *yin* culture and identity is assumed to be male, because the practice of *yin* often constituted political action in defiance of a bad or illegitimate government that could only be initiated by

---

Zheng Man suffered from harsh interrogations but he refused to admit he was guilty. As his accusers were stepping up in their desperate search for "witnesses" to consolidate the case against Zheng Man and persuade the emperor to execute him, Zheng asked one of his sons to help compile the autobiography. He claims that this would be subject to the judgment of literati readers of later generations. Zheng Man, *TSZXNP*, 495-99.

24   Zheng Man, *TSZXNP,* 484-85.

male subjects. During the Ming-Qing transition, a new gender identity was emerging for the recluse. Wu Weiye 吳偉業（1608-1671）observed the changed lifestyle of *yin*, saying that unlike the hermits of old, contemporary hermits do not leave behind their parents or wife and children.[25] This transformation was also connected to gentry's increasing interest in lay-Buddhist pursuits. In this sense, lay-Buddhist devotion not only provided a space for literati to gather for their favored cultural practices, it also provided a new cultural venue for married life in gentry society.[26] But literati-officials still had to accommodate their lay-Buddhist pursuits within Confucian morality, especially its terms of familial and political duty. It is therefore understandable that in Zheng Man's account of his parents' Buddhist pursuits, he stresses their harmonious spousal relationship and their emphasis on filial piety as the Zhengs' central family value.

Lastly, by stressing the unity of the Zheng father and son's political reputation and moral accomplishments, Zheng Man could debunk the popular theory that he had faked filial piety to deceive Donglin colleagues. He ends the remembrance of his parents with a mention of two Donglin icons and good friends, Huang Daozhou and Wen Zhenmeng 文震孟（1574-1636）:

> Many years ago, Huang Shizhai 石齋（Huang Daozhou）took a

---

[25] Wu Weiye, "Chen Quean zunren qi shi xu" 陳確菴尊人七十序, *Meicun jia cang gao*, 37.5a-6a.

[26] Brook, *Praying for Power*, 105.

leave to accompany my Aunt [Huang]²⁷ to the south. At that
time Father and Mother were still alive. Shizhai performed the
shengtang rite.²⁸ Father had for a long time shied away from
visitors. Among those in my *jinshi* cohort, he only received
Zhanchi 湛持 (Wen Zhenmeng) and Shizhai, partly because
they insisted on paying him visits. Later when Shizhai was on
his way back to the capital, he mourned my father. His wife paid
a visit to my mother and stayed with her for ten days. The next
time they came, they had to mourn my mother.²⁹

By this time, Huang and Wen had come to symbolize the upright
Donglin man. In his representation of these friendships, Zheng Man enlists
the two friends as key witnesses. They not only admired the Zheng father's
political integrity but also shared with Zheng Man a strong sense of filial
devotion. He quotes officials who defended him and Wen Zhenmeng, after
they memorialized against the powerful eunuch Wei Zhongxian 魏忠賢:
"The offspring of loyal officials would only want to become loyal
officials!"³⁰

---

27 Shizhai is Huang Daozhou's literary name. Here, Zheng Man uses *bomu* 伯
    母, literally meaning aunt, to refer to Huang Daozhou's mother.
28 *Shengtang zhi li* 升堂之禮 is often referred to as *shengtang bai mu* 升堂拜母.
    In pre-modern China, when one intimate friend visited another, they usually
    went to the back hall and to greet their friend's mother. This etiquette was
    called *shengtang bai mu*.
29 Zheng Man, *TSZXNP*, 491.
30 Zheng Man, *TSZXNP*, 488.

It is unclear how widely this autobiography was disseminated during the one year between its completion and Zheng Man's execution. Nonetheless, it reiterated and elaborated on Zheng's previous claims about his parents, which had already been presented to the emperor in memorials as his self-defense. We cannot absolutely exclude the possibility that Zheng Man, even if he did not beat his mother, might have moral defects as an individual. Limited space here does not allow for a comprehensive analysis of the case. Still, the accusations and defense put forth by the various sides reveal that the discursive connection between public and personal moralities according to the Confucian formulation generated both opportunities and limitations for political actors.

Early Qing Representations

Almost as soon as the Donglin emerged as a political force in the late Wanli reign, factional rivals labeled their Confucian scholarship "false teaching," and denied the Donglin its claim to moral exemplarity. But after the eunuch faction's bloody persecution of Donglin-identified officials during the Tianqi reign, the popular image of the Donglin was a faction of moral exemplars. Still, many argued that opportunists had sneaked into the Donglin camp and corrupted its moral purity. Zheng Man's case became a hot topic because it could be appropriated by all sides to make a point about the Donglin. As I have pointed out elsewhere, even before the Chongzhen emperor made up his mind to execute Zheng Man, some in the Donglin-Fu She community—such as Chen Zilong 陳子龍（1608-

1647)—had already contemplated severing ties with Zheng to protect the Donglin claim to the moral high ground. The Fu She activist Zhang Zilie 張自烈 (1597-1673) even advocated a unified Donglin-Fushe stance on this issue, thereby silencing those who had expressed admiration for Zheng Man because they did not support "the pure element's judgment" (*bu he qingyi* 不合清議).[31] Similarly, in the post-1644 era, many literati disseminated unverified information and made hasty moral judgments about Zheng Man in order to clarify their own political stance.

Among the literati-produced historical works in the early Qing, most agree that Zheng Man was a victim of Grand Secretary Wen Tiren's conspiracy against the growing power of the Donglin, especially the combined forces of iconic figures such as Wen Zhenmeng and Huang Daozhou. But writers had differing views on the charges against Zheng Man and the veracity of his Donglin status. Jiang Pingjie 蔣平階 (1616-1714), a disciple of Chen Zilong, records that rival officials attacked Zheng Man's moral character because they wanted to use his case to prevent Wen Zhenmeng and Huang Daozhou from gaining more power in the government.[32] Li Xunzhi 李遜之 (?-1677), son of the widely recognized Donglin leader Li Yingsheng 李應昇 (1593-1626), echoes Jiang's view that Zheng Man's misconduct in his hometown allowed Wen

---

31 Zhang Zilie, "Zai fu Shen Meisheng shu" 再復沈眉生書, *Qishan wenji*, 116-17. Zhang, "Politics and Practice of Moral Rectitude."

32 Jiang Pingjie, *Donglin shimo*, 27. Part of the contents is the same as Ji Liuqi's *Ming ji bei lue*. Jiang Pingjie was a member of Ji She, a literary society that had a very close but complicated relationship with the Fu She.

Tiren to create a dilemma for the upright Donglin officials and made Wen Zhenmeng and Huang Daozhou politically vulnerable.[33] These historical works circulate other literati's documentation and hearsay; they all contain obviously false information about Zheng Man's case. Taken together, however, they presented an influential perspective and supported a sweeping argument that evil anti-Donglin partisans employed horrendous strategies to attack and persecute the morally impeccable Donglin. They did not verify Zheng Man's moral defects but simply used the case to make their own points.

Another telling example can be found in an early Qing historical novel on late Ming politics, *Qiaoshi tongsu yanyi* 樵史通俗演義. As the modern historian Meng Sen 孟森 suggests, the author, apparently a Ming loyalist, had an explicit agenda to eulogize the Donglin officials and condemn anti-Donglin factions.[34] Zheng Man appears in this novel as a moral deviant attaching himself to the "gentlemen's faction."[35] The author's representation of Donglin history and moral exemplarity reflected and perpetuated a popular, politically convenient attitude toward Zheng Man's case. He accomplished this by using late Ming sources selectively. For instance, among the historical works of the late Ming which the author

33   Li Xunzhi, *Chongzhen chao ji shi*, 509.
34   Meng Sen, "Chong yin *Qiaoshi tongsu yanyi xu*" 重印樵史通俗演義序, in Jiangzuo qiaozi, *Qiaoshi tongsu yanyi*, 1a-6a. Huazhao qiaozi, "Qiaoshi xu" in *Qiaoshi tongsu yanyi*, no page number. In the preface, the author uses the name Huazhao qiaozi 花朝樵子.
35   Jiangzuo qiaozi, *Qiaoshi tongsu yanyi*, 3.13b-14a.

claimed to be consulting, one finds *Song tian lu bi* 頌天臚筆, a massive volume penned and published by the literatus Jin Risheng 金日升 (fl. 1620s) at the beginning of the Ming Chongzhen reign. Aiming to provide comprehensive documentation of officials' brave resistance to Wei Zhongxian during the Tianqi reign and the new emperor's swift actions against the eunuch faction, this book came into print as soon as the Chongzhen emperor was enthroned and had dismantled the eunuch power machine. Jin Risheng praises Zheng Man as an upright official and in particular points out his exemplary filial devotion.[36] The author of *Qiaoshi tongsu yanyi*, by ignoring this kind of biographical detail, betrays his determination to purge men like Zheng Man from Donglin roster.

In the early Qing, Zheng Man's case was also employed by some to question the Donglin's image of moral perfection. Li Qing 李清 (1602- 1683), who served in the Chongzhen government and then the Southern Ming Hongguang court, was one of them. He did not join the Qing government and enjoyed much authority as a historian because of both his insider status in the late Ming and his *yimin* 遺民 ("remnant subject," or Ming loyalist) identity in the early Qing. In his most influential work, *San yuan biji* 三垣筆記, Li Qing depicts Zheng Man as an evil man, his account allegedly informed by "local knowledge" provided by the official Wang Zhang 王章 (d. 1644), also a native of Wujin. Li reports that the Donglin official Sun Shenxing was deceived by Zheng Man's phony

---

36   Jin Risheng, *Song tian lu bi*, 690.

intellectual quality.[37] He also documents how, according to "some righteous natives" of Wujin, Zheng Man put on a mask of filial piety to impress Huang Daozhou, another Donglin figure. By the time Li Qing published this work, Wang Zhang had already died: He was one of the officials who committed suicide upon the fall of Beijing in 1644. The official record says that Wang Zhang did not know anything about Zheng Man's family matters. More importantly, Wang allowed his name to appear as one of the proofreaders of Zheng Man's collected works, specifically, a volume of poems that Zheng had composed in prison.[38] This can only be interpreted as an important gesture of recognition. Such contradictions aside, Li Qing presents no evidence to substantiate his remarks that the late Chongzhen emperor made a resolute and wise decision to execute Zheng because he had seen through his faked moral image.[39] This is not "first-hand information," as Li claims, but merely a representation of the Chongzhen emperor as an astute ruler who did not back down in dealing with a morally corrupt man. Li Qing's bias against Zheng reflected the continued bitterness among former Ming officials caused by factionalism in the last decades of the Ming. Li complains that factionalism hurt many officials by dividing them into Donglin and non-Donglin camps, his father being one of the latter. In his petition on behalf of his father, who was punished for his connection with the eunuch faction, Li Qing seems particularly unforgiving toward certain controversial Donglin figures,

---

[37]   Li Qing, *San yuan biji*, 18.
[38]   Zheng Man, *MYCTSJ*, 682.
[39]   Li Qing, *San yuan biji*, 72.

especially those who were not morally perfect.[40] In *San yuan biji*, he cites one of his own old memorials to argue that the Donglin did not represent moral perfection: commenting on Zheng Man's defending of Wen Zhenmeng's criticisms of eunuch power at the Tianqi court, Li bitingly refers to Zheng as a *xiaoren* 小人 who has attached himself to a gentleman.[41]

The abovementioned authors all focus on what Zheng Man's case reveals about the Donglin faction. They are all vague about his alleged moral defects themselves. But their claims are predicated on and helped perpetuate the impression generated by the sensationalistic stories circulated in popular sources. Take, for example, Zheng's image as a sexually immoral man.

If the officials defended Zheng Man by focusing on how Confucian principles should be understood and observed, popular literature and public imagination tended to fix on sensational elements, especially the flimsy "inner-chamber" details. What made Zheng Man vulnerable and his domestic life a ready target of rumor was the complex composition of the Zheng household. When Zheng Man's wife failed to conceive in the first six years of their marriage, the family followed the local wisdom of "raising girls to bear boys" (*ya nü sheng nan* 壓女生男) to fulfill the filial duty of continuing the patrilineal line. Zheng's grandmother, Madam Dong, had his wife adopt a girl from the Dong family.[42] Then Zheng Man

---

40   Wen Bing, *Jia-yi shi an*, 510.
41   Li Qing, *Nan du lu*, 161 & 171.
42   Li Qing, *Nan du lu*, 486.

and his wife adopted two infant girls from her remote relatives, girls who
would have been drowned after their births due to their families' poverty.
The couple's Buddhist piety might have inspired these charitable
adoptions. Thus Zheng already had three adopted daughters by the time he
turned thirty.[43] Over the years, Zheng's wife and two concubines together
produced six daughters. (They also gave births to a total of five sons.) In
addition, Zheng Man's daughter-in-law, Miss Han, lost her parents at the
tender age of twelve and became seriously ill. The Zhengs welcomed her
into their household although she was too young to be officially married.
She died soon afterwards. How all these women had entered into Zheng's
household fairly reflected the gendered social and religious realities in
their world. In a sense, they represented the concerns, decisions, and
lifestyle typical of gentry households. But they did not look like the family
of the Donglin man, whose idealized image of moral purity had been
established by Donglin sympathizers.

The joint operation of moralism and sensationalism permeated early
Qing accounts of Zheng Man, as the boundaries between historical and
literary writings further blurred and intellectual standards grew confused.
Instead of checking the sources, some early Qing literati writers simply
suggested that women of various ages and social strata—including maids
and nannies—resided in Zheng Man's house and that this had planted the
seed of disorder and scandal. One author, Ji Liuqi 計六奇 (1616-?),
argued that the Zhengs' messy domestic arrangements alone suggested that

---

43 Li Qing, *Nan du lu*, 486.

the charge of raping the daughter-in-law could be true.[44]

In fact, Ji's historical work, *Mingji bei lüe*《明季北略》(An Outline of the Late Ming), borrowed from literary sources, including the abovementioned *Qiaoshi tongsu yanyi*.[45] The entry on Zheng Man, entitled "Zheng Man benmo" 鄭鄤本末 (A Complete Account of Zheng Man's Life, "Complete Account" hereafter), came from "Miyang shi hui 崧陽事會" (Key Issues in Zheng Man's Case), a piece in an early Qing collection of anecdotes.[46] Likely Ji Liuqi had gotten this source from the literatus Zhang Xia 張夏 (fl. 17th c.), to whom the editorship of *Yuqiaohua* 漁樵話 (Chat between a Fisherman and a Woodman), a collection of material on Zheng Man, is attributed. Both men hailed from Wuxi 無錫, where the Donglin Academy was located. When Ji Liuqi was writing his book, Zhang Xia traveled with him to track down sources.[47] On one of these trips in 1670, Ji and Zhang visited the ancestral hall of the loyalist martyr Du Yinxi 堵胤錫 (1601-1649) and saw the wooden figures

---

44   Ji Liuqi, "Zheng Man ben mo," *Mingji bei lue*, 261.

45   Also see Ye Jun, "Zheng Man yanjiu," 17 fn. 9.

46   Compiler's notes to "*Yuqiaohua* Zheng Man benmo," Tang Juanshi, *Zheng Man shiji* III, 5a.

47   For example, Ji notes in an entry on the rebel leader Li Zicheng 李自成: "Feng Jipu, a literatus from Jiangyin, followed a Wuxi gentry Zhang Fu and traveled to Gongchang, Shanxi. He had returned from the trip. I thought he must have learned much about [Li] Zicheng [in Shanxi] and attempted to visit him. But I could not find the time until the winter of Kangxi 9. Zhang Qiushao (Zhang Xia) and I made a trip to see him. The account above came from this interview with Feng." Ji Liuqi, *Mingji beilue*, 651.

Du had made to express his filial piety.[48] Their intellectual collaboration explains why Ji's "Complete Account" is identical to Zhang's "*Yuqiaohua Zheng Man benmo*" 漁樵話鄭鄤本末（Complete Account of Zheng Man's Life from the *Yuqiaohua*, the "*Yuqiaohua* Complete Account" hereafter）. Locally, Zhang Xia enjoyed much greater fame and more resources than did Ji Liuqi. Whereas Ji's documentation took the form of short entries, Zhang seems to have compiled longer works on similar topics. For instance, Zhang composed a chronological biography on the aforementioned Du Yinxi, *Du Wenzhonggong nianpu* 堵文忠公年譜（Chronological Biography of Du Yinxi）, and he edited the *Yuqiaohua* collection on Zheng Man.[49] We shall examine Zhang Xia's intellectual and

---

48　Ji Liuqi, *Mingji beilue*, 412.

49　*Yuqiaohua* is a collection of material on Zheng Man's case. The National Library of Beijing keeps a hand-copied version. It is attributed to Zhang Xia. It seems that this particular manuscript is not exactly what Zhang Xia put together but might have been based largely on his compilation. In the early twentieth century, the bibliographer Sun Dianqi 孫殿起 recorded a hand-copied version of this title in *Fanshu ouji* 販書偶記 and noted the "compiler" (*bian* □) as "Wuxi Zhang Xia" 無錫張夏（Sun Dianqi, *Fanshu ouji*, 299）. The compiler of *Zheng Man shiji* 鄭鄤事跡, Tang Juanshi 湯絹石, also claims "Complete Account of Zheng Man's Life" is from *Yuqiaohua* and that it draws upon "Key Issues in Zheng Man's Case." See Tang's notes to "Zheng Man shiji III," 5a.（Some scholars have confused Tang Juanshi with Tang Xiuye 湯修業, author of *Zheng Man yuanyu bian* 鄭案冤獄辯 and *Zheng an chuanxin lu* 鄭案傳信錄）. In fact these are two different men. Tang Juanshi has made a reference to Tang Xiuye, from the same county, in his notes to "Zheng Man shiji I," 24a.）*Yuqiaohua* includes some historical documentation such as Wen Bing 文秉's（1609-69）historical work *Liehuang xiao zhi* 烈皇小識, and original sources such as *Qian Lucan* 錢陸燦（1612-98）, "Miyang caotang shu jing gao xu" 峚陽草堂書經稿序；Hu Xie 胡瀣, "Miyang caotang

social activities later in the article. Here we will first look at the similarities and differences between the two versions of "The Complete Account of Zheng Man's Life" and their source, "Key Issues in Zheng Man's Case."

Zhang Xia and Ji Liuqi were among the early Qing writers who drew on "Key Issues in Zheng Man's Case," authored by someone pen-named "Huacun kan xing shizhe" 花村看行侍者 (Huacun hereafter). This piece offers very detailed explanations and exposes the falsity of the three major moral charges against Zheng Man: that he beat his mother, seduced his daughter-in-law, and raped his sister. The author Huacun begins the account with these cautionary lines: "In this world many incidents originate from trivial and vague things. Once women become involved, disasters are sure to occur. Zheng Man's ruined reputation and horrific death presents the most prominent and extreme of such cases!"[50] At the end of his analysis, Huacun writes, "There exists no limit to the evil

---

shu jing gao xu" 崒陽草堂書經稿序; Zhao Ding 趙鼎, "Fujia bu gong zhuan Zheng Miyang *Shangshu* gao xu" 附駕部公撰鄭崒陽尚書稿序; Zhao Ding 趙鼎, "Miyang xiansheng shi ji xu" 崒陽先生詩集序; Fu Shu 馮舒, "Hou yuzhongcao xu" 後獄中草序. It has also collected sensational accounts such as *Fulun xinshi* 放鄭小史 as well as the aforementioned biographies of Miss Han, *Minjie waishi*, *Han lienu zhuan*, and *You zhuan*. However, the copy of *Yuqiaohua* in the National Library collection also contains a couple of items that could only have been composed after Zhang Xia himself had died, by authors such as Gong Wei 龔煒 (1704- after 1769) and Qian Renlin 錢人麟 (1689-1772). The person who hand-copied this book might have added a couple of accounts to the original version.

50   Hua cun kan xing shizhe, *Hua cun wang tan* 花村往談, 1.25a. In "Miyang shi hui," the author indicates that this was composed about thirty years after Zheng Man's execution (29a). That puts the time of the work around 1669.

women can do," giving voice to conventional fears about women causing trouble for men. But he highlights the main focus: he warns that people enjoy spreading gossip about matters of the inner chambers and this threatens the political order.[51] "Complete Account of Zheng Man's Life" in *Ming ji bei lue* and *Yuqiaohua* both retain the above cautionary lines from Huacun's account. But a careful comparison of their accounts of Zheng Man's ethical problems shows the authors' very different editorial concerns.

"Key Issues in Zheng Man's Case" differs from the two versions of "Complete Account" on one crucial point. From the author's comments on the tragedy, we can tell that he means to articulate a lesson from the failure of late Ming politics, one which is consistent with the point of his whole book.

Chen Meigong 陳眉公 writes in *Dushu jing*《讀書鏡》:[52] In the Song dynasty, Zhao Shuping and Ouyang Wenzhonggong[53] both served in the Hanlin Academy. Ouyang looked down upon Zhao because he was reserved and not a prolific writer. Soon, an incident involving Ouyang's nephew triggered gossip. Officials who did not like Ouyang reported them to the emperor. The emperor grew very angry, but no one at court defended

---

51　Hua cun kan xing shizhe, *Hua cun wang tan* 花村往談, 1.28b.
52　Chen Meigong refers to the late Ming literatus Chen Jiru 陳繼儒（1558-1639）, a prolific writer and well-recognized connoisseur. *Dushu jing* is a book on history.
53　Zhao Shuping 趙叔平 refers to Zhao Gai 趙槩（996-1083）. Ouyang Wenzhonggong 歐陽文忠公 refers to Ouyang Xiu 歐陽修（1007-1072）. They served as Hanlin Academicians at the same time.

Ouyang. Only Zhao memorialized: "[Ouyang] Xiu became close to your Majesty because of his outstanding literary skills. He should not be humiliated by attacks citing dubious matters of the inner chambers. [Ouyang] Xiu and I do not socialize with each other much; he does not treat me well. What I want to save is the integrity of the court." Thanks to this memorial, the criticisms of Ouyang faded. A prosperous country is blessed with such loyal and sincere views. Unfortunately, the Chongzhen court did not have anyone like this. Officials threw unverifiable things into their memorials, scandalizing their superiors and insulting respected officials. This is the most serious symptom of a failing government.[54]

A victim of Song factionalism, Ouyang Xiu was once accused of incest with his daughter-in-law. It was also said that Ouyang Xiu had an affair with a very young niece and wrote a poem expressing sexual interest in her when she was merely seven.[55] But instead of using the historical reference to Zhao Gai's insistence on principle, as does Huacun in the above passage, the two versions of "Complete Account of Zheng Man's Life" invoke the reference to Ouyang Xiu for a completely different reason. They contain the same single sentence that reminds the reader, "Ouyang Xiu's reputation was ruined by one *ci* poem."[56] In other words, their invocation of Ouyang Xiu's case means to reiterate the point that Zheng's tragedy should be understood as a personal moral lesson, not a

---

54 "Miyang shi hui" in *Hua cun wang tan,* 1.31a.

55 Liu Tzu-chien, *Ouyang Xiu de zhixue yu congzheng*, 198-213 and 248-51.

56 Ji Liuqi, "Zheng Man benmo," *Mingji bei lue*, 261; Zhang Xia, "*Yuqiao hua Zheng Man benmo*," in *Zheng Man shiji*, 2b.

political lesson for the government. Zheng Man himself should be blamed for what happened to him. Even his physical appearance is invoked to suggest the cause of his misfortune: "Zheng Man was very fat, like a pig. He must have craved money and sex!"[57] Hence these two authors have omitted Huacun's observation that the most important lesson is the danger of bringing private matters into political discussions. Not only did Ji Liuqi and Zhang Xia fail to comprehend the important lesson of following Confucian principles in political communication and historical writing, they helped perpetuate the sensationalism around Zheng's life by casting his case as one of personal moral failure. It was upon such negative images of Zheng Man and his household that many literati writers based their historical documentation of late Ming politics and one of its main players, the Donglin faction.

Politics, History, and Scholarship

What makes the *Yuqiaohua* version of the "Complete Account" particularly interesting for us is that it implicitly attempts to distance the Donglin from Zheng Man. It describes how Zheng Man faked filial piety and deceived the moral paragon and Donglin icon Huang Daozhou.[58] It concludes with a comment that frames Zheng's case as one of personal moral failure, which throws into question his status as a Donglin partisan: "How sad that to the present day when people talk about Zheng Man, they

---

57   Ji Liuqi, "Zheng Man benmo," 263.
58   Ji Liuqi, "Zheng Man benmo," 263.

still consider him a Donglin!"[59]

Zhang Xia's account is representative of the false information and theories about Zheng Man that circulated widely. For example, it claims: "The stepmother of Hanlin Academician Zheng Man was a sister of the grand secretary Wu Zongda 吳宗達 (*jinshi* 1604)."[60] The high Qing literatus Tang Xiuye 湯修業 (1730-1799), a harsh critic of Zhang Xia, has pointed out the same mistake being made by Wang Runan 王汝南, author of *Ming ji biannian*《(續補)明紀編年》(1660):

Madam Wu (Zheng's mother) was Taichu's (Zheng's father) official wife and remained so [until Zheng died]. Taichu died in Chongzhen 1 (1628) and Madam Wu died in Chongzhen 4 (1631). Taichu never married another wife. How could [Zheng Man] have a "stepmother?"... *Ming ji biannian* includes an assertive account of Zheng Man's arrest. But the very first sentence of that account, 'The stepmother of Hanlin Academician Zheng Man was the sister of the grand secretary Wu Zongda,' gets the facts wrong! How can we say such history books are reliable?[61]

Tang was also highly critical of historical work influenced by the

---

59   Zhang Xia, "*Yuqiaohua* Zheng Man benmo," 4b.
60   Zhang Xia, "*Yuqiaohua* Zheng Man benmo," 1a.
61   Tang Xiuye's footnotes to Zheng Man's chronological autobiography, in Tang Juanshi, *Zheng Man shiji* I, 12b. (Tang Juanshi explains to the reader that when he published this collection of sources, he included Tang Xiuye's footnotes. *Zheng Man shiji* I, 24a.) See the above-quoted sentence in Wang Runan, *Xu bu Ming ji biannian*, 207.

popular theory that Zheng Man faked filial performance to deceive his
Donglin colleagues, as we will see below.

　　Tang Xiuye's intellectual authority derives from the tremendous effort
he put into finding and studying sources on Zheng Man and his case. His
Zheng an chuanxin lu《鄭案傳信錄》（Reliable Sources on the Zheng
Case）collected all the primary sources he was able to hunt down over
many years of research. It comprises four *juan* and more than 160 pages of
original sources.[62] In the preface to this book, Tang Xiuye singles out
Zhang Xia for criticism because Zhang especially demonized Zheng Man
in his historical scholarship:

> Those who wronged Miyang（Zheng Man）clearly were Ming
> *yimin* like Zhang Qiushao 張秋紹（Zhang Xia）. They harbored
> no personal grievance toward Zheng, but based their accounts
> on gossip without verification. As a result, their accounts
> inevitably lack cohesiveness and suffer from self-contradiction.
> Even knowledgeable men trusted the wrong sources. Gu

62　Tang Xiuye, "*Zheng an chuanxin lu* xu" 鄭案傳信錄序, in *Laiguzhai wenji*,
　　148-49. In this preface, Tang Xiuye details what he has compiled into this
　　four-*juan* book. Several documents in this collection show he and the
　　renowned scholar-official Zhu Gui had many exchanges concerning the
　　writing of Ming history. It seems that this book never made it to print, in part
　　because the manuscript got lost as it was circulated among the literati. Tang
　　was only able to recover some of it. For an examination of Tang Xiuye's
　　family from the perspective of women's history, see Mann, *Talented Women*,
　　esp. chapter 2.

Ningren 顧寧人 (Gu Yanwu 顧炎武), for instance, composed a poem to ridicule [Zheng Man]. Editors of our own dynasty adopt a problematic classification system. They not only deliberately exclude Zheng Man's essays [from compilations], but also, in literary commentary on others' works, criticize Zheng. They condemn him harshly and express disapproval of the righteous officials who "were deceived" by Zheng.[63]

In this passage, Tang Xiuye sheds light on how sensational stories about Zheng Man got recycled as trustworthy historical evidence: These began with late Ming literati in the Jiangnan region, then spread further in the early Qing through *yimin* circles and eventually entered the historical record as reliable accounts. Qing scholars accepted biased theories and perpetuated them, going so far as to, on this basis alone, erase Zheng Man from the history of outstanding officials and writers.

Zhang Xia's *yimin* identity made it easy for literati readers to trust the damaging stories of Zheng Man that Zhang helped disseminate. Gu Yanwu's fame as a meticulous researcher and moral paragon also played no small part in destroying Zheng's image. The poem Tang Xiuye mentions, in which Gu Yanwu condemns Zheng Man, was published in Gu's collected poems. Therein, Gu notes that a literatus named Lu Laifu 陸來復 visited him and described how he had helped a key "witness," Xu Xi 許曦 (fl. 1630s), put together the incriminating memorial that

---

63   Tang Xiuye, "*Zheng an chuanxin lu* xu."

contributed to Zheng Man's arrest and execution. Gu considers both Xu Xi and Lu Laifu to be "chivalrous men" (*xiashi* 俠士).[64] Although Tang Xiuye blames Lu Laifu for misleading Gu Yanwu, he also makes it clear that Gu was one of the many early Qing literati who did not realize the serious consequences of passing on unverified information.

Men like Lu Laifu, who claimed to have insider information, cultivated a market among the literati reading public in the late Ming and also found themselves a special position in the social world of the *yimin*. Take, for instance, the account of Ye Shaoyuan 葉紹袁 (1589-1648), a former Ming official living as an *yimin* in the early Qing. During the days when Ye lived outside the city to avoid Qing soldiers (in 1646), a friend brought to his place a man surnamed Han 韓. It was said that this man was a son of the Wujin Han family and the older brother of Miss Han, Zheng Man's daughter-in-law whom he allegedly attempted to rape. In this meeting, Han informed Ye Shaoyuan that his sister, at the age of 16, committed suicide to resist Zheng Man's sexual aggression. Subsequently, the Han family submitted a request to the Chongzhen emperor asking for imperial recognition of her chastity. Ye Shaoyuan documented this in his diary as a case of pending petition for the imperial *jingbiao* 旌表 award.[65]

64　Gu Yanwu, "Lu gongshi Laifu shu xi nian dai Xu sheren Xi cao shu gong Zheng Man shi" 陸貢士來復述昔年代許舍人曦草疏攻鄭鄤事, in Gu Yanwu, *Tinglin shiji*, 808.

65　Ye Shaoyuan, *Jia xing rizhu* (entry Shunzhi 3/12), 170-72. For a discussion about the Ming *jingbiao* system and practice, esp. literati's interests in petition cases, see Fei, "Writing for Justice."

However, this "first hand information" is false. Zheng Man's second son, to whom the Han daughter was engaged, had been born in 1622. The Han daughter was one year younger than Zheng's son.[66] In 1634 when she died, Zheng's son was 13 and she was 12 (according to the traditional way of counting age), not 16. The inaccuracy itself is less important for our purpose than the lesson that had Ye Shaoyuan and his *yimin* friend followed the principle of not discussing others' domestic affairs, they would have immediately dismissed a man who was eager to openly talk about a sexual aggression against his late sister. That man's account simply repeated a storyline from the scandalous biographies of Miss Han. Ye and his friend, however, counted him as a reliable source.

Tang Xiuye was keenly aware that the cultural-political authority assigned to *yimin* allowed them to transmit rumors easily. These men's Ming loyalism was so admirable that people were willing to trust their words. Tang did not soften his criticism of Zhang Xia because of Zhang's *yimin* identity. On the contrary, he recognized in Zhang's works a serious political and intellectual problem of the historiography of the late Ming:

> Even children have heard of Zheng Man. But so few people—
> even among senior masters and accomplished Confucianists—
> know the complete history of Zheng Man's tragedy. There is
> only one explanation: they allow themselves to be guided by a

---

66   "Zheng Miyang xia shi die wu jie" 鄭崇陽下石疊誣揭, in *Zheng an chuanxinlu yuangao*, no page number.

strong first impression. Shallow men enjoy talking about Zheng Man's case with great relish as if savoring the after-taste of a delicacy. When asked about their source of information, they merely refer to the accounts provided by *Fang Zheng xiaoshi* 放 鄭小史 and the like.[67] One can tell they lack in-depth knowledge. ... The literati dismiss slander about [Ouyang Xiu]'s domestic life, but they accept the same kind of slander about [Zheng Man]. Why? Because the former did not fall as a result of political troubles but the latter did. The results of their political struggles end up determining [how their personal lives are interpreted]. Stories of Zheng Man's "indecent behavior" are so widespread, even commoners on the street can recount them. In contrast, while Ouyang Xiu had a number of similar charges against him, senior masters and accomplished Confucianists spend their whole lives reading books but know nothing about those charges.[68]

Tang Xiuye was motivated to pursue research on Zheng Man's case because the sensational rumors had come to be considered historical sources. Self-identified Confucianists applied Confucian ideas superficially and selectively. They allowed their political self-positioning to affect their historical writing, casting judgment based on a historical figure's political

---

67　*Fang Zheng xiaoshi* was one of the novels concocted and presented to the emperor to incriminate Zheng Man.

68　Tang Xiuye, "Zheng Miyang yuanyu bian 5," *Laiguzhai wenji,* 137.

success or failure instead of on moral principle or honest research. This betrayed the fundamental Confucian teachings. Their lack of interest in probing into the inconvenient truth encouraged sensational negative accounts of Zheng Man to run rampant.

Many of Tang Xiuye's criticisms took aim at Zhang Xia, and those criticisms might surprise those who are familiar with the cultural-social circle coalesced around the Donglin Academy in the early Qing. Though not nationally famous, Zhang Xia was an important figure in the Jiangnan area, especially in Wuxi 無錫 where the Donglin Academy was located. He studied with the aforementioned Donglin official Ma Shiqi in their hometown, Wuxi, and then entered the Donglin Academy to further his study. Ma Shiqi committed suicide upon the fall of Beijing. Zhang Xia followed another mentor, Gao Shitai 高世泰 (*jinshi* 1637), nephew of Gao Panlong 高攀龍 (1562-1626). Gao Shitai withdrew from politics and revived the Donglin Academy in the early Qing, committing himself to Neo-Confucian studies and grounding the intellectual authority of the Donglin Academy in the Cheng-Zhu tradition. Later, after Gao died, Zhang Xia himself was elected to fill the position of the chief lecturer at this great institution. Zhang was considered by some a *yimin*. But after the Qing took over Jiangnan, he cooperated with officials in the local government and taught at an official academy in Suzhou. He received recognition from the Qing as a serious Confucian scholar, which can be seen by the inclusion of his works into the *Siku quanshu* 四庫全書 project.[69]

---

69   Qin Songling, "Zhang Guchuan xiansheng zhuan" 張菰川先生傳, *Donglin*

Zhang Xia himself knew very well the essential principle for literati biographical writing, which he claims to have followed in his publications: "When composing a biography, one should omit the person's errors while illuminating his good deeds."[70] But he obviously did not apply this principle to the discussion about Zheng Man's case. How should we understand Zhang Xia's interest in Zheng Man and in disseminating unverified information about him? I would argue that precisely due to his self-consciousness as a successor to the Donglin, Zhang Xia might have felt compelled to define the fallen Zheng Man in contrast to—rather than as one of—the Donglin.

A friend prefacing Zhang Xia's work writes, "[Zhang Xia]'s Confucian scholarship follows orthodoxy. He has inherited the legacy of the Donglin Academy and taken upon himself the mission of elucidating Confucian doctrines for many years."[71] A student of the Donglin Academy and one of its post-1644 leaders, Zhang Xia promoted himself as a true Donglin Confucianist by depicting the academy as the main intellectual force that helped restore the Cheng-Zhu orthodoxy. As part of this effort,

---

shuyuan zhi, 12.39a-40a; Qian Yiji comp., *Bei zhuan ji*, 648; Xu Chengli, *Xiao tian ji zhuan buyi*, 781. The two works by Zhang Xia included in the *Siku* project are: *Luomin yuan liu lu* 雒閩源流錄 and *Song Yang Wenjinggong Guishan xiansheng nianpu er juan* 宋楊文靖公龜山先生年譜二卷. As a Qing compilation, *Xijin kaosheng* 錫金考乘, points out, many Qing sources identify Zhang Xia as a Ming loyalist. Zhou Youren, *Xijin kaosheng,* 280. For Zhang's biography, see Sun Jing'an, *Ming yijin lu, juan* 5.

70　Zhang Xia, "Fanli" in *Luomin yuan liu lu,* 363.
71　Peng Long, "Luomin yuan liu lu xu" 雒閩源流錄序, in Zhang Xia, *Luomin yuanliu lu,* 353.

he compiled a chronological biography for the great Song Confucian scholar and the original founder of the Donglin Academy, Yang Shi 楊時 (Guishan 龜山, 1053-1135). He also completed *Luomin yuanliu lu* 雒閩 源流錄, biographies of Ming Neo-Confucian thinkers. He and his friends attributed the early Ming prosperity to its adherence to the Cheng-Zhu Neo-Confucianism, and the Ming demise to heterodox teachings in circulation since the mid-Ming.[72] One of them suggests that the Qing state's promotion of orthodox Confucianism encouraged Zhang Xia to write this work in support of benevolent governance and restoration of proper human relations.[73] Although Zhang Xia did not denounce Wang Yangming and respects some of Wang's followers whom he considers not radical or heterodox, he harshly condemned those who had attacked the Cheng-Zhu school.[74]

Zhang Xia seemed to strive to maintain some kind of distinction between the Donglin Academy and the Donglin political faction. In the compilation of *Luomin yuanliu lu*, he labels the founders of the Ming Donglin Academy—Gu Xiancheng 顧憲成, Qian Yiben 錢一本, Gao Panlong 高攀龍, etc.—as adhering to the orthodoxy (*zhengzong* 正宗). Meanwhile, he places a few of those who had been commonly recognized as Donglin officials—such as Liu Zongzhou and Huang Daozhou—in the

---

[72] Huang Shengxie, "Luomin yuan liu lu xu" 雒閩源流錄序, in Zhang Xia, *Luomin yuan liu lu,* 355.

[73] Zhang Xia, *Luomin yuan liu lu,* 354-57.

[74] See for instance, Zhang Xia, "Luomin yuanliu lu zixu" 雒閩源流錄自序, *Luomin yuanliu lu*, 358-60; "Fanli," *Luomin yuanliu lu*, 365.

three chapters on the Yangming school. Zhang Xia's attempt to differentiate the Donglin Academy and the Donglin faction also explains his decision to exclude some prominent Donglin factional officials—such as Zhao Nanxing 趙南星（1550-1627）, Yang Lian 楊漣（1571-1625）, Miao Changqi 繆昌期（1562-1626）, and Li Yingsheng 李應昇（1593-1626）—from the collection. He points out that these extraordinary men best fit in a collection of biographies of loyal officials; it is not proper to include them in this intellectual history, because not every virtuous official excels in scholarship.[75]

Zhang Xia's limited attempts to differentiate the Donglin Academy from the Donglin faction found few sympathizers. The updated edition of the gazetteer of the Donglin Academy, completed and published by Zhang Xia's successors in 1732, clearly sidelined that distinction.[76] Commenting on Zhang's decision to exclude famous Donglin officials from *Luomin yuanliu lu* because they were undistinguished by scholarship, editors of the *Siku quanshu* 四庫全書 mockingly retorted: "Does the Cheng-Zhu school only teach people how to compile books of quotations?!"[77] They also pointed out that, in the chronological biography compiled by Zhang Xia for Yang Shi, the Song founder of the Donglin Academy, Zhang had misrepresented some facts due to his strong identification with the late Ming Donglin faction.[78]

75　Zhang Xia, "Fanli," 364.

76　Gao Tingzhen et al., *Donglin shuyuan zhi*.

77　Zhang Xia, *Luomin yuan liu lu*, 304-05.

78　"Yang Wenjing nianpu er juan tiyao" 四庫全書總目楊文靖年譜二卷提要,

Even though Zhang Xia strongly defies the accusation that his intellectual historical work had been compromised by factionalist bias, he admits that officials without an excellent moral reputation should be omitted from the history of Ming Neo-Confucian scholarship.[79] Indeed, by creating an impeccable record for the Donglin Academy where he studied and taught, like many others during the Ming-Qing transition, Zhang Xia contributed to consolidating the Donglin image of moral superiority. Zhang Xia's attempt to elevate the Donglin-identified figures to the highest moral-intellectual levels is reflected in how he portrayed Zheng Man and Zheng's fellow Wujin natives differently. Zhang Xia personally composed the proposal to install the tablets of some Wujin natives in the hall of the Donglin Academy, one of whom was Sun Shenxing, the Zheng father and son's close friend.[80] Deep connections of the Zhengs with Sun Shenxing threatened to complicate the history of the Donglin faction and Donglin Academy.[81] It was thus natural for Zhang Xia to insist on a moral contrast between the Zhengs and Sun in the "*Yuqiaohua* Complete Account of Zheng Man," and to ignore the memorials submitted by Huang Daozhou and Liu Zongzhou as well as the epitaphs written by Huang Daozhou and

---

attached to Zhang Xia, *Yang Wenjinggong nianpu*, 627.

[79] Zhang Xia, "Luomin yuanliu lu zixu," 359.

[80] Zhang Xia, "Sun Yun liang xiangsheng congsi Donglin Shuyuan yi" 孫惲兩先生從祀東林書院議, *Wujin xianzhi* (Qianlong ed.), 715-16. This proposal nominated two Wujin natives, the other being Yun Richu 惲日初 (1601-1678).

[81] Tang Xiuye refutes the theory that Sun Shenxing was deceived by the Zhengs in "Zheng Miyang yuanyu bian."

Huang Zongxi, all of which strongly defended Zheng Man.

Zhang Xia's intellectual activities—and others' reactions to them—shed light on the deep entanglement of politics and scholarship, alerting us to the complicated ways in which the representations of "small men" like Zheng Man and the historiography of the Donglin are mutually constructed. Many seventeenth- and eighteenth-century literati presumed the connection between the Donglin Academy and the moral exemplariness of Donglin officials. The Donglin Academy as a symbol of intellectual orthodoxy had to be constantly clarified and sometimes reified by the political performance of some of the figures associated with it. This same framework also affected those who did not share Zhang Xia's negative view on Zheng Man. For instance, the high Qing literatus Lu Jilu 陸繼輅（1772-1834）, who believed in Zheng's innocence, claimed Zheng had studied at the Donglin Academy.[82] It should be noted that Liu's words then entered the Guangxu 光緒 edition of the Wujin gazetteer（1879）, which, to give Zheng Man a place in its local history, asserts Zheng's intellectual connection with the academy.[83]

In the Name of Defending Confucian Principles

As we have seen above, literati historians' accounts of Zheng Man's life demonstrate not only their varied understandings of Confucian

---

[82]　Lu Jilu, *Hefei xueshe zhaji* 合肥學舍札記, quoted in *Gu Tinglin shiji huizhu*, 809.

[83]　*Guangxu Wujin Yanghu xianzhi*（Guangxu 5）, 525.

principles but also how they practiced them selectively in politics and scholarship. Self-appointed guardians of Confucian teachings such as Zhang Xia did not necessarily practice Confucian principles thoroughly or consistently. Tang Xiuye's work, *Reliable Sources on the Zheng Case,* completed by the 1780s, attempted to expose the harm done by these tendencies. In particular, quite boldly, Tang distinguishes "those who uphold public judgment fairly" (*zhuchi qingyi zhi dezhong zhe* 主持清議 之得中者) from those who do so irresponsibly, a category to which Zhang Xia seems to belong.[84] Aiming to present reliable evidence rather than hearsay, in addition to presenting his own analysis of the whole case, Tang's *Reliable Sources* includes original documents such as officials' memorials, public posters, official biographies, and Zheng Man's own poems that are documentary in nature.[85] Those who saw the manuscript all thought highly of it. So much so that the renowned official Zhu Gui 朱珪 (1731-1806) had an assistant hand-copy it.[86] When asked how he had scrutinized the vast volume of historical material that mentioned Zheng Man and the overwhelming amount of detail they contained, Tang Xiuye replied:

> We uphold Confucian teachings with the help of two tools: the law and history. ... Lü Xinwu 呂新吾 (Lü Kun 呂坤, 1536-

---

84   Tang Xiuye, "Zheng an chuanxinlu xu," 148.

85   Tang Xiuye, "Zheng an chuanxinlu xu," 148.

86   Notes by the copier on the first page of *Zheng an chuanxinlu yuangao*, no page number.

1618）once said: "The pure element's judgment (*qingyi* 清議)
is harsher than the law. Those who wield this judgment are
harsher than those in charge of punishment. If someone were
wronged by legal procedure he could still rely on "the pure
element's judgment" to clear his reputation. Even if he lost his
life, he could still live on in spirit. However, if one has been
wronged by "the pure element's judgment," it would be nearly
impossible to reverse the verdict. Therefore, gentlemen hesitate
to criticize others, because they are afraid of wronging others.
… I hope I resort to *qingyi* to prove Zheng Man's innocence; I
dare not use it to wrong him.[87]

Tang Xiuye called particular attention to how "the pure element's
judgment" misguided the historiography of the Donglin. For this reason he
appreciated the early Qing scholar Qian Renlin's 錢人麟（1689-1722），
who had set out to correct for excessive zeal and sloppy historical research
on the Donglin. Tang wrote:

As［Qian Renlin］argues, historically［in the Song］, Cai Jing
蔡京 erected the Stele of Factionalists in order to suppress the
worthy men in the country. Meddlesome men followed his lead
when composing biographies. Evaluations of Donglin officials
resembled those in the Song Yuanyou 元祐 era. … Those who

87　Tang Xiuye, "Zhen an chuanxinlu xu," 148-49.

participated in writing the official *Ming History* had limited access to sources and did not have time to verify everything. Even renowned scholars cannot be error-free. Mr. Qian's book thus provides what is missing from *Donglin liezhuan* 東林列傳 (Biographies of Donglin Officials) by Chen Dingjiu 陳定九 (Chen Ding 陳鼎)... [88]

Qian Renlin's work has survived as *Donglin biesheng* 東林別乘 (Alternative Genealogy of the Donglin), a compilation of anti-Donglin blacklists created by the so-called eunuch faction in the late Ming.[89] Self-identified as an "offspring of the Donglin" (*Donglin yiren* 東林裔人),[90] Qian researched these lists and also wrote an introduction to each of them for the publication. He believes the historian should present the sources as they are instead of making arbitrary changes in the name of defending Confucian principles. He challenges some scholars' approach to the Donglin roster: "[Chen Ding] has adopted very strict guidelines but his list [of Donglin officials] still contains errors. Might he have added and

---

88   Tang Xiuye, "Qian Zhu'an xiansheng Donglin jishi xu" 錢鑄庵先生東林紀事序, *Laiguzhai wenji*, 149.

89   These lists are: *Donglin pengdang lu* 東林朋黨錄; *Donglin tongzhi lu* 東林同志錄; *Donglin jiguan* 東林籍貫; *Donglin dianjiang lu* 東林點將錄; *Daobing Donglin huo* 盜炳東林夥; *Donglin dangren bang* 東林黨人榜; *Huohuai fengjiang lu* 夥壞封疆錄; and *Tianjian lu* 天鑒錄. Qian Renlin, *Donglin biesheng*.

90   Qian Renlin's discussion of *Donglin dianjiang lu*, in *Donglin biesheng*, 16b.

deleted names according to his own likes and dislikes?"[91]

Why were Qian Renlin and Tang Xiuye so critical of Chen Ding? What is in fact missing in Chen Ding's twenty-four-chapter biographical account of the Donglin officials, *Biographies of Donglin Officials*? The answer lies in Chen Ding's editorial agenda, which seems to aspire to exemplify the "pure element's judgment." *Biographies of Donglin Officials* claims to pass on stories of the "loyal and fearless" Donglin men during the Ming-Qing transition.[92] In the preface, Chen Ding explicitly describes his historical project as "biased" against moral imperfection. Chen's long list of Donglin men includes most of the names that appear on the notorious "Seven Lists" (*qilu* 七錄)[93] that anti-Donglin forces generated to persecute their political enemies in the Tianqi reign and at the Southern Ming Hongguang court. However, Chen Ding did not include everyone on the original blacklists because he insisted on maintaining the highest standard: "Some people have appeared in these Seven Lists but I do not include their biographies in this book if they did not make any meaningful suggestions to the emperor, did not suffer persecution by the eunuch faction, or did not have an impeccable moral character."[94] Chen laid out his principles for selection this way:

---

91 Qian Renlin, Introduction to *Donglin dangren bang*, in *Donglin biesheng*, 49a.
92 Chen Ding, *Donglin liezhuan,* 003.
93 Chen Ding, "Fanli" 凡例 of *Donglin liezhuan*, 005-007. These seven lists are: 七錄者曰天鑒曰雷平曰同志曰薙稗曰點將曰蠅蚋曰蝗蝻".
94 Chen Ding, "Fanli", 007-008.

This collection of biographies excludes men who, although they appeared in the Seven Lists and "Dangren bang" 黨人榜 (List of [Donglin] Partisans),[95] started right but ended wrong— started as *junzi* but ended up *xiaoren*—or whose despicable behavior belied their moral statements. Posthumously judged by their character, they either deserved a miserable end or their character and behavior did not qualify them as exemplary righteous literati-officials (*qingliu* 清流, "pure element"), even if the powerful eunuch faction once labeled them "Donglin."[96]

Chen Ding's omission of Zheng Man, whose name appeared in the blacklists, seems to have occurred in his application of these principles. Zheng's alleged lack of filial piety and sexual immorality, although unverified, were declared punishable by the emperor Chongzhen and led to his execution. Chen Ding seems to have been one of those who rushed to embrace the so-called "pure element's judgment" and so excluded Zheng from the Donglin roster. In contrast, Qian Renlin examined more sources with a more critical attitude. Moreover, elsewhere, he explicitly points out—in line with the Confucian principle of refraining from discussing others' domestic matters—that scholars should have denounced Zheng Man's accusers who brought to the court those sensational stories about

---

95   This list was compiled by Wei Zhongxian's follower Lu Chengqin 盧承欽 and submitted in the form of a memorial in 1625. It includes about the names of three hundred literati-officials.

96   Chen Ding, "Fanli," 011.

his sexual life.[97]

Chen Ding's attempt to erase names from the Donglin lists and history itself exemplifies the efforts of certain Qing literati to "restore" Neo-Confucian orthodoxy. He explains the editorial principles of this massive project as follows:

> This collection of biographies concerns itself with Confucian teachings. It strictly excludes those who ended up in Buddhist or Daoist pursuits. However, it acknowledges those who originally followed Buddhist or Daoist teachings but eventually returned to Confucian orthodoxy, for example, Xiong Kaiyuan 熊開元 and Jiang Cai 姜垛. Men like Fang Yizhi 方以智 were in the beginning righteous literati-officials but turned themselves into monks in old age. This book does not include them. Others such as Zhang Rujin 章如金 grew up Daoist but became Confucian and engaged in Confucian scholarship. Therefore men of this kind are included.[98]

Zheng Man's interest in Buddhism and Daoism would definitely disqualify him from Chen Ding's list of Donglin men. Zheng Man's professed strong interest in various religions, including his interaction with

---

97   Qian Renlin, comment section of "Zheng Man zhuan" 鄭鄤傳, included in the hand-copied *Yuqiaohua*, no page number.

98   Chen Ding, "Fanli," 011. All these men were late Ming officials.

Christian missionaries, made him appear unorthodox.[99] In fact, the whole scandal surrounding the Zheng family derived from gossip around their religious practices. Even if the charge of beating his mother were false, it was undeniable that Zheng Man frequently socialized with both Daoist and Buddhist figures of his time. Thus Zheng Man did not fit the image that Chen Ding, and the many literati like him, wished to construct for Donglin officials—that of noble figures who endeavored to restore orthodox Neo-Confucianism in society and government.

Conclusion

The discussion and representations of Zheng Man's case in the seventeenth and eighteenth centuries demonstrate how Confucian ideals, such as filial piety, loyalty, and proper gender separation were negotiated in everyday political and historical practices. This study has examined some of these representations to show the diverse ways in which certain Confucian moral-political principles were understood and pursued by the literati in their particular political, social, and cultural situations. For instance, when evaluating officials' performance of filial piety, other principles such as avoidance of commenting on personal matters or on those of superior status also had to be taken into consideration. In historical writing, too, the literati should have insisted on these principles instead of manipulating records based on historical figures' political

---

[99]   Ye Jun, "Zheng Man yanjiu," chap. 4, esp. section 2.

success or failure.

However, even though the literati were educated in the same system, their understandings of Confucian principles clearly varied. The complexity and richness of the Confucian system itself resulted from these diverse approaches. Meanwhile, literati appropriation of Confucian moral rhetoric in their writings—biographies, vernacular literature, and historical work— during this period shows that many of them applied moral criteria superficially and expediently. This not only affected how literati authors selected and presented their sources but also how they documented political history. The impact of these tendencies was more difficult to offset due to the flourishing print culture and the appetites of a broader readership. The representations of Zheng Man's "scandal" in the seventeenth and eighteenth centuries examined in this study, though with a seemingly narrow focus on Confucian values, demonstrate how the literati engaged in dynamic debates about important questions such as "public opinion" and political and intellectual "objectivity" in the new socio-economic, cultural, and political conditions.

道德準則與醜聞：
從十七、十八世紀關於鄭鄤杖母案之紀聞談起

張穎

摘要

　　一度被看作東林人物的庶吉士鄭鄤，因遭政治對手揭發"杖母"、"姦媳"等惡行而鋃鐺入獄，最終被處以凌遲極刑。這是晚明政治史上一大離奇事件。以往研究僅止關注這樁案件如何反映明末政治之混亂。本文則將此案置於一個更複雜的時空情境中。文章將首先討論崇禎朝一些東林人士對鄭鄤的辯護。其次將分析清初幾篇具有代表性的對此案的描述、評價以及它們的政治道德含意。最後，通過深度考察幾位清初士人在散布鄭鄤負面形象中的作用，本文探討政治立場與東林史寫作之間的關聯、以及有關史料如何生成。這些史料的形成過程，顯示了士人在政治、社會、學術層面上對儒家政治道德原則的理解與實踐的多樣與差異。

關鍵詞：東林、黨爭、明清之際、政治史、儒家思想

Bibliography

Abbreviations

MDZJCK   Zhou Junfu 周駿富 ed., *Ming dai zhuanji congkan*《明代傳記叢刊》.
          Taipei: Mingwen shuju, 1991.
SKJH   *Siku jinhui shu congkan* 四庫禁燬書叢刊. Beijing: Beijing
          chubanshe, 2000.
SKCM   *Siku quanshu cunmu congshu*《四庫全書存目叢書》Jinan: Qilu
          shushe, 1996.
TWWXCK   Taiwan yinhang jiji yanjiu shi ed., *Taiwan wenxian congkan*《臺灣文
          獻叢刊》Taipei: Taiwan yinhang jinji yanjiushi. 1959-1972.
XXSKQS   *Xu Xiu Siku quanshu*《續修四庫全書》. Shanghai: Shanghai guji
          chubanshe, 2002.

Brook, Timothy. *Praying for Power: Buddhism and the Formation of Gentry
    Society in Late-Ming China*（Cambridge, Mass.: Harvard University Press,
    1993）.
Chen Ding 陳鼎. *Donglin liezhuan*《東林列傳》（*MDZJCK* ed.）.
Dardess, John. *Blood and History in China: The Donglin Faction and Its
    Repression, 1620-1627*. Honolulu: University of Hawai'i Press, 2002.
Epstein, Maram. *Competing Discourses: Orthodoxy, Authenticity, and Engendered
    Meanings in Late Imperial Chinese Fiction.*（Cambridge, MA: Harvard
    University Asia Center, 2001）.
Fan Shuzhi 樊樹志. "Donglin shuyuan de shitai fenxi: 'Donglin dang' lun zhiyi"
    〈東林書院的實態分析：「東林黨」論質疑〉, *Zhongguo shehui kexue* 2001
    （2）: 188-208.
Fei, Siyen. "Writing for Justice: An Activist Beginning of the Cult of Female
    Chastity in Late Imperial China." *The Journal of Asian Studies*, 71（2012）:
    991-1012.
Gao Tingzhen 高廷珍 et al. *Donglin shuyuan zhi*《東林書院志》（Taipei:
    Guangwen shuju, 1968）.
Gu Yanwu 顧炎武. *Tinglin shiji*《顧亭林詩集彙注》（Shanghai: Shanghai guji
    chubanshe, 2006）
Hua cun kan xing shizhe〈花村看行使者〉. *Hua cun wang tan*《花村往談》

（*Shiyuan congshu*《適園叢書》edition）

Huang Zongxi 黃宗羲. *Nanlei wen ding*《南雷文定三集》（*Sibu beiyao* ed.）
（Shanghai: Zhonghua shuju, 1927-1936）.

Hucker, Charles O. "The Tung-lin Movement of the Late Ming Period." In *Chinese Thought and Institutions,* ed. J. K. Fairbank（Chicago: University of Chicago Press, 1957）, 132-62.

Ji Liuqi 計六奇. *Ming ji bei lue*《明季北略》. Ed. Wei Deliang 魏得良 and Ren Daobin 任道斌（Beijing: Zhonghua shuju, 2006）.

Jiang Pingjie 蔣平階. *Donglin shi mo*《東林始末》（*TWWXCK* ed.）.

Jiangzuo qiaozi 江左樵子. *Qiaoshi tongsu yanyi*《樵史通俗演義》（rpt, Beijing: Zhongguo shudian, 1988）.

Jin Risheng 金日升. *Song tian lu bi*《頌天臚筆》（*SKJH* ed.）

Li Qing 李清. *San yuan biji*《三垣筆記》（Beijing: Zhonghua shuju, 1997）

____. *Nan du lu*《南渡錄》, in Huang Zongxi ed. 黃宗羲, *Nan Ming shi liao ba zhong* 南明史料八種（Nanjing: Jiangsu guji chubanshe, 1997）.

Li Xunzhi 李遜之. *Chongzhen chao ji shi* 崇禎朝記事（*SKJH-shi* 6）.

Liu Tzu-chien 劉子健. *Ouyang Xiu de zhixue yu congzheng*《歐陽修的治學與從政》（Hong Kong: Xiya yanjiusuo, 1963）.

Lu Shiyi 陸世儀. *Fushe ji lue*《復社紀略》in *Donglin yu Fushe zhu jia*《東林與復社諸家》（*TWWXCK* ed.）

Ma Shiqi 馬世奇. *Danningju wenji* 澹寧居文集（*SKJH-ji* 113）.

Mann, Susan. *The Talented Women of the Zhang Family*（Berkley: University of California Press, 2007）.

Miller, Harry. "Opposition to the Donglin Faction in the Late Ming Dynasty: the Case of Tang Binyin." *Late Imperial China* 27: 2（2006）: 38-66.

____. "Newly Discovered Source Sheds Light on Late Ming Faction: Reading Li Sancai's *Fu Huai xiao cao.*" *Ming Studies* Vol. 47（Spring, 2003）: 126-40.

Ono Kazuko 小野和子. *Mingji dangshe kao*《明季黨社考》. Trans. Li Qing 李慶 and Zhang Rongmei 張榮湄（Shanghai: Shanghai guji chubanshe, 2006）.

Qian Renlin 錢人麟. *Donglin biesheng*《東林別乘》（reprint）（Guangzhou: Guangdong sheng Zhongshan tushuguan, 1958）.

Qian Yiji 錢儀吉 comp. *Bei zhuan ji*《碑傳集》, *Qing dai bei zhuan quanji*《清代碑傳全集》（Shanghai: Shanghai guji chubanshe, 1987）.

Sieber, Patricia. *Theaters of Desire: Authors, Readers, and the Reproduction of Early Chinese Song-Drama, 1300-2000*（New York: Palgrave MacMillian, 2003）.

Sun Dianqi 孫殿起. *Fanshu ouji*《販書偶記》（Shanghai: Shanghai guji chubanshe, 1999）.

Sun Jing'an 孫靜庵, ed. *Ming yijin lu*《明遺民錄》（Shanghai: Shanghai xin zhonghua tushuguan, 1912）.

Tang Juanshi 湯狷石. *Zheng Man shiji*《鄭鄤事蹟》, *Guxue huikan* 古學彙刊（Shanghai: Shanghai guocui xue bao she, 1912）.

Tang Xiuye 湯修業. *Laiguzhai wenji*《賴古齋文集》, *Qingdai shiwen ji huibian*《清代詩文集彙編》（Shanghai: Shanghai guji chubanshe, 2013）.

____. *Zheng an chuanxinlu yuangao*《鄭案傳信錄原稿》（hand-copied manuscript）. National Library of Beijing.

Vitiello, Giovanni. *The Libertine's Friend: Homosexuality & Masculinity in Late Imperial China*（Chicago: University of Chicago Press, 2011）.

Wang Hung-tai 王鴻泰. "Shehui de xiangxiang yu xiangxiang de shehui"〈社會的想像與想像的社會〉. In *Wan Ming yu Wan Qing: Lishi chuancheng yu wenhua chuangxin*《晚明與晚清：歷史傳承與文化創新》, eds. Chen Pingyuan, Wang Dewei, and Shang Wei（Wuhan: Hubei jiaoyu chubanshe, 2001）, 133-47.

____. "Ming-Qing de zixun chuanbo, shehui xiangxiang yu gongzhong shehui"〈明清的資訊傳播，社會想像與公眾社會〉. *Mingdai yanjiu*［Taipei］12（June 2009）: 41-92.

Wang Nunan 王汝南. *Xu bu Ming ji biannian*《續補明紀編年》（*SKJH* ed.）.

Wang Qigan 王其淦 and Wu Kangshou 吳康壽 comp. *Guangxu Wujin Yanghu xianzhi*《光緒武進陽湖縣志》（Guangxu ed.）, *Zhongguo difangzhi jicheng Jiangsu fuxianzhi ji*《中國地方誌集成・江蘇府縣志輯》（Nanjing: Jiangsu guji chubanshe, 1991）.

Wen Bing 文秉. *Jia-yi shi an* 甲乙事案 in Huang Zongxi ed. 黃宗羲, *Nan Ming shi liao ba zhong* 南明史料八種（Nanjing: Jiangsu guji chubanshe, 1997）.

Wu Shanjia 吳山嘉. *Fu She xingshi zhuanlue*《復社姓氏傳略》（Nangaitang 南陔堂 ed., Daoguang 11）.

Wu Weiye 吳偉業. *Mei cun jia cang gao*《梅村家藏槀》（*SBCK* ed.）.

Wu Yuancui 伍袁萃. *Yi'antang gao*《貽安堂稿》（Wanli ed.）. Shanghai Library.

Xu Chengli 徐程禮. *Xiao tian ji zhuan buyi*《小腆紀傳補遺》（*Qing dai zhuanji congkan* ed.）.

Ye Jun 葉軍. *Zheng Man yanjiu: jian lun Ming dai hou qi dangzheng*《鄭鄤研究：兼論明代後期黨爭》（Ph.D. diss., Fudan University, 2002）.

Ye Shaoyuan 葉紹袁. *Jia xing ri zhu*《甲行日注》, *Li dai riji cong chao*《歷代日

記叢鈔》Vol. 10（Beijing: Xueyuan chubanshe, 2006）.

Yu Mingqiu 虞鳴球 and Dong Chao 董潮 comp. *Wujin xianzhi*《武進縣志》（Qianlong ed.）, *Xijian Zhongguo difangzhi huikan*《稀見中國地方誌彙刊》（Beijing: Zhongguo shudian, 1992）.

Zhang Pu 張溥. *Qiluzhai shiwen he ji*《七錄齋詩文合集》（Taipei: Weiwen tushu gongsi, 1977）.

Zhang Xia 張夏. *Luomin yuan liu lu*《雒閩源流錄》（*XXSKQS* ed.）.

＿＿＿. *Song Yang Wenjinggong Guishan xiansheng nianpu er juan*《宋楊文靖公龜山先生年譜》二卷（*SKCM*）.

＿＿＿. *Yuqiaohua*《漁樵話》（hand-copied manuscript）. National Library of China.

Zhang, Ying. "The Politics and Practice of Moral Rectitude." *Late Imperial China* 34:2（Dec. 2013）: 52-83.

Zhang Zilie 張自烈. *Qishan wenji*《芑山文集》（*SKJH* ed.）.

Zheng Man 鄭鄤. *Miyang caotang wenji*《崟陽草堂文集》（*MYCTWJ*）（*SKJH* ed.）

＿＿＿. *Miyang caotang shiji*《崟陽草堂詩集》（*MYCTSJ*）（*SKJH* ed.）

＿＿＿. *Tianshan zi xu nianpu*《天山自敍年譜》, in *Miyang caotang wenji*.

Zhou Youren 周有壬. *Xijin kaosheng* 錫金考乘, reprinted in *Wuxi wenxian congkan*《無錫文獻叢刊》vol. 5（Taipei: Taibei shi Wuxi tongxianghui, 1981）.

Zhou Zhikui 周之夔. *Qi cao er ji*《棄草二集》（詩集七卷、文集八卷）（*SKJH* ed.）

【論著】

Later Reflections on the Revolution in France:

Changing British Interpretations from 1815 to the Present

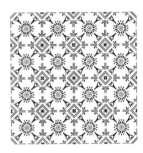

Harry T. Dickinson

Teaching for forty years at the University of Edinburgh, Harry T. Dickinson has been an Emeritus Professor there since 2006. He has lectured in the UK, the USA, Europe and Asia and has published in seven languages in fourteen countries. He is the author or editor of well over two hundred publications, including, *Bolingbroke, Walpole and the Whig Supremacy, Caricatures and the Constitution, 1760-1832, Liberty and Property in Eighteenth-Century Britain,* and *The Politics of the People in Eighteenth-Century Britain*

Later Reflections on the Revolution in France:
Changing British Interpretations from 1815 to the Present

Harry T. Dickinson

Abstract

The French Revolution, which began in 1789, had a profound effect on Britain, dividing the British elite and even ordinary people into those excited by and sympathetic to French principles and those opposed to and alarmed by these principles. The most intellectually profound and politically influential conservative critique of French principles was Edmund Burke's *Reflections on the Revolution in France*, written as early as 1790. Many scholars have examined British views of the French revolution from its origins to the defeat of Napoleon in 1815. This article breaks new ground by attempting an overview of British reflections on the French Revolution from 1815 to 2015. It explores three aspects of these later reflections: the major changes in the historiography of the Revolution produced by British scholars from 1815 to the present; the cultural responses to the Revolution produced by British poets, novelists, playwrights and film makers; and the impact on British political opinions of the Revolution forged by political parties and organizations on the left, right and center of politics.

Keywords: historiography; historians; Walter Scott; Thomas Carlyle; Lord Acton; Alfred Cobban; Simon Schama; poets and novelists; Samuel Taylor Coleridge; Robert Southey; William Wordsworth; Percy Shelley; Jane Austen; Mary Shelley; Charles Dickens; Baroness Orczy; films; caricatures; Whigs; Tories; radicals; Chartists; Bronterre O'Brien.

The French Revolution of 1789 proved to be so dramatic, traumatic and significant that it was later regarded as a watershed marking the change from the ancien regime to the modern world.[1] It has undoubtedly had a profound impact on all subsequent French history. In Britain, it inspired a prolonged and intense ideological debate between those hoping to see Britain emulate the example of France and those who greatly feared that the Revolution would destroy Britain's cherished political and social order. It influenced the policies and actions of the British government and Westminster Parliament and motivated radicals and loyalists across the British Isles. It brought Britain into a war unprecedented in scale and posed a major threat to the country's overseas trade, colonial possessions and very survival as an independent state. Not surprisingly, therefore, the French Revolution remained a subject of debate and dispute within British society long after it ceased to pose a direct threat. To appreciate how the French Revolution continued to have an influence on Britain and lingered long in the historic memory of the British people, we need to look at how British historians have studied and interpreted it, how it has been represented in a wide range of cultural media, and how it affected the attitudes and constitutional principles of British politicians and political commentators.

---

[1] F.L. Ford, "The Revolutionary-Napoleonic Era: How much of a Watershed?," *American Historical Review*, 69 (1963), pp. 18-29.

I
British Historians and the French Revolution

Many of the most famous and most gifted French historians, from the early nineteenth century to the present, have attempted to explain, interpret and understand the significance of the French Revolution of 1789. From Thiers to Furet, through the likes of Michelet, Taine, Mathiez and Lefebvre, they have published a huge number of studies and yet widely different interpretations of the Revolution.[2] All the best, most influential and most controversial works on the Revolution produced by French scholars have been translated into English and have had a profound impact on British historians. They have not, however, always been accepted uncritically. Throughout much of the nineteenth century British historians were suspicious of the political motives and intellectual bias of many of the leading French historians writing on the Revolution, but few of them discovered new sources on the scale of Aulard or offered grand new interpretations in the manner of Mathiez. While they might claim to stand more aloof from the Revolution, British historians were in fact greatly influenced by its impact, which included its effects on Britain. In the

---

[2]　See, for example, G.P. Gooch, *History and Historians in the Nineteenth Century* (2nd edn., London: Longmans Green and Co, 1952), pp. xvii-xx, 151-196, 214-240; J. McManners, "The Historiography of the French Revolution," in *The New Cambridge Modern History, Volume VIII: The American and French Revolutions 1763-1793* (Cambridge: Cambridge University Press, 1965), pp. 618-652; and N. Hampson, "The French Revolution and its Historians," in *The Permanent Revolution: The French Revolution and its Legacy*, ed. G. Best (London: Fontana Press, 1988), pp. 211-234.

nineteenth century most British historians believed that the abuses and corruption of the ancien regime had justified demands for reform, but they were invariably critical of the way the Revolution had degenerated into violence and terror. They tended to ignore the influence of economic and social forces on the course of the Revolution. They were often convinced of the follies and crimes of the Girondins and the Jacobins, but they tended to neglect the impact that foreign military intervention had on the conduct of these revolutionaries. While acknowledging that the consequences of the Revolution had been profound, they were reluctant to accept its more constructive achievements.[3]

Historical accounts of the French Revolution were produced by writers both inside and outside the academy. William Smyth, Regius Professor of History at the University of Cambridge from 1807 to 1847, was the first academic scholar in Britain to attempt a disinterested study of the French Revolution. He read widely, though uncritically, among the sources, both reliable and unreliable, that were beginning to be published in France. He blamed the outbreak of the Revolution on the abuses of the ancien regime and the failure to reform the royal finances. While sympathetic to the early French efforts to establish a limited, constitutional monarchy along British lines, he criticised even these early revolutionaries for being too ready to rely on visionary theories and to place too much trust in human reason. While critical of the counter-revolutionary

---

3   H. Ben-Israel, *English Historians on the French Revolution* (Cambridge: Cambridge University Press, 1968).

intentions of Louis XVI and the Austrians, he placed great stress on the follies and crimes of the Girondins and the Jacobins. He rejected the claims of Thiers and Mignet that the descent into the Terror was virtually inevitable and he did not accept Guizot's view that great principles were at work in the Revolution.[4]

In 1825, the conservative poet and novelist Walter Scott began work on a biography of Napoleon. By the time it was completed, as *The Life of Napoleon Buonaparte: Emperor of the French*, in 1827, it stretched to nine volumes and over one million words. Before beginning his study of Napoleon's career, Scott produced an opening volume on the earlier stages of the French Revolution. In it he revealed his debt to Edmund Burke's hostile views on the Revolution. He proclaimed the benefits of an hierarchical society, his interest in defending private property, and his conviction that the Christian religion was of great social value. He acknowledged that the Revolution was primarily caused by the weaknesses and rigidity of the ancien regime, but he did not accept that the course taken by the Revolution was inevitable or that the leading revolutionaries had strong popular support. A more able monarch, with better advisers, could have avoided the descent into violence and terror. Agreeing strongly with Burke, Scott attacked rash appeals to abstract natural rights and lamented the doomed attempts to create an egalitarian society. He

---

4　Ibid., pp. 71-97; H. Ben-Israel, "William Smyth, Historian of the French Revolution,"*Journal of the History of Ideas*, 21 (1960), pp. 571-585; and K.T.B. Butler, "A "petty" Professor of Modern History: William Smyth (1765-1849)," *Cambridge Historical Journal*, 9 (1948), pp. 217-238.

condemned the unwitting role played by Voltaire and other French philosophes in stoking the political ambitions of both the restless bourgeoisie and the lawless mob. He made martyrs out of Louis XVI and Marie Antoinette, and denounced the Girondins as weak and the Jacobins as satanic.[5]

The conservative bias of Scott's volume on the French Revolution did not go unchallenged. John Stuart Mill severely criticised it in a very substantial and painstaking review,[6] while the essayist and literary critic William Hazlitt rushed to respond to Scott's work by producing his own study of *The Life of Napoleon* in four volumes, between 1828 and 1830. As a young man, Hazlitt had been attracted to the radical political views of William Godwin. He later castigated in print James Mackintosh, Samuel Coleridge, Robert Southey and William Wordsworth for abandoning their earlier enthusiasm for the French Revolution. Hazlitt was never a convinced democratic republican, but he hated the political power exercised by divine right monarchies and the landed aristocracy throughout Europe. He attacked Edmund Burke's views of the French Revolution as

---

5   R.C. Gordon, "Scott among the Partisans: A significant bias in his "Life of Napoleon Buonaparte"," in *Scott Bicentenary Essays*, ed. A. Bell (Edinburgh: Scottish Academic Press, 1973), pp. 115-133; M.A. Weinstein, "Sir Walter Scott's French Revolution: the British Conservative View," *Scottish Literary Journal*, 7 (1980),pp. 31-40; and B.R. Friedman, *Fabricating History: English Writers on the French Revolution* (Princeton, NJ: Princeton University Press, 1988), pp. 67-108.

6   *Westminster Review*, 9 (1828), pp. 251-303. It was published as a separate pamphlet in the same year as *A Critical examination of the Preliminary View of the French Revolution, prefixed to Scott's 'Life of Bonaparte'*.

pernicious, condemned the decision of the British government to wage a counter-revolutionary war against France, and was appalled when the Bourbon monarchy was restored in France in 1814-15. Hazlitt particularly admired the role that Rousseau had played in influencing the French revolutionaries. He blamed the abuses of the ancien regime for causing the Revolution and he believed that timely concessions could have avoided the subsequent violence. The Revolution's descent into violence and terror was partly due to flaws in the French character (the French people were in his view too devoted to abstract ideas and wild speculation), but it was also due to the unjust interference in the internal affairs of France by foreign counter-revolutionary forces. Hazlitt did not admire Robespierre, but he did regard Napoleon as the saviour of the Revolution and credited him with giving unity and stability to the French state. Britain, by contrast, he regarded as vindictive and hypocritical, and primarily responsible for the rise and fall of Napoleon.[7]

The 1830s saw the publication of two very influential histories, which were to reach a great many readers and to have a profound effect on the popular image of the French Revolution in Britain. Archibald Alison, a

---

7　B.R. Friedman, *Fabricating History*, pp. 67-108; S. Deane, *The French Revolution and Enlightenment in England, 1789-1832* (Cambridge, MA: Harvard University Press, 1988), pp. 130-157; M.A. Garnett, "Hazlitt against Burke: Radical versus Conservative?," *Durham University Journal*, 81 (1989), pp. 229-239; C. Salvesen, "Hazlitt and the French Revolution," in *Tropes of Revolution: writers' reactions to real and imagined revolutions 1789-1989*, ed. C.C. Barfoot and T. D'haen (Amsterdam: Rodopi, 1991), pp. 55-71; and P. Harling, "William Hazlitt and Radical Journalism,"*Romanticism*, 3 (1997), pp. 53-65.

conservative Scottish lawyer, began writing on the French Revolution as early as 1829 and produced his multi-volume *History of Europe from the Commencement of the French Revolution in 1789 to the Restoration of the Bourbons in 1815* between 1833 and 1842. Ten editions of this work, including an abridged version for use in schools, had appeared by 1860.[8] In the mid and later nineteenth century his was the best-selling history of the French Revolution in both Britain and the USA. Although striving for impartiality, Alison was in fact a professed conservative and he consciously endeavoured to warn his readers of the dangers of too much democracy. While he accepted that the French people had many reasons to dislike the ancien regime, he criticised the propertied elite for not standing up to popular violence. He believed that the absence of a large and influential middle class in France had made it impossible to prevent the growth of royal absolutism during the ancien regime and to defeat popular violence from 1789 onwards. Irreligious men, craving power and deluded by wild democratic theories, had led the descent into violence that inevitably resulted in a military dictatorship.[9]

---

[8]   An on-line version of the complete text was produced by Cambridge University in 2011.

[9]   H. Ben-Israel, *English Historians on the French Revolution*, pp. 99-102, 151-153; M. Michie, *An Enlightened Tory in Victorian Scotland: The Career of Sir Archibald Alison* (East Linton: McGill-Queen's Press, 1997), pp. 130-158; M. Milne, "Archibald Alison: Conservative Controversialist," *Albion*, 27 (1995), pp. 419-443; and C.A. Simmons, "Disease and dismemberment: Two conservative metaphors for the French Revolution," *Prose Studies: History, Theory, Criticism*, 15 (1992), pp. 208-224.

Thomas Carlyle began his work, *The French Revolution: A History*, about the same time as Alison and completed it in three volumes in 1837. It was a greater critical success and it remained for many years the most famous British study of the Revolution. Even if no longer widely read, it succeeded in fixing in the British mind a particular view of the French Revolution. Carlyle wrote only about the aspects of the Revolution that evoked in him the strongest reactions. His history is episodic and lacks proportion because he deliberately set out to write a very vivid and human history of the Revolution. He was dissatisfied with those historians who offered grand theories rather than specific information. He relied heavily on his imagination, adopted a dramatic narrative form, wrote regularly in the first person, offered innumerable anecdotes, and produced brilliant if unreliable character vignettes. There is little in his history on economic and constitutional developments, administrative and legal reforms, the events in provincial France, or the reactions to the Revolution across Europe. Carlyle was preoccupied with the effect his prose would have on his readers and so he strove to enable his readers to see, hear, and feel what was happening in revolutionary Paris. His writing was most powerful when describing the dramatic scenes of death and terror when the guillotine was being over-used.

Carlyle stressed the grievous social, economic and political injustices of the ancien regime, which, un-redressed, inevitably led to the Revolution. He also criticised the French philosophes for encouraging change and all the revolutionary groups who tried to implement radical reforms. He did not, however, believe that the Revolution was a conspiracy hatched by intellectuals and he pitied rather than blamed the revolutionary leaders. The early reforms offered no remedy for the sickness affecting the French monarchy and, after the death of Mirabeau, there was no one to suggest effective policies to improve the situation. Attempts at universal suffrage and unlimited liberty continued rather than ended the political sickness affecting France. The Parisian sans-culottes strove to achieve a lofty ideal, but were ill equipped to achieve success. Carlyle refused to condemn the Terror because he believed it was the work of the many not the few. The Terror was a violent punishment of France for past abuses and was the means to destroy sick, corrupt and decaying institutions. It was terrible and destructive, but it was natural, even necessary, and might yet prove productive of good. Carlyle therefore suspended judgement on the ultimate significance of the Revolution. After the death of Robespierre he lost interest in the Revolution and his study ends in 1795.[10]

---

[10] H. Ben-Israel, *English Historians on the French Revolution*, pp. 127-150; H. Ben-Israel, "Carlyle and the French Revolution,"*Historical Journal*, 1 (1958), pp. 115-135; B.F. Friedman, *Fabricating History*, pp. 109-144; L.T. Frye, ""Great Burke", Thomas Carlyle and the French Revolution," in *The French Revolution Debate in English Literature and Culture*, ed. L.P. Crafton (Westport, Conn. Greenwood Publishing Group, 1997), pp. 83-106; A. Cobban, "Carlyle's French Revolution," *History*, 48 (1963), pp. 306-316; C.F. Harrold, "Carlyle's General Method in the French Revolution," *Publications of the Modern Language Association*, 43 (1928), pp. 1150-1169; H.M. Leicester, "The Dialectic of Romantic Historiography: Prospect and Retrospect in "The French Revolution"," *Victorian Studies*, 15 (1971), pp. 5-17; and C. Heyrendt-Sherman, "Re-presenting the French Revolution: the impact of Carlyle's work on British society and its self-representation," *Revue française de civilization Britannique*, 15 (2000), pp. 29-41.

Carlyle and other writers in the early to mid-nineteenth century had used some primary sources for their accounts, but the first British historian to recognise the difficulty of establishing the facts about the Revolution and to use primary sources well in the manner of a genuine researcher was John Wilson Croker. He was a fierce critic of the flood of spurious and unreliable memoires, which were published after the Bourbon restoration of 1815, and he was outraged at the shallowness of the research underpinning Alison's history of the Revolution. Partly because he recognised that the available sources were inadequate for a complete understanding of the Revolution, Croker never produced a complete narrative or coherent history of it. Instead, he composed very extensive reviews of published accounts claiming to provide first-hand evidence and he compiled individual essays on particular episodes. About thirty of these reviews and essays appeared in the conservative *Quarterly Review* between the early 1820s and the early 1850s. The best eight were subsequently reissued as *Essays on the Early Period of the French Revolution,* in 1857. Croker was a great admirer of Edmund Burke and a staunch conservative who revered the monarchy and the aristocracy, disliked abstract political theories, feared revolution spreading to Britain, and hated Napoleon. He tried hard, however, to prevent these prejudices affecting his judgement too much when writing as an historian on the early years of the Revolution. Always horrified by the violence of the Revolution, he did moderate his tone in his later, revised essays. He did come to recognise that the Revolution had been caused by the great social, legal and moral grievances of the French people under the ancien regime, and he did appreciate the need for some reforms in 1789. Although he believed that Louis XVI had made grave mistakes in 1789, he nevertheless believed that an irresistible democratic tide had defeated all the efforts of the ablest political leaders from Lafayette to Danton. While utterly deploring the Terror, he accepted that Robespierre possessed ability and integrity, was incorruptible, and was not responsible for all the crimes of the Terror. He recognised how Robespierre made the Jacobin Club the source of his power and how he exploited popular opinion in Paris. Yet he ignored Rousseau's influence on Robespierre and he showed no real psychological understanding of Robespierre's motives. Within the wider context, Croker largely ignored the constructive legal, administrative and constitutional reforms achieved by the Revolution and he barely mentioned the impact on the Revolution of foreign military interventions into the internal affairs of France.[11]

By the later nineteenth century, leading French historians were producing more impressive research on the Revolution. Their scholarly achievements were first introduced to the British public by H. Morse Stephens. In his two volumes on *A History of the French Revolution* (1886, 1892), Stephens essentially summarized this recent research by French scholars within a narrative account of the internal developments in revolutionary France, but he made no effort to offer his own overall

---

[11] H. Ben-Israel, *English Historians on the French Revolution*, pp. 151-153, 165-170, 175-202; and W. Thomas, *The Quarrels of Macaulay and Croker: Politics and History in the Age of Reform* (Oxford: Oxford University Press, 2000), pp. 162-209.

interpretation of the Revolution. French research also began to inform the scholarly activity of other British writers and academics. From 1895 to 1899 Lord Acton lectured at the University of Cambridge on the French Revolution; his efforts were later published as *Lectures on the French Revolution* in 1910. While Acton did not engage in primary research himself, he did make use of much of the new research recently produced by French scholars. He offered a narrative of events, combining detailed evidence with bold generalizations. He was at his best in examining political actions and motives, and in assessing the leading personalities of the Revolution. He acknowledged that the Revolution was produced by many causes, including economic factors, but he placed particular stress on the ideas and influence of the French philosophes and on the example of the earlier American Revolution. He acknowledged the importance of the French Revolution, but not because it was caused by particular material grievances (which French historians were stressing at this time), but because it rejected established authority and fought for liberty on principle. In his opinion, however, the Revolution failed because it ignored the importance of religion. While he was able to approve of some achievements of the Revolution, he was typical of most British historians of his time in condemning the crimes and folly of the leading revolutionaries and deploring the Terror in particular.[12]

From the late nineteenth century and through the twentieth century,

---

12　H. Ben-Israel, *English Historians on the French Revolution*, pp. 236-241, 245-273.

research and writing on the Revolution in France became increasingly professionalised, institutionalised and specialised. The best histories of the Revolution were now researched and written by scholars working in French universities and grandes écoles, rather than by French politicians seeking to influence current affairs. The work of historians such as Albert Mathiez, Georges Lefebvre, and Albert Soboul paid much greater attention to the mental world of rural peasants and urban sans-culottes, to the activities of Robespierre and other Jacobins, and to the impact of the Revolution on the French provinces. An emphasis on the economic and social factors affecting the causes and course of the Revolution established a new and persuasive overall interpretation of the Revolution. Clearly influenced by a Marxist approach, leading French historians came to regard the Revolution as, in essence, a bourgeois revolution. What became almost an orthodox or classic interpretation of the French Revolution emphasised the importance of class conflict, the role of the bourgeoisie in sweeping away many of the principal features of the ancien regime, and the growth of a capitalist economy. In this analysis of the Revolution the plebeian sans-culottes played a major role in assisting the bourgeoisie to overturn the monarchy and to destroy the feudal privileges of the aristocracy, but they did not develop sufficiently as a coherent working class to reap many political, social and economic rewards for themselves.

This overall interpretation of the French Revolution dominated how British as well as French historians approached the study of the Revolution for several decades. It greatly influenced the research and publications of leading British historians studying the Revolution, such as Richard Cobb,

George Rudé, Olwen Hufton, R.B. Rose, and Gwynne Lewis.[13] It first came under attack in Britain when Professor Albert Cobban gave his inaugural lecture at the University of London in 1954, entitled 'The Myth of the French Revolution'.[14] His criticisms were developed more fully in his book, *The Social Interpretation of the French Revolution* (1964). Cobban raised several major objections to the prevailing left-wing interpretation of the Revolution. He maintained that feudalism had disappeared in France long before the Revolution and yet, after 1789, France still remained essentially a rural economy. The sans-culottes in the towns were not a single class, but rather a loose coalition of disparate

---

13　See, for example, Richard Cobb, *Les armées révolutionnaires* (2 vols., Paris: Mouton & Co, 1961-63); Cobb, *Terreur et Subsistances, 1793-1795* (Paris: Clavreuil, 1965); Cobb, *The Police and the People: French Popular Protest, 1789-1820* (Oxford: Oxford University Press, 1970); Cobb, *Reactions to the French Revolution* (Oxford: Oxford University Press, 1972); Cobb, *Paris and the Provinces, 1792-1802* (Oxford: Oxford University Press, 1975); George Rudé, *The Crowd in the French Revolution* (Oxford: Oxford University Press, 1959); Rudé, *Robespierre: Portrait of a Revolutionary Democrat* (London: Viking, 1975); Olwen Hufton, "Women in Revolution 1789-1796," in Douglas Johnson ed., *French Society and the Revolution* (Cambridge: Cambridge University Press, 1976); Hufton, *Women and the limits of citizenship in the French Revolution* (Toronto: University of Toronto Press, 1992); R.B. Rose, *The making of the sans-culottes: Democratic ideas and institutions in Paris, 1789-92* (Manchester: Manchester University Press, 1983); Gwynne Lewis, *Life in revolutionary France* (London: Putnam Pub Group Juv, 1972); and Lewis, *The Second Vendée: the continuity of counter-revolution in the Department of the Gard, 1789-1815* (Oxford: Oxford University Press, 1978).

14　It was later published in a collection of Cobban's essays, *Aspects of the French Revolution* (London: Jonathan Cape Ltd, 1968), pp. 90-111.

social groups. The French bourgeoisie were bureaucrats rather than industrial capitalists and the Revolution did not advance and may even have retarded the growth of a capitalist economy. The war certainly severely damaged French commerce. Finally, in Cobban's view, the French Revolution was primarily a political rather than a social or economic revolution. It was a struggle for power and its most significant achievement was the overthrow of the old monarchical system and the creation of different forms of government.

Cobban's views initially came in for considerable criticism and for some years they made little headway against those historians who rushed to defend and justify the orthodox (left-wing) view of the French Revolution.[15] A few British historians began to adopt and expand Cobban's criticisms, but it was the French historian François Furet who did most to advance what became known as the revisionist interpretation of the French Revolution.[16] Furet rejected what he regarded as a Marxist

---

[15] B. Behrens, "Professor Cobban and His Critics," *Historical Journal*, 9 (1966), pp. 236-241; G.J. Cavanaugh, "The Present State of French Revolutionary Historiography: Alfred Cobban and Beyond," *French Historical Studies*, 7 (1972), pp. 587-606; and A. Cobban, 'The French Revolution, Orthodox and Unorthodox: A Review of Reviews,' *History*, 52 (1967), pp. 149-159.

[16] F. Furet et D. Richet, *La Révolution: des* états *généraux au 9 thermidor* (2 vols., Paris: Realites Hachette, 1965); Furet, *Penser la Révolution française* (Paris: Gallimard, 1978); Furet, *La Révolution, de Turgot à Jules Ferry : 1770-1880* (Paris: Hachette, 1988); and *Dictionnaire critique de la révolution française*, ed. Furet and M. Ozouf (2 vols., Paris: Flammarion, 1992).

interpretation of the French Revolution. He denied that 1789 marked a major watershed that saw the destruction of the old world and the beginning of the modern society of bourgeois capitalism. He opposed the claims of those historians who believed that the Revolution was primarily about the underlying social and economic conditions of the French people, that class conflict played a major role in the development of the Revolution, and that the Revolution did much to develop a capitalist economy in France that was promoted and controlled by the bourgeoisie. Furet did acknowledge that the French Revolution was a great event, but he believed that it had gone astray when the revolutionary emphasis on equality undermined the efforts to promote liberty. The Revolution established a new kind of absolute authority empowering the state at the expense of the rights of the individual citizen. The legislature claimed to be the embodiment of popular sovereignty and the sole interpreter and judge of its own will. This led inevitably to the kind of abuse of authority seen in totalitarian regimes in the twentieth century.

　　Furet's intervention in the debate on the French Revolution had a much greater impact on historians in France, and in Britain, the USA, and elsewhere, than had Cobban's work. By the time the Revolution's bicentenary was being celebrated in 1989 it was being widely claimed that Furet and his revisionist allies had won the historiographical debate and that the left-wing interpretation of the French Revolution was in full retreat.[17] Three colloquia held at Chicago in 1986, Oxford in 1987, and

---

17　J.R. Censer, "Commencing the Third Century of Debate," *American Historical*

Paris in 1988, led to the appearance of four very large volumes of collected essays, published between 1987 and 1994, entitled *The French Revolution and the Creation of Modern Political Culture*, that were dominated by revisionist historians.[18] In the Anglophone world the revisionist case was most forcibly advanced when Simon Schama, a British historian based in the USA, produced, in time for the bicentenary, *Citizens: A Chronicle of the French Revolution* (New York, 1989). Schama maintained that the ancien regime in France had been full of vitality and moderate men might have reformed its weaknesses. The Revolution destroyed much of value, but failed to achieve much good because the preference for equality above liberty encouraged the sans-culottes to ever more violence. The Revolution was born in violence from its origins in 1789 and violence marked its whole course until it ended in a military dictatorship. In Schama's view the Revolution was an unmitigated disaster. Its central importance was not the Declaration of the Rights of Man and the Citizen, but the belief that the untrammelled reason and the unrestrained will of man was more important than the rule of law and the search for justice for all. It led in France to the kind of abuse of power seen in totalitarian regimes in the twentieth

---

Review, 94 (1989), pp. 1309-1325; I. Woloch, "On the Latent Illiberalism of the French Revolution," *American Historical Review*, 95 (1990), pp. 1452-1470; and W. Doyle, "Reflections on the Classic Interpretation of the French Revolution," *French Historical Studies*, 16 (1990), pp. 743-748.

18 These four volumes were published by the Pergamon Press in Oxford in 1989. The first and fourth volumes were edited by Keith Michael Baker (a British-trained scholar based in the USA), the second by Colin Lucas of Oxford University, and the third jointly by François Furet and Mona Ozouf.

century.

Schama's book was well received by the popular press and it sold large numbers of copies, but it came in for considerable criticism from better-informed academic reviewers.[19] While the French Revolution remains a major subject of historical enquiry, which still attracts some of the finest and most engaged historians in Britain (as it does in France and the USA), much recent research has been content to be narrowly focused and highly specialised. There has been a reluctance to advance a new overall interpretation of the Revolution. It has even been argued that the area of French revolutionary studies has become splintered and atomised to the confusion of new students seeking to enter the field.[20] Some major British historians, such as Colin Jones, Gwynne Lewis, and Olwen Hufton continued to publish on the kind of subjects that previously interested

---

[19] For favourable reviews of *Citizens* in the popular media in the USA, see the *New York Times Book Review*, 19 March 1989, *Newsweek*, 3 April 1989, and the *New Yorker*, 17 April 1989. For academic criticism, see M. Slavin's review in *Annales historiques de la Révolution française*, 277 (July-Sept. 1989), pp. 27-30; and R. Forster's review in *French Politics and Society*, 7 (1989), pp. 150-156. See also, A. Sa'adah, "Recent Writings on the French Revolution: Violence, Democratic Politics and "Modernity"," *Polity*, 22 (1990), pp. 731-743; G. Lewis, "Revolution, Revision and Reaction," *Historical Journal*, 33 (1990), pp. 711-722; and A.B. Spitzer, "Narrative Problems: The Case of Simon Schama," *Journal of Modern History*, 65 (1993), pp. 176-192.

[20] J.R. Censer, "Social Twists and Linguistic Turns: Revolutionary Historiography a Decade after the Bicentennial," *French Historical Studies*, 22 (1999), pp. 139-167; R.L. Spang, "Paradigms and paranoia: How Modern is the French Revolution," *American Historical Review*, 108 (2003), pp. 119-147; and L. Hunt, "The World We Have Gained: The Future of the French Revolution," *American Historical Review*, 108 (2003), pp. 1-19.

Georges Lefebvre and Albert Soboul, while not being tied to a strict Marxist interpretation of the Revolution. They have pointed out that these French historians were, in fact, willing to produce evidence that ran counter to a left-wing interpretation of the Revolution and also acknowledged that not all the bourgeoisie were capitalists. They have also tended to shift interest from Paris to the provinces and from social conflict to cultural transformations, such as the development of new social conventions, the growth of the press, and the strengthening of public opinion. Other leading British historians writing on the French Revolution, such as William Doyle, Keith Michael Baker, and Colin Lucas, who are usually counted as being in the revisionist camp, have not entirely accepted François Furet's overall interpretation of the Revolution. Doyle in particular, is more eclectic, empirical and balanced, and less theoretical.[21]

In the field of historical writing, therefore, the French Revolution has continued to stimulate opinion and controversy among informed Britons. The contemporary concerns and preoccupations of British authors,

---

[21]   W. Doyle, *Origins of the French Revolution* (3rd edn., Oxford: Oxford University Press, 1999); and W. Doyle, *The Oxford History of the French Revolution* (2nd edn., Oxford: Oxford University Press, 2002). See also, Colin Lucas, *The Structure of the Terror: The Example of Javogues and the Loire* (Oxford: Oxford University Press, 1973); Lucas, "Nobles, Bourgeois and the Origins of the French Revolution," *Past and Present*, 60 (1973), pp. 84-126; and Keith Michael Baker, *Inventing the French Revolution: Essays on French Culture in the Eighteenth Century* (Cambridge: Cambridge University Press, 1990).

both academic historians and others, have influenced how they have understood and interpreted the Revolution. A similar pattern can be observed in the cultural responses to, and political legacy of, the French Revolution in Britain, discussed below.

II
Cultural Responses to the French Revolution

The French Revolution inspired contemporary responses from many creative artists in Britain – poets, novelists, dramatists and caricaturists. It continued to do so across the nineteenth century and beyond. Most of these works appeared in the first half of the nineteenth century, particularly during and shortly after the Napoleonic wars, but some were produced long after. Some of these creative works were sympathetic to French revolutionary principles and defensive of French actions, but most were hostile. The latter in particular have left an indelible impression of how a powerful but restricted image of the French Revolution has been produced in Britain over more than two centuries.

The French Revolution inspired poetic responses from some of Britain's greatest poets as well as many lesser versifiers during the 1790s. An unprecedented number of poems continued to be published in Britain in the early nineteenth century in response to the threat posed by Napoleonic France.[22]   Napoleon's aggressive policies persuaded some

---

22   H.F.B. Wheeler and A.M. Broadley, *Napoleon and the Invasion of England* (2 vols., London, 1908-1911); *The Warning Drum: The British Home Front*

leading British poets, who had been supportive of French revolutionary principles in the 1790s, to express their disillusionment with the turn of events in France. William Blake never entirely lost his sympathy for French principles, but he ceased to support them openly in the early 1800s. His caution was no doubt influenced in part by his alarm at being charged with sedition in 1803, even though he was acquitted.[23]   The radicalism he continued to display in such works as *Milton* (1804-08) and *Jerusalem* (1804-20) owed more to his belief that change would come from a person's inward, spiritual transformation rather than from the kind of political changes advocated by the French in the early 1790s.[24]

The three young British poets most excited by the French Revolution in the early 1790s, Samuel Taylor Coleridge, Robert Southey, and William Wordsworth, had all become seriously disillusioned with events in France by the early nineteenth century and became increasingly conservative in their political principles and writings. By 1798, in *France an Ode* and in *Fears in Solitude*, Coleridge condemned the French invasion of Switzerland and claimed that Britain was justified in waging war against

---

faces Napoleon, ed. F. J. Klingberg and S.B. Hustvedt (Berkeley, CA: University Of California Press, 1944); and *British War Poetry in the Age of Romanticism, 1793-1815*, ed. Betty T. Bennett (New York: Keats-Shelley Association of America, Inc., 1976).

23   J. Mee and M. Crosby, ""This Soldierlike Danger": The Trial of William Blake for Sedition," in *Resisting Napoleon: The British Response to the Threat of Invasion, 1797-1815*, ed. M. Philp (Aldershot, 2006), pp. 111-124.

24   D. V. Erdman, *Blake: Prophet against Empire* (revised edn., New York: Dover Publications, 1969), pp. 422-438, 457-487.

French aggression. In perhaps his most famous poem, *The Rime of the Ancient Mariner*, written the same year, Coleridge implied that man should not challenge the providential order of nature and could not improve his condition by his own efforts, but needed God's grace to achieve salvation.[25] In his periodical, *The Friend* (1809-10) Coleridge attacked the ideas of Voltaire and Rousseau, and the revolutionary principles they inspired. While Coleridge continued to acknowledge that all men were endowed with reason and should be accorded the same moral status, he now came to the conclusion that they should not possess the same political rights because they had not benefited from the same experiences, talents, or education. Moreover, he now accepted that governments were created to protect property and, since property was held unequally, then so should political power. To produce a better society, Coleridge increasingly turned to the Christian religion and traditional moral values. In his two *Lay Sermons* (1816-17) he urged men in the upper and the middling classes in Britain to use their influence to improve the moral standards of the nation and he attacked rash demagogues who were promoting radical ideas. In his most famous pamphlet, *On the Constitution of the Church and State* (1829), Coleridge insisted that the bible was the best political guide for those seeking a better society and he advised the clergy and educated laymen to work together to strengthen Britain's existing constitution and safeguard its social hierarchy. Like Edmund Burke, he had now become a

---

25　P. Kitson, "Coleridge, the French Revolution, and "The Ancient Mariner": Collective Guilt and Individual Salvation," *The Yearbook of English Studies*, 19 (1989), pp.197-207.

fierce opponent of atheism, political radicalism, and all major innovations. He wished to defend the authority of the landed elite and he stressed the duties rather than the rights of man.[26]

Robert Southey trod a similar path from admiration for French revolutionary principles to a conservative defence of Britain's constitution and social structure. He never abandoned his belief that the French Revolution had been an unavoidable and necessary response to the abuses and corruption of the ancien regime, but he came to regard the Jacobin Terror as a monstrous abuse of power and Napoleon's military ambitions as intolerable. His faith in the French Revolution was first shaken by the coup d'état of Brumaire 1799, but it was not until the threat of a French invasion in 1803-05 that he became a firm advocate of the war against France. The Spanish uprising of 1808 convinced him that Britain must fight a total war against France. His attitude to the war encouraged him to produce some of his most popular works. His two-volume *Life of Nelson*

---

26 L. Patton, "Coleridge and Revolutionary France," *South Atlantic Quarterly*, 31 (1932), pp. 321-330; I.R. Robertson, ""Things As They Are": The Literary Response to the French Revolution 1789-1815," in *Britain and the French Revolution, 1789-1815*, ed. H.T. Dickinson (Basingstoke: MacMillan, 1989), pp. 229-249; A.S. Link, "Samuel Taylor Coleridge and the Economic and Political Crisis in Great Britain, 1816-1820," *Journal of the History of Ideas*, 9 (1948), pp. 323-338; M. Francis and J. Morrow, *A History of English Political Thought in the Nineteenth Century* (London:Palgrave Macmillan , 1994), pp. 123-138; P. Edwards, "Coleridge on Politics and Religion: The Statesman's Manual, Aids to Reflection, on the Constitution in Church and State," in *The Oxford Handbook of Samuel Taylor Coleridge*, ed. F. Burwick (Oxford: Oxford University Press, 2012), pp. 235-253.

（1812-13）extravagantly praised Britain's greatest naval hero in this war, and it was so successful that it has remained in print ever since.[27] Southey followed up this historical biography with a three-volume *History of the Peninsular War* (1823-32) and the first volume of a series on *Lives of the British Admirals* (1833). Although he was made Poet Laureate, Southey became more famous as a writer of prose. He became one of the most famous and influential authors of essays and reviews in the leading conservative periodical, the *Quarterly Review*. He continued to show concern for the harsh conditions facing the labouring poor, advocating the creation of public works to provide employment opportunities, increased expenditure on the country's system of poor relief, and a national system of education, but he became a fierce opponent of radical political reforms. He campaigned against parliamentary reform and demanded a stringent censorship of the radical press.[28]

William Wordsworth, the finest and most prolific of these three poet friends, followed a similar political trajectory from radical sympathy for French principles to a conservative reaction against revolutionary ideas.

---

[27] D. Eastwood, "Patriotism personified: Robert Southey's *Life of Nelson* reconsidered," *Mariner's Mirror*, 77 (1991), pp. 143-149.

[28] D. Eastwood, "Robert Southey and the Intellectual Origins of Romantic Conservatism," *English Historical Review*, 104 (1989), pp. 308-331; K. Gilmartin, *Writing against Revolution: Literary Conservatism in Britain, 1790-1832* (Cambridge: Cambridge University Press, 2007), pp. 207-252; and W.A. Speck, "Robert Southey's Contribution to the Quarterly Review," in *Conservatism and the Quarterly Review : A Critical Analysis*, ed. J.B. Cutmore (London, 2007), pp. 165-177.

He traced his political development in *The Prelude*, one of his longest and most impressive poems.[29] In this autobiography in verse Wordsworth accepted that the abuses and corruption of the ancien regime had justified French reformers in seeking to improve France's political system and social structure. Their efforts at moderate reform, however, had been frustrated by foreign military intervention in the affairs of France. This attempted counter-revolution led to the Jacobin reaction and the Terror. While deploring these, Wordsworth tried to understand the motives behind them and did not immediately give up hope of a return to moderate political reform. It was the rise of Napoleon, his destruction of Venetian and Spanish independence, and his attempted invasion of Britain, that led Wordsworth to support the war against France. In his pamphlet, *The Convention of Cintra* (1809) he criticised this agreement as being too generous to France and he celebrated the defeat of Napoleon in his poem, *The Excursion* (1812-14). In his later years he admitted that Burke had been right to condemn the French Revolution and he came a staunch defender of the British constitution, the Church of England, and government by the landed elite. In his uncompleted poem, *The Recluse*, he stressed the importance of tradition, religion and nature as the best means

---

29 Wordsworth worked on this poem for many years. He constantly revised it, but did not publish a substantial version of it during his lifetime. A version of it appeared posthumously in 1850, but literary scholars now prefer the original draft of the 1805 version, which was not published until 1926. This presents the clearest statement of Wordsworth's political philosophy and is regarded as fresher and more vigorous verse.

of promoting moral regeneration.[30] Like Coleridge and Southey, he lamented the damaging social and economic effects of urbanization and industrialization, and sought to ameliorate them by advocating, in *The Excursion*, Book IX, for example, a national system of education. He was, however, opposed to parliamentary reform.[31]

While Coleridge, Southey and Wordsworth were in the process of abandoning their sympathy for French revolutionary principles, two younger poets, Percy Bysshe Shelley and George Gordon, Lord Byron, were attempting to keep alive British admiration for the radical principles of the early French Revolution. Shelley was a political radical from his early years, being expelled from Eton and Oxford for expressing atheistic views and attacking the Christian religion. Captivated by the political views of William Godwin, he eloped, although married, with Godwin's daughter Mary and lived a very irregular personal life thereafter. In his first major poem, *Queen Mab* (1813), Shelley attacked monarchy, aristocracy, and religion, protested against the exploitation of the poor, and envisioned

---

30　K.R. Johnston, "Wordsworth and *The Recluse*: The University of the Imagination," *Publications of the Modern Language Association*, 97 (1982), pp.60-82.

31　A.V. Dicey, *The Statesmanship of Wordsworth* (Oxford: Oxford University Press, 1917); F.M. Todd, *Politics and the Poet t: A Study of Wordsworth* (London: Methuen, 1957); E.C. Batho, *The Later Wordsworth* (Cambridge: Cambridge University Press, 1933); V.G. Kiernan, "Wordsworth and the People" in *Marxists in Literature*, ed. D. Craig (London: Penguin, 1975), pp. 161-206; and E.L. Stelzig, ""The Shield of Human Nature": Wordsworth's Reflections on the Revolution in France," *Nineteenth-Century Literature*, 45 (1991), pp.415-431.

the creation of a new golden age. In 1817, he published under a pseudonym, *A Proposal for Putting Reform to the Vote*, a pamphlet in which he recommended holding a referendum of the British people on the question of parliamentary reform. In his poem *The Revolt of Islam* (1818) he admitted his disillusionment with the way the French Revolution had degenerated into violence, but he still expressed the hope that political progress might be achieved by more gradual and more peaceful means. In another political pamphlet, *A Philosophical View of Reform* (1819), which he decided not to publish,[32] Shelley commented more favourably on the French Revolution and expressed the desire to see a democratic republic established in Britain relatively soon and, in the more distant future, an egalitarian state erected. The collapse of the French Revolution into violence and terror appears to have convinced him that rushing into radical reform could be dangerous, but he still clearly had hopes of a much better future for mankind. In his lyrical drama *Prometheus Unbound* (1820) he produced a grand vision of progressive historical forces leading eventually to a golden age of liberty.[33] In *The Mask of Anarchy*, written in response to the forcible dispersal of a mass radical meeting at Manchester, in 1819, Shelley urged the men of England to rise from their slumber, break their chains and strive for political liberty.[34] He sent it for publication, but it remained unpublished until 1832, ten years after his death.

---

32   This pamphlet was not published until 1920.
33   K.N. Cameron, "Shelley and the Reformers," *ELH*, 12 (1945), pp.62-85.
34   A.S. Walker, "Peterloo, Shelley and Reform," *Publications of the Modern Language Association*, 40 (1925), pp.128-164.

The French Revolution exerted no such direct influence on Lord Byron, and yet he can be regarded as the heir of the British literary Jacobins of the early 1790s in his belief in the power of reason, his hatred of monarchical government, his devotion to individual liberty, and his sympathy for the politically oppressed. Regarded by his enemies as a supporter of anarchy and upheaval, he never actually favoured a revolution in Britain, disliked political agitators such as William Cobbett and Henry Hunt, and favoured only a moderate measure of parliamentary reform. Throughout his short life, however, he liked to pose as the apostle of revolt and a rebel against all constituted authority. While not believing in democracy or equality, he did oppose all forms of tyranny and all attempts by rulers to restrict the lives of their subjects. In Canto III of his first major work, *Childe Harold's Pilgrimage* (1812), he expressed sympathy for the ideas of Voltaire and Rousseau. In Canto IV, he used the imagery of the French Revolution to construct a vision of a better future. He expressed admiration for the principles of the early French Revolution and he condemned the opposition to it of all the monarchs of Europe. He even attacked Britain for waging war against Napoleon, and lamented the restoration of the Bourbon monarchy in 1814-15 and the strengthening of ancien regimes throughout Europe. In his poem *Don Juan* (1819-24) he castigated Coleridge, Southey, and Wordsworth for their political apostasy and attacked the British aristocracy for their hypocrisy, cruelty, and indolence. He went into exile in 1816, hoping that he might return in triumph after a successful revolution, but his hopes were dashed. Disillusioned, he produced two verse plays in 1821, *Marino Faliero* and

The Two Foscari, which depicted the failure of revolutionary republicans and other attempts at major political innovations.[35]

The French Revolution had inspired a considerable number of British authors to produce novels in the 1790s that were either supportive or critical of French revolutionary principles.[36] By the early nineteenth century there were no explicitly Jacobin or anti-Jacobin novels published in Britain and yet the French revolution can still be shown to have had an indirect influence on some of the leading novelists of the age. William Godwin's *Fleetwood: Or, the New Man of Feeling* (1805) can be seen as a criticism of Rousseau's ideas on education and it does depict the passing of a great age of civil liberty, but it is set in mid-seventeenth-century England. In his last novel, *Mandeville* (1817), Godwin deals with the psychological impact on the individual of violent revolutionary excesses and severe civil unrest, but again the story is set in mid-seventeenth-century England. In both novels, Godwin is no longer optimistic about political changes.[37] Frances Burney's last novel, *The Wanderer: Or,*

---

35 D.V. Erdman, "Byron and Revolt in England," *Science and Society*, 11 (1947), pp. 234-248; D.V. Erdman, "Lord Byron and the Genteel Reformers," *Publications of the Modern Language Association*, 56 (1941), pp. 1065-1094; and J.D. Gonsalves, "Byron's Venetian Masque of the French Revolution," in *Byron and the Politics of Freedom and Terror*, ed. M.J.A. Green and P. Pai-Lapinski (Basingstoke: Palgrave Macmillan, 2011), pp. 47-63.

36 G. Kelly, *The English Jacobin Novel, 1780-1805* (Oxford: Clarendon Press, 1976); and M.O. Grenby, *The anti-Jacobin Novel: British conservatism and the French Revolution* (Cambridge: Cambrisge University Press, 2001).

37 P. Clemit, *The Godwinian Novel: The Rational Fictions of Godwin, Brockden Brown, Mary Shelley* (Oxford: Clarendon Press, 1993), pp. 95-102.

Female Difficulties (1814), deals very largely with the difficulties women faced in early nineteenth-century British society, but the heroine had fled from revolutionary France, where she had been forced into a marriage with a French official in order to save her guardian from the guillotine. In Britain she faces competition for the affections of Albert Harleigh from a rival who has been educated in France, where she has absorbed dangerous moral principles and has adopted lax standards of behaviour. Her belief in unbridled liberty leads her into irrational actions and morally reprehensible conduct in defiance of the social conventions accepted in Britain. Becoming a slave to her desires and lost to shame, she fails to convert Harleigh to her extreme views.[38]

The last novels of Godwin and Burney were much criticised and failed to attract the number of readers who had welcomed their earlier novels. By contrast, the two most admired and widely read novelists of the early nineteenth century, Jane Austen and Walter Scott, were much more successful in promoting conservative attitudes and patriotic values, while appearing to ignore the French Revolution. Although many literary critics have praised her prose, Jane Austen has been criticised for focusing very narrowly on the daily lives, courtship rituals and marriage arrangements of

---

[38] D. Silverman, "Reading Frances Burney's *The Wanderer: Or, Female Difficulties*: The Politics of Women's Independence," *Pacific Coast Philology*, 26 (1991), pp. 68-77; J. Crump, ""Turning the World Upside Down": Madness, Moral Management and Frances Burney's *The Wanderer*," *Eighteenth-Century Fiction*, 10 (1998), pp. 325-340; and H. Thompson, "How *The Wanderer* works: Reading Fanny Burney and Bourdieu," *ELH*, 68 (2001), pp. 965-989.

the English gentry living in small rural communities. Critics have accused her of studiously ignoring the wider political context in which her heroines lived in the 1790s and early 1800s. A few admirers, however, have pointed out that these critics have failed to recognise how the French Revolution and the French Wars do impact on her stories. Her principal characters are shown in a good light whenever they seek to exercise a benevolent paternalism over, and to preserve social stability and cohesion in, their local communities. Moreover, soldiers, sailors and militia officers appear in several of her novels. In *Mansfield Park* (1814), the conduct and actions of officers in the Royal Navy are praised by those characters in the novel, whom readers are expected to admire. In *Emma* (1815), an explicit contrast is drawn between the two rivals for Emma's affections. George Knightly possesses the conventional English virtues of integrity, candour and a strong sense of duty, whereas Frank Churchill, who has absorbed French manners and appearances, is devious, self-indulgent and lacking in substance. Emma's growing maturity and improved judgement of character are demonstrated by her eventual recognition of Churchill's weaknesses and Knightly's strengths.[39]

Walter Scott was the best-selling poet and novelist of the early

---

39 W. Roberts, *Jane Austen and the French Revolution* (London: Macmillan, 1979), pp. 31-48, 99-108; W. Hellstrom, "Francophobia in Emma," *Studies in English Literature, 1500-1900*, 5 (1965), pp.607-617; G. Russell, "The Army, the Navy, and the Napoleonic Wars," in *A Companion to Jane Austen*, ed. C.L. Johnson and C. Tuite (Oxford: Wiley-Blackwell, 2009), pp. 261-271; and M. Butler, *Jane Austen and the War of Ideas* (Oxford: Oxford University Press, 1975).

nineteenth century and, in both literary forms, he revealed his fierce opposition to French military aggression and his firm commitment to conservative values. His best-selling poems, *The Lay of the Last Minstrel* (1805), *Marmion* (1808) and *The Lady of the Lake* (1810), while depicting martial heroism in the wars between England and Scotland in the sixteenth century, praised the martial spirit of this earlier period in order to rally the British people behind the war against Napoleonic France. He highlighted the glory rather than the horror of war in order to inspire the British people into fighting an unremitting war with France.[40] When Scott turned to writing novels he was just as successful with the reading public, while adopting a similar approach to using the past to influence contemporary opinion in Britain. Almost all his novels, from *Waverley* (1814) to *The Bride of Lammermoor* (1819), were set in times of rebellion or civil conflict, but in late seventeenth or early eighteenth-century Scotland. Only *The Antiquary* (1816) was set during the recent Napoleonic Wars, when invasion threatened. In all these novels, however, Scott's heroes display the kind of chivalry, which Edmund Burke so admired. They all learn the wisdom of renouncing fanaticism and turning away from dangerous leaders in order to seek peace and to promote good relations between the different social classes. Scott shows social and ideological differences to be folly in times of peace and dangerous

---

[40] S. Bainbridge, *British Poetry and the Revolutionary and Napoleonic Wars: Visions of Conflict* (Oxford: Oxford University Press, 2003), pp. 120-147 and 159-170.

delusions in times of civil upheaval.[41]

Much more directly linked to the principles and impact of the French revolution was Mary Shelley's novel, *Frankenstein* (1819). The daughter of William Godwin and Mary Wollstonecraft, and the mistress and then wife of Percy Shelley, Mary had very strong personal links with optimistic believers in the value of human reason and committed advocates of political liberty. In *Frankenstein*, however, she clearly reacted against these influences and wrote a very pessimistic novel. On one level, *Frankenstein* is a study in how an ambitious, rational idealist could produce unintended consequences that were terrifyingly violent. In the novel, Dr Frankenstein is depicted as an ambitious, rational man, striving to achieve an impossible goal by ill-conceived and irresponsible means. He seeks to create a new, superior species of man from body parts stolen from charnel houses and paupers' graves. The link with the dangerously utopian ambitions of the early French revolutionaries is made quite explicit. Frankenstein was born in Geneva, the birthplace of Rousseau, and he conducts his dangerous experiment in Ingolstadt, where the Illuminati, held responsible for plotting to spread violent revolution across Europe, were believed to have begun their evil conspiracy.[42] Dr Frankenstein is seeking to create a new, superior race of men by rational experimentation, but his efforts, like those of the Jacobin revolutionaries, end in disaster, as

---

41   M. Butler, *Romantics, Rebels and Reactionaries: English Literature and its Background, 1760-1830* (Oxford: Oxford University Press, 1981), pp. 110-111.

42   On this, see Abbé Barruel, *Memoirs Illustrating the History of Jacobinism* (London: T. Burton & Co., 1797).

his new creature turns into a murderous, vengeful monster, who wreaks terrible harm on his creator and on the doctor's loved ones. There is, however, another political layer to the novel that is not quite so obvious. Soon after he is created, the creature claims the rights of man and the citizen. He demands that Dr Frankenstein, his creator, makes a female partner for him. When this claim is denied, and he is also denied the society of an admired family of French émigrés, the creature grows to feel isolated, unloved, and alienated. In his distress, like an alienated revolutionary, the creature resorts to violence and terror. The end result is the mutual destruction of both the doctor and his creature.[43]

The flaws in the principles underpinning the French Revolution undoubtedly influenced Mary Shelley's *Frankenstein*. The cruel, unjust, and violent actions attributed to the French revolutionaries are also central to Charles Dickens's novel, *A Tale of Two Cities* (1859). Much influenced by Thomas Carlyle's history of the French Revolution, this novel has probably done most to shape popular British attitudes towards events in France during the Terror. In the novel, Dickens portrays the savage instincts and murderous actions of the Parisian sans-culottes. He does not

---

43　P. Clemit, *The Godwinian Novel*, pp. 139-174; *The Endurance of Frankenstein: Essays on Mary Shelley's Novel*, ed. G. Levine and U.C. Knoepflmacher (Berkeley, CA, 1979), pp. 3-30, 143-171; J. O'Rourke, ""Nothing More Unnatural": Mary Shelley's revision of Rousseau," *ELH*, 56 (1989), pp.543-569; D. Reese, "A Troubled Legacy: Mary Shelley's Frankenstein and the Inheritance of Human Rights," *Representations*, 96 (2006), pp. 48-72; and J.V. Douthwaite, *The Frankenstein of 1790 and other lost chapters from revolutionary France* (Chicago: University Of Chicago Press, 2012), pp. 91-97.

do so in an effort to compare the violent, volatile French with the civilised, peaceful British, because he implies that a revolutionary situation was simmering just below the surface of society in London. A careful reading of the novel can reveal that Dickens feared that a corrupt, unjust, and uncaring government, whether in Paris or London, could provoke a violent revolution from the oppressed masses, but it is likely that most readers would note more easily the violence in Paris as the guillotine goes to work and as revolutionary tribunals unjustly condemn the innocent to death. A careful reading can also show that, while Dickens does not mention a single constructive reform that the French Revolution had achieved, he does appear to have wished to convey the suggestion that some good might come from the Revolution. Hence, when his flawed hero, Sydney Carton, is just about to sacrifice his wasted life on the guillotine, in order to save the virtuous Charles Darnay, he has a vision of evil gradually disappearing and the people's struggle to be free eventually ending in triumph. Like Carlyle, Dickens appears to have believed, or at least hoped, that the French Revolution might in some inexplicable way turn out to be a regenerative force that was in the process of benefiting mankind. For many readers, however, Carton's last act is more like a deathbed religious conversion leading to eternal salvation.[44]

A Tale of Two Cities, despite being a work of creative fiction, is

---

44   B.R. Friedman, *Fabricating History*, pp. 145-171; I. Collins, "Charles Dickens and the French Revolution," *Literature and History*, 1 (1990), pp.40-57; and *Charles Dickens, 'A Tale of Two Cities' and the French Revolution*, ed. C. Jones, J. McDonagh and J. Mee (Basingstoke: Palgrave Macmillan, 2009), pp. 1-58.

credited with doing more to shape British impressions of the French Revolution than any other book. Paradoxically, this may, in part, have been due to the fact that many readers have failed to appreciate the more subtle points that Dickens was attempting to make. It probably owes more, however, to the fact that the novel was adapted by other media, which heightened its more melodramatic features, ignored the potential for revolution in London, and stressed the almost Christ-like sacrifice made by Sydney Carton. The novel was adapted as a play for the London stage as early as 1860. It was later transformed into an even more melodramatic play, *The Only Way*, by John Martin Harvey, who performed the role of Sydney Carton for forty years (1899-1939) across Britain and Canada. In 1917 the Twentieth Century Fox film studio produced a silent film of *A Tale of Two Cities*. In a 1925 film version John Martin Harvey played the part of Sydney Carton. In 1935 a leading British film star, Ronald Colman, played the role of Carton in a film produced by MGM studio. Some sympathy for the French Revolution was created in this production, but mob violence was still shown as inevitably getting out of control and the final climax concentrates on the bravery and nobility of Carton's personal sacrifice rather than on the suggestion that the Revolution might yet lead to some good. In 1958, Dirk Bogarde, another leading British film star, played the role of Carton in a film produced by the Rank Organization. This time there was even more emphasis on the violence in revolutionary France and no attempt was made to understand the political significance of the events taking place in France. Even more radical alterations were made to the original story when *A Tale of Two Cities* was made into a mini-series for Granada TV and then sold as a DVD. In all of these versions, the final personal sacrifice of Sydney Carton was retained, but his final words and vision have been converted into a moral rather than a political statement.[45]

Throughout much of the twentieth century an even more melodramatic and partisan version of the French Revolution was offered to the British public through the novels of Baroness Emmuska Orczy and their adaptation for films and TV. Baroness Orczy wrote in *The Scarlet Pimpernel* of the brave efforts of her fictional hero, Sir Percy Blakeney, a British secret agent, to rescue aristocratic French men and women from the guillotine during the French Terror. Blakeney and his friends repeatedly outwit the evil but bungling French revolutionary bureaucrat Chauvelin, and bring those they have rescued back to Britain, where real liberty and true justice survive compared to the injustice and violence of the French Terror. No attempt is made to understand the causes, course, or achievements of the French Revolution. Instead, France is simply shown to be a country dominated by violence and injustice, with the threat of execution hanging over many innocent individuals. *The Scarlet Pimpernel* originated as a play, which opened on the London stage in 1905, eventually playing for more than two thousand performances and becoming one of the most popular theatrical shows in Britain. Baroness Orczy quickly converted her play into a novel, which proved so popular that eleven sequels were published between 1908 and 1940 and these were

---

45 *Charles Dickens, 'A Tale of Two Cities' and the French Revolution*, ed. Jones, McDonagh and Mee, pp. 126-187.

translated into sixteen languages. Several silent and talking films based on the novels were produced from 1917 onwards. The most famous adaptation appeared in 1934, with the leading British film star, Leslie Howard, playing the role of Sir Percy Blakeney. A fictional biography of Blakeney, *Life and Exploits of the Scarlet Pimpernel: A Gay Adventurer*, was published in New York in 1935. It was written by 'John Blakeney', a pseudonym for John Orczy Barstow, the son of Baroness Orczy, who provided a Foreword to it. Television adaptations of the Scarlet Pimpernel appeared in Britain in 1950, 1955-56, 1960, 1982, and 1999-2000 and a musical version was staged on Broadway in 1997.[46]

The repeated and highly popular adaptations of *A Tale of Two Cities* and *The Scarlet Pimpernel* into films and TV series aimed at mass viewers have, without doubt, given a great many Britons who have seen them and have never read a serious work of historical scholarship on the subject, a highly distorted view of the French Revolution. To most Britons, the French Revolution is associated above all else with mob violence, the injustice of the revolutionary tribunals, and the guillotining of large numbers of innocent victims. Britain's greatest caricaturists created this image during the 1790s, and these popular films and TV shows reinforced it. It was therefore not surprising that when the British Museum mounted an exhibition to mark the bicentenary of the French Revolution in 1989, it was entitled *The Shadow of the Guillotine*.[47] The exhibition included a

---

46　See the entry on Baroness Orczy in the *Oxford Dictionary of National Biography* and the entry on the Scarlet Pimpernel in the on-line Wikipedia.

47　D. Bindman, *The Shadow of the Guillotine: Britain and the French Revolution*

great many caricatures, paintings, ceramics and wax models produced in the 1790s highlighting the violence of France during the Terror and the agony experienced by so many innocent victims, whether aristocratic, bourgeois or plebeian. Illustrative material depicting Britain's heroic resistance to Napoleon's foreign wars and internal authoritarian regime dominates a more recent exhibition, mounted at the British Museum to mark the bicentenary of the battle of Waterloo in 2015, and entitled Bonaparte and the British.[48] British caricaturists, poets, novelists, and essayists of the early nineteenth century would have agreed with much that was presented in it for public display. Thus, the more constructive and positive achievements of the French Revolution have been and increasingly are ignored in British popular culture, even while British historians make great efforts to do the Revolution full justice.

III
The Political Legacy of the French Revolution

The French Revolution of 1789 triggered a political earthquake in France that caused deep fissures, which help to explain why France has experienced three monarchies, two empires, and five republics from then to the present. Today the tricolour still flies over all public buildings in

---

(London: Published for the Trustees of the British Museum by British Museum Publications, 1989).

48   T. Clayton and S. O'Connell, *Bonaparte and the British: Prints and Propaganda in the Age of Napoleon* (London: British Museum Press, 2015).

France, the revolutionary ideals of 'Liberty, Equality, and Fraternity' are carved in stone in towns across the entire country, and Bastille Day (14 July) is still one of the most important public holidays enjoyed by French citizens. The seismic shocks created by the French Revolution were felt across all Europe, not least in Britain as the sections above have shown. The impact of these shocks was also profound and long lasting, particularly on British politics. By the early nineteenth century the French Revolution, and the ideological response to it led by Edmund Burke, had helped to create a new Tory party, which has gone on to be the most successful political organization in British history. Initially, the French Revolution did much to destroy the credibility of the Whig party, but efforts were subsequently made to refine the Whig interpretation of the Revolution in such a manner that it could emerge as the more liberal of the two parties and go on to dominate Parliament for much of the middle decades of the nineteenth century. The descent of the French Revolution into anarchy, terror, and war, combined with government repression, did much to silence the radical campaign which had been advocating parliamentary reform through the last third of the eighteenth century. When radicalism revived in Britain, and became a major political force, it had learned the wisdom of pursuing political change by constitutional reform rather than by threatening revolutionary violence. Together, these developments helped to create a situation in which gradual evolutionary development marked the political history of Britain in sharp contrast to the quite frequent sharp changes of political direction in France. This encouraged British politicians and political commentators to have great confidence in the country's constitutional principles and practices.

By the late 1790s the French Revolution and the revolutionary war had persuaded most of the propertied elite in Britain and a great many ordinary Britons to abandon support for political changes and to rally behind the existing constitution and social order. Government repression undoubtedly aided this development. It was also strengthened by the long war with Napoleonic France in the early nineteenth century, when Britain faced the prospect of invasion and defeat. This long, bitter and expensive conflict persuaded the political alliance built up in Parliament by William Pitt and led later by his disciples, that it was worth paying almost any price to defeat Napoleon's ambitions. This alliance adopted a conservative stance at home, in defence of the existing constitution and social order. Labelled a new Tory party by its critics, it soon accepted the title. These Tories continued to castigate those who opposed the war against France as unpatriotic and near treasonous. In Parliament, they steadfastly resisted any pressure for reform and were ready to adopt, when necessary, repressive measures to persecute radical propagandists and popular agitators who threatened political stability at home.

Tory ideologues and propagandists also waged a prolonged ideological campaign to counter French principles and to silence calls for reforms within Britain. Edmund Burke's critique of French revolutionary principles, which had seemed excessive in 1790, was very widely accepted by Tory propagandists in the early nineteenth century. Loyalist periodicals, such as the *Anti-Jacobin Review*, continued to produce ultra-conservative propaganda until 1821. In 1809, when liberal opinions once again seemed to present a serious challenge, several loyalists established the *Quarterly Review*, which rapidly became the most influential conservative defender of church and state. Its major contributors, including Robert Southey, Walter Scott, and John Wilson Croker, regularly attacked French revolutionary principles, staunchly supported the war with France, and condemned demands for political reforms within Britain. In the *Quarterly Review*, the French Revolution was still held to be the most dangerous threat to monarchy, aristocracy, social order, and the Christian religion. Long after the fall of Napoleon, its contributors were still expressing deep-seated fears that the French example might encourage the poor in Britain to emulate the French in supporting a violent revolution against the propertied elite. British radicals were frequently equated with French Jacobins and it was firmly believed that popular radical agitators were engaged in a conspiracy to bring revolution to Britain.[49]

This conservative ideology, combined with the prestige which victory

49   G. Newman, "Anti-French Propaganda and British Liberal Nationalism, in the Early Nineteenth Century: Suggestions toward a General Interpretation," *Victorian Studies*, 18 (1875), pp. 385-418; *Conservatism and the Quarterly Review*, ed. J.B. Cutmore (London: Pickering & Chatto, 2007); K. Wheatley, "Paranoid Politics: The Quarterly and Edinburgh Reviews," *Prose Studies: History, Theory, Criticism*, 15 (1992), pp.319-343; W. Thomas, "Religion and Politics in the *Quarterly Review*, 1809-1853," in *History, Religion and Culture: British Intellectual History 1750-1950*, ed. S. Collini, R. Whatmore and B. Young (Cambridge: Cambridge University Press, 2000), pp. 136-155; and P. Harling, ""The perils of French philosophy": Enlightenment and revolution in Tory journalism, 1800-1832," in *Enlightenment, Revolution and the Periodical Press*, ed. H.-J. Lüsebrink and J.D. Popkin (Oxford: Voltaire Foundation, 2004), pp. 199-220.

over Napoleon brought to their party, helped successive Tory ministers to weather a serious radical challenge in the 1810s and to retain power until 1830. When the party began to split in the late 1820s on the question of conceding equal political rights to Protestant Dissenters and Roman Catholics, the ultra-Tories remained alarmed at the threat of revolution in Britain. These fears were increased when the Bourbon monarchy in France was overthrown by the 1830 Revolution. When, in 1831, a Whig administration brought in a bill for a moderate reform of Britain's electoral system, John Wilson Croker, now an MP, spoke and wrote of his fears that Parliament was in danger of repeating the mistakes that the aristocratic elite in France had made in the late 1780s. In Croker's view the French Revolution of 1789 owed much to the weakness of the French aristocratic elite when faced with a political challenge from the middling and lower orders of France. He did his best to warn the British elite not to make the same mistake.[50] His fears were genuinely held, but proved to be exaggerated because the reform bill was a moderate measure and reformers outside Parliament, while encouraged by the French Revolution of 1830, had no wish to emulate what had happened in France in the early 1790s.

The French Revolution and the revolutionary war came close to destroying the Opposition Whigs during the 1790s as a large segment of the party rejected the liberal political views advanced by Charles James

---

[50] W. Thomas, *The Quarrel of Macaulay and Croker: Politics and History in the Age of Reform* (Oxford: Oxford University Press, 2000), pp. 7-31, 162-209.

Fox and his closest associates and accepted William Pitt's suggestion that they join his supporters in doing everything possible to combat French principles. The Whigs loyal to Fox were not to command a majority in the House of Commons until 1830,[51] very largely because of their attitude towards the French. As early as 1802, however, there were signs of a modest liberal revival among the propertied, educated classes, when Francis Jeffrey and others established the *Edinburgh Review*. From its inception, this lively periodical challenged the claim so frequently made by British conservatives that Voltaire, Rousseau, and other French philosophes had encouraged a conspiracy against the ancien regime that led to the French Revolution of 1789. Instead, the contributors to the *Edinburgh Review* claimed that it was the abuses and corruption of the despotic ancien regime and the failure of Louis XVI and the French aristocracy to offer timely and meaningful concessions that provoked widespread popular disturbances and ultimately a violent revolution. If the Tory government in Britain did not address the legitimate grievances of the middling and lower orders at home, it was in danger of provoking a similar violent revolution. While the *Edinburgh Review* was always critical of the French Terror, its contributors frequently attacked British conservatives for supporting oppressive legislation and opposing all demands for moderate reforms at home. They maintained that the French bourgeoisie had

---

51   A few Whigs were in office for just over a year in 1806-7, in the so-called Ministry of All the Talents, but this coalition was led by Lord Grenville, who had been Pitt's Foreign Secretary during the French Revolutionary War and who still differed with Fox and his allies over whether to make peace with Napoleon.

supported the Revolution because they had largely been excluded from political power and influence under the ancien regime. French society, even under Napoleon, was more meritocratic than society in Britain and the armies of Napoleon could be seen as a reforming force because of their destruction of some of the most oppressive feudal and absolutist regimes in Europe.[52]

The *Edinburgh Review* was a literary and commercial success before it began to wield influence over the Whig party in Parliament from about 1809. Together the Whigs in Parliament and the contributors to the *Edinburgh Review* combined to attack the government's conduct of the war against France and to accuse Tory ministers of presiding over corrupt practices at home. The war effort was seen to be enriching government ministers, war contractors, and financial speculators, while Tory ministers were urging the British people to spill their blood and waste their money on an unnecessary and unsuccessful conflict. Some contributors to the *Edinburgh Review* were beginning to raise the question of a moderate reform of the electoral system before the Whig party in Parliament plucked up sufficient political courage to revive their interest in proposals for parliamentary reform, a strategy that had caused them so much political damage in the 1790s. The case for a moderate measure of parliamentary reform was promoted by a handful of radical MPs in the House of Commons and by a more liberal periodical, the *Examiner*, edited weekly

---

[52]   J. Clive, *Scotch Reviewers: The Edinburgh Review, 1802-1815* (London: Harvard University Press, 1957), pp. 86-123.

by Leigh Hunt from 1808 to 1821. Appealing to educated middle-class readers, Leigh Hunt rejected natural rights arguments for reform and accused the French Jacobins of being anarchists, who had destroyed all attempts to achieve political stability and social order in France during the French Revolution. Blatantly chauvinistic, he extolled British virtues and compared them to the immorality of the French. He claimed to be defending the historic rights of free Britons and to be seeking to restore the British constitution to its true principles. He preferred to attack the corrupt practices of the governing elite rather than advocate any specific measure of parliamentary reform.[53]

Throughout the 1810s the Whig party in Parliament routinely attacked the handful of radical MPs campaigning for a moderate measure of electoral reform. The Whigs were even more critical of popular radicals outside Parliament whom they accused of fomenting mob violence. The fear engendered by the Tory accusations that the Whigs were too sympathetic to French principles hindered the Whigs from contemplating parliamentary reform at this stage. By the late 1820s, however, a number of younger, reform-minded Whigs in Parliament were coming to the conclusion that Britain had experienced such great social and economic changes, connected with urbanization and industrialization, since the late eighteenth century that it was no longer wise to resist enfranchising more of the propertied middle classes in the larger towns.

53　P. Harling, "Leigh Hunt's *Examiner* and the Language of Patriotism," *English Historical Review*, 111 (1996), pp.1159-1181; and N. Roe, *Fiery Heart: The First Life of Leigh Hunt* (London: Pimlico, 2005), pp. 93-171.

By 1827, Thomas Babington Macaulay, for example, was claiming that the refusal of ultra-Tories to concede moderate parliamentary reform risked uniting the disgruntled middle classes with the impoverished urban poor into a potentially revolutionary alliance as had occurred in France in the early 1790s. Wishing for order without despotism and liberty without anarchy, Macaulay believed that revolution could be averted only by timely concessions to middle-class men of wealth and talent. The Whigs supported the repeal of the Test and Corporation Acts to satisfy Protestant Dissenting opinion in 1828 and supported Roman Catholic Emancipation in 1829 to extend equal political rights to this religious body. When the French Revolution of 1830 quickly removed the Bourbon monarchy from power, middle-class opinion in Britain began to swing behind the Whig party's recent conversion to the cause of moderate parliamentary reform.[54] Victories in successive general elections in 1830 and 1831 enabled the Whigs to pass an important, if moderate, parliamentary Reform Act in 1832. In the prolonged debates on this measure Whigs such as Macaulay urged Parliament to reform itself in order to preserve the essential features of the British constitution while avoiding radical change.[55] In his historical

---

[54]   R. Quinault, 'The French Revolution of 1830 and Parliamentary Reform', *History*, 79 (1994), pp. 377-393.

[55]   W. Thomas, *The Quarrel of Macaulay and Croker: Politics and History in the Age of Reform* (Oxford: Oxford University Press, 2000), pp. 7-31, 162-209; J. Clive, "Macaulay and the French Revolution," in *The French Revolution and British Culture*, ed. C. Crossley and I. Small (Oxford: Oxford University Press, 1989), pp. 103-122; and J. Hamburger, *Macaulay and the Whig Tradition* (Chicago: University of Chicago Press, 1976).

study *Napoleon and the Restoration of the Bourbons* (1830-31), Macaulay
described the French Revolution of 1789 as a necessary evil, which was
justified by its elimination of greater evils. In spite of its violence, follies,
and crimes, the French Revolution of 1789 had proved to be a great
blessing to mankind. Napoleon had consolidated some of the achievements
of the Revolution, but it was only after the Bourbons had been restored
that it became clear that the feudal abuses and unjust aristocratic privileges
of the ancien regime had been permanently abolished by the Revolution
and middle-class men of wealth and talent had achieved the legitimate
political influence which they had been denied before 1789. The French
Revolution, therefore, had been a great step forward, and the more recent
Revolution of 1830 had confirmed the fact that the power of public opinion
was irresistible. Macaulay's advice was heeded and, although the Reform
Act of 1832 disappointed radical opinion in Britain, it showed that the
British political system could reform itself when public opinion was
effectively marshalled and well expressed. It was a lesson learned by the
governing elite of all political parties in Britain.

By the end of the 1790s government repression and a powerful loyalist
reaction against French principles and French power had silenced most of
the radicals who had been enthusiastic supporters of the Revolution in the
early 1790s. Hostility to the authoritarian regime of Napoleon and patriotic
resentment at the threat of a French invasion made it very difficult to
achieve a radical revival in the early nineteenth century. Some of the
leading radical ideologues and propagandists of the 1790s had died,
emigrated, or given up the cause of reform. Others found it difficult to

voice their opinions. Daniel Isaac Eaton was imprisoned from 1803 to 1805 and again from 1812 to 1813 because of his seditious publications.[56] Thomas Spence emerged from prison in 1802, wrote a few radical tracts, which reached only a tiny coterie of admirers in London, and died impoverished in 1814.[57] William Godwin made a brief, but extremely unsuccessful return to political pamphleteering with his *Letters to Verax* in 1815. This pamphlet expressed admiration for the abilities of Napoleon and wished to see him restored to power now that the French people had clearly rejected the restored Bourbon monarchy and had rallied in support of Napoleon after his escape from Elba. Godwin urged Britain not to oppose Napoleon's return to power, believing that he could now be trusted to act as a constitutional monarch under a liberal form of government. Godwin's first letter was published in the Whig *Morning Chronicle* on 25 May 1815. He composed a second letter, hoping the two might be published as a separate pamphlet. Advertised for sale on 1 July, Godwin's optimism was dashed when news arrived in London of Napoleon's defeat at Waterloo on 18 June.[58]

Popular radicalism began to revive in the early 1810s and flourished until 1821 and was active again from 1830 to 1832 and for much of the period from 1836 to 1848. It did so because of the widespread economic

---

56   See the entry on Eaton in the *Oxford Dictionary of National Biography*.

57   *The Political Works of Thomas Spence*, ed. H.T. Dickinson (Newcastle upon Tyne: Avero, 1982), p. xvi.

58   B.R. Pollin, "Godwin's *Letters of Verax*," *Journal of the History of Ideas*, 25 (1964), pp. 353-373.

266 Harry T. Dickinson 思想史 5

distress caused by the war with Napoleonic France, the deep post-war depression after 1815, and the recurring economic crises caused by rapid urbanization and industrialization. Some modern historians have claimed that Britain came close to revolution during these crises.[59] There was certainly some widespread, large-scale and serious outbreaks of disorder, but the worst of these, such as the Luddite industrial disputes of 1811 to 1813 and the violent protests of large numbers of impoverished agricultural labourers in 1830, had primarily economic causes and sought mainly economic remedies to alleviate severe distress.[60] Only a handful of incidents occurred that that can be classified as attempts at political insurrection or armed revolt, and these were all small-scale, badly led, ill-coordinated, and poorly armed.[61] Successive governments employed spies, informers, and agents provocateurs, passed repressive legislation, and, as a last resort, employed armed force to defeat such ill-judged attempts at applying physical force to achieve political ends.

The popular radical movement that flourished at times between 1812

---

[59] The most famous of these is Edward Thompson in *The Making of the English Working Class* (New edn., London: Penguin Books, 1991).

[60] See, in particular, M.I. Thomis, *The Luddites: Machine Breaking in Regency England* (Newton Abbot: David & Charles, 1970); E. Hobsbawm, "The Machine Breakers," *Past and Present*, 1 (1952), pp. 55-70; E.J. Hobsbawm and G. Rudé, *Captain Swing* (revised edn., London: Penguin Books, 1973); and C.J. Griffin, *The Rural War: Captain Swing and the Politics of Protest* (Manchester: Manchester University Press, 2012).

[61] For example, the Spa Fields riots in London in November 1816 and December 1817, the Prentrich rising of 1817, the Cato Street Conspiracy of 1820, the Glasgow rising of 1820, and the Newport rising of 1839.

and 1850 was very largely moderate, peaceful, and constitutional in its methods and ultimate objectives. Most radical leaders had learned the political lesson taught them by the example of the French Revolution's descent into violence, terror and military despotism. They explicitly denied that they wanted to provoke a revolution on the French model. They did not attack monarchy, aristocracy, or the social hierarchy. They made no serious attempt to erect a democratic republic or to create an egalitarian society. They campaigned almost exclusively for the kind of parliamentary reforms that would democratise the House of Commons, and they did so very largely by the peaceful constitutional means of mass petitions to parliament, public marches, and meetings to hear speeches and to demonstrate the extent of their support, and the setting up of clubs and societies designed to educate the people about their political rights. They rested their demands largely on historic precedents drawn from the British past rather than on any claim to universal natural rights. They claimed that Britain had once possessed an ancient constitution in which all adult males had been able to vote for the people's representatives sitting in the House of Commons. For inspiration they looked back to the radicals of seventeenth-century England or to the more recent American Patriots rather than to the French Revolution.[62]

---

62 P. Spence, *The Birth of Romantic Radicalism: War, popular political English radical reformism, 1800-1815* (Aldershot: Scolar Press, 1996); J. Belchem, "Republicanism, Popular Constitutionalism and the Radical Platform in early Nineteenth-Century England," *Social History*, 6 (1981), pp. 1-32; J.A. Epstein, "The Constitutional Idioms: Radical Reasoning, Rhetoric, and Action

There were, however, some indications that the French Revolution had made some impression on the British radicals of the first half of the nineteenth century. Tricolour flags, red caps of liberty, and French revolutionary songs appeared at several political meetings between 1815 and 1819. The government responded by seeking through the Six Acts of 1819 to ban the use of such revolutionary emblems in future.[63] A few extreme radical propagandists, such as John Wade and Richard Carlile reminded their readers of the benefits which the revolutionaries had brought to France in the early 1790s.[64] Most Chartists were committed to support for the People's Charter, advocating an extensive reform of the electoral system principally by means of mass petitioning campaigns

in early Nineteenth-Century England," *Journal of Social History*, 23 (1990), pp. 553-574; C. Flick, *The Birmingham Political Union and the Movement for Reform in Britain 1830-1839* (Hamden, Conn.: Shoe String Press Inc., 1978); D. Thompson, *The Chartists* (London: Pantheon, 1984); J. Epstein, *The Lion of Freedom: Feargus O'Connor and the Chartist Movement* (London: Croom Helm Ltd, 1982), chapters 3 and 4; and M. Chase, *Chartism: A New History* (Manchester: Manchester University Press, 2007).

[63] J.A. Epstein, "Understanding the Cap of Liberty: Symbolic Practice and Social Conflict in Early Nineteenth-Century England," *Past and Present*, 122 (1989), pp. 75-118; J.A. Epstein, *Radical Expression: Political Language, Ritual and Symbol in England, 1790-1850* (Oxford: Oxford University Press, 1994), pp. 70-99; and J. Ann Hone, *For the Cause of Truth: Radicalism in London 1796-1821* (Oxford: Clarendon Press, 1982), p. 264.

[64] See John Wade, in *The Gorgon*, 14 November and 26 December 1818, and Richard Carlile, in *The Republican*, 24 September 1819. For Richard Carlile, see E. P. Thompson, *The Making of the English Working Class* (Harmondsworth: Penguin Books, 1968 edn.), pp. 720-734, 762-768; and J. H. Wiener, *Radicalism and Free Thought in Nineteenth-Century Britain: The Life of Richard Carlile* (Westport, Conn.: Greenwood Press, 1983).

mounted between 1839 and 1848. James Bronterre O'Brien was the most influential Chartist propagandist, who believed that the British radical cause had much that it could learn from the French Revolution. He spoke French and visited France several times in order to collect material on the French Revolution. In 1836, he published an annotated translation of Philippe Buonarroti's *History of Babeuf's Conspiracy*. Two years later he published what he intended to be the first volume of a biography of Robespierre, the *Life and Character of Maximilian Robespierre*. He never completed this task, but he regularly presided over events celebrating Robespierre's birthday. And he later published a short pamphlet, *Elegy on the Death of Robespierre* (1857) and a more substantial *Dissertation and Elegy on the Life and Death of the Immortal Maximilian Robespierre* (1859). O'Brien never wrote on Robespierre's role during the Terror, but he did blame the Terror on the military intervention of Austria and Prussia in France's internal affairs and he lamented Britain's entry into the war. He always insisted that Robespierre remained true to his democratic and egalitarian principles. He greatly admired the French constitution of 1793 and regarded the constitution of 1795 as a betrayal of France's revolutionary principles. He was greatly dissatisfied with the Great Reform Act of 1832 and he was soon disillusioned with the French Revolution of 1848 and the Second Republic. While praising the French revolutionaries of 1789 for being willing to use force to achieve their political aims, he was careful to avoid recommending such violent activities to British radicals.[65]

---

[65]   J.R. Dinwiddy, "English Radicals and the French Revolution, 1800-1850," in

George Julian Harney, a younger Chartist, was more attracted to the violent, insurrectionary aspects of the French Revolution and he occasionally implied that British radicals might need to follow the French example. He praised the French insurrections of 20 June and 10 August 1792. He identified himself with Marat and, writing as 'The Friend of the People' in the *London Democrat*, he advised his readers that in the approaching revolution in England, they should avoid the errors but imitate the heroic deeds of the French republicans of the early 1790s. At the Chartist Convention of 1837 he wore the bonnet rouge as the emblem of victory over tyranny and urged other members to follow his example. His advice caused considerable resentment. He was greatly excited when the French Revolution of 1848 broke out and he expressed the hope that the French constitution of 1793 might be restored. He continued to admire the ideas and merits of Robespierre and Saint Just and, as late as 1850, he launched the *Red Republican* periodical. Although he liked to think of himself as a revolutionary, Harney possessed sufficient self-knowledge to admit privately that he lacked the courage and the energy to lead a revolution himself. His private judgement was more in tune with the

---

The French Revolution and the Creation of Modern Political Culture: Volume III, The Transformation of Political Culture 1789-1848, ed. F. Furet and M. Ozouf,(Oxford: Pergamon Press) pp. 455-459; M.J. Turner, "Revolutionary Connection: "The Incorruptible" Maximilian Robespierre and the "Schoolmaster of Chartism" Bronterre O'Brien," *The Historian*, 75 (2013), pp. 237-261; and A. Plummer, *Bronterre: A Political Biography of Bronterre O'Brien 1804-1864* (London: Allen and Unwin, 1971), pp. 66-71, 236-248.

attitude of the great majority of Chartists than was his public rhetoric.[66]

While France and several other European countries experienced revolution in 1848, the political challenge posed by the Chartist campaign of that year was relatively easily rebuffed. Widespread distress and mass support for parliamentary reform were not sufficient to cause a revolution in Britain as many conservatives had feared might well be the case since the first French Revolution of 1789. Ever since, historians have speculated why a Britain experiencing widespread popular distress and severe social tensions managed to avoid revolution over these decades. The explanation that for a long time attracted most support from historians, was that religion saved Britain from revolution. Whereas it was maintained that the French philosophes had undermined the traditional authorities in church and state with their religious scepticism and anti-clericalism, it was religion that did so much to sustain the authority of monarchy, aristocracy and social hierarchy in Britain. The clerical leaders of the established Church of England and the Church of Scotland constantly preached the need to obey the existing powers in the state and taught the poor to be deferential to their social superiors.[67] The ordinary evangelical clergy in

---

66 J.R. Dinwiddy, "English Radicals and the French Revolution, 1800-1850," pp. 459-464; and A.R. Schoyen, *The Chartist Challenge: A Portrait of George Julian Harney* (London: Heinemann, 1958).

67 G.F.A. Best, "The Protestant Constitution and its Supporters, 1800-1829," *Transactions of the Royal Historical Society*, 5th series, 8 (1958), pp. 105-127; and I.F. Maciver, "Moderates and Wild Men: Politics, Religion and Party Divisions in the Church of Scotland, 1800-1843," in *The Scottish Nation: Identity and History : Essays in Honour of William Ferguso*, ed. Alexander

both churches were more interested in teaching their congregations how to merit eternal salvation rather than in encouraging them to campaign for political changes in this world. If individuals wished to act in a public capacity they should support such moral crusades as the abolition of the slave trade and the practice of slavery or join such organizations as the Society for the Suppression of Vice or the missionary work of the British and Foreign Bible Society.[68]

The religious group given the greatest credit for saving Britain from revolution was Methodism. Elie Halévy, the eminent French historian, first made this claim.[69] He pointed to the political conservatism constantly preached by John Wesley, the movement's founder, in the later eighteenth century, and then by the clerical oligarchy of leading ministers who governed the movement though Annual Conferences after Wesley's death in 1791. There can be no doubt that the clerical leaders of Methodism in the earlier nineteenth century, dominated by the formidable Jabez

---

Murdoch (Edinburgh: John Donald Publishers Ltd, 2007), pp. 104-119.

[68]   G.F.A. Best, "The Evangelicals and the Established Church in the early Nineteenth Century," *Journal of Theological Studies*, new series, 10 (1959), pp. 63-78; V.G. Kiernan, "Evangelicalism and the French Revolution," *Past and Present*, 1 (1952), pp. 44-56; and M.J.D. Roberts, "The Society for the Suppression of Vice and its Early Critics, 1802-1812," *Historical Journal*, 26 (1983), pp. 159-176.

[69]   Halévy initially advanced his hypothesis in two articles in the *Revue de Paris* published in 1906. He elaborated his thesis in the first volume of his *History of the English People: England in 1815*, which appeared in France in 1913 and then in England in 1924. Halévy included the smaller number of other Protestant Dissenting evangelicals (the Independents and Baptists) with the Methodists.

Bunting,[70] repeatedly urged their congregations to be loyal to the king and his government through the decisions taken at the movement's Annual Conferences. This has been enough to convince some historians to accept Halévy's claims for the political influence of Methodism,[71] but others have challenged it. Eric Hobsbawm has pointed out that there were simply not enough Methodists in the earlier nineteenth century to have saved Britain from revolution and, besides, there is clear evidence that radicalism was strong in some parts of the country where Methodism was also strong.[72] Other historians have claimed that, whereas the clerical leadership of Methodism was undoubtedly politically conservative, this was not necessarily the case with lay preachers and other influential lay members who dominated the movement at the local level.[73] Alan Gilbert has

---

70   *The Early Correspondence of Jabez Bunting, 1820-1829*, ed. W.R. Ward (London: RHS, 1972); and *Early Victorian Methodism: The Correspondence of Jabez Bunting, 1830-55*, ed. W.R. Ward (Oxford: Oxford University Press, 1976).

71   See, for example, B. Semmel, "The Halévy Thesis," *Encounter*, 37:1 (1971), pp. 44-55; B. Semmel, *The Methodist Revolution* (London: Heinemann Educational Publishers, 1974), pp. 127-137; and R. F. Wearmouth, *Methodism and the Working-Class Movement of England 1800-1850* (London: Epworth Press, 1937). E.P. Thompson has acknowledged that Methodism did attempt to inhibit the activities of popular radicals and it acted as the opium of the people, attracting members when radical hopes were crushed. See his famous chapter 11 in *The Making of the English Working Class*.

72   E.J. Hobsbawm, "Methodism and the Threat of Revolution in Britain," *History Today*, 7:2 (1957), pp. 114-124; reprinted in *Labouring Men: Studies in the History of Labour* (London: Weidenfeld and Nicolson, 1964), pp. 23-33.

73   W.R. Ward, 'The Religion of the People and the Problem of Control, 1790-1830', *Studies in Church History*, 8 (1972), 237-257; W.R. Ward, *Religion*

accepted this claim, but has gone beyond it. He believes that Methodism
did indeed act as a safety valve, as Halévy implied, because the
independence of local chapels and the active role played by lay preachers
enabled local Methodists to voice criticism of the existing order in church
and state, while the religious emphasis on good behaviour advised by the
Annual Conferences and preached by the itinerant ministers of the
movement inhibited the kind of conduct which might have promoted a
violent revolution.[74]

Any attempt to understand why Britain avoided the kind of revolution
that France experienced in 1789 needs, however, to go beyond the
religious evidence employed by Halévy and others. While it is certainly
the case that the middling and lower orders in Britain in the late eighteenth
and first half of the nineteenth century did not live in an entirely fair, just,
egalitarian, or democratic society, they did enjoy much better
circumstances than the French experienced under the ancien regime. The
monarch did not possess absolute power and the aristocracy did not enjoy
a range of feudal privileges nor exemption from some taxes. The House of
Commons was elected by several hundred thousand middle-class adult

and Society in England 1790-1850 (London, 1972), chap. 4; and D. Hempton, *Methodism and Politics in British Society, 1750-1850* (London: Harper Collins Publishers Ltd., 1984), chaps. 3 and 4.

74   A.D. Gilbert, "Methodism, Dissent and Political Stability in Early Industrial England," *Journal of Religious History*, 10 (1979), pp. 380-399; and A.D. Gilbert, "Religion and political stability in early industrial England," in *The Industrial Revolution and British Society*, ed. P.K. O'Brien and R. Quinault (Cambridge: Cambridge University Press, 1993), pp. 79-99.

males and was not immune to public opinion.[75] Parliament represented the powerful interests in the state, passed many laws to promote the economic interests of the middling orders, and proved capable of reforming the electoral system. A growing proportion of the population lived in towns where there were opportunities for industrial and commercial activities, more amenities, better chances of regular employment, and higher wages. Towns gave many Britons access to a flourishing, expanding and uncensored press and also enabled middle-class men in particular to form voluntary societies, which could promote their economic and social interests and enable them to petition Parliament and lobby MPs for the redress of grievances.[76] A growing number of working-class Britons could protect their interests by joining trade unions to put pressure on their employers and paying into Friendly Societies to insure themselves against the consequences of unemployment, injury, sickness, and old age.[77] Parliament passed many acts to improve the working conditions of the

---

75   F. O'Gorman, *Voters, Patrons and Parties: The Unreformed Electorate of Hanoverian England, 1734-1832* (Oxford, 1989).

76   D. Eastwood, "Contesting the politics of deference, 1820-1860," in *Party, State and Society: electoral behaviour in Britain since 1820*, ed. J. Lawrence and M. Taylor (Aldershot: Scolar Press, 1996), pp. 27-49; R.J. Morris, "Voluntary Societies in British Urban Elites, 1780-1850; An Analysis," *Historical Journal*, 26 (1983), pp. 95-118; and H.T. Dickinson, "How Democratic were British Politics from the Wilkesites to the Chartists (1760s-1840s)?," *Intellectual History*, 5 (2015), pp. 226-273.

77   A.E. Musson, *British Trade Unions 1800-1875* (London: Macmillan, 1972); M. Chase, *Early Trade Unionism: Fraternity, Skill and the Politics of Labour* (Aldershot: Scolar Press, 2000); and P.H.J.H. Gosden, *The Friendly Societies in England, 1815-75* (Manchester: Manchester University Press, 1961).

industrial poor.[78] Moreover, despite periods of economic recession, the British economy expanded steadily across this period, and the standard of living of the poor slowly rose rather than fell.[79] The overwhelming majority of those advocating radical change or organising popular protests did not seek to promote a violent revolution in Britain.[80] Finally, the governing elite in Britain never lost their nerve as Louis XVI and the French aristocracy had done. They proved very determined to avoid making major concessions and yet were flexible enough to give way before very strong pressure from below. The period has justly been labelled 'The Age of Improvement'.[81]

From the mid-nineteenth century onwards Britain enjoyed greater political stability than almost any other country in the world. British politicians and political commentators increasingly emphasised how stable Britain had been and still was in comparison with France. They contrasted

---

[78] J. Ward, *The Factory Movement, 1830-1855* (London: Macmillan, 1962); and A.E. Peacock, "The successful prosecution of the Factory Acts, 1833-1855," *Economic History Review*, 2nd series, 37 (1984), pp.197-210.

[79] R.M. Hartwell, "The Rising Standard of Living in England, 1800-1850," *Economic History Review*, new series, 13 (1961), pp. 397-416; R.M. Hartwell, "The Standard of living," *Economic History Review*, news series, 16 (1963), pp. 135-146; and J.E. Williams, "The British Standard of Living, 1750-1850," *Economic History Review*, new series, 19 (1966), pp. 581-606.

[80] M. Thomis and P. Holt, *Threats of Revolution in Britain 1789-1848* (London: Archon Books, 1977); and E. Royle, *Revolutionary Britannia? Reflections on the threat of revolution in Britain, 1789-1848* (Manchester: Manchester University Press, 2000).

[81] The most famous and influential book using this title is Asa Briggs, *The Age of Improvement 1783-1867* (2nd edn., London: Longman, 2000).

the French appeal to abstract natural rights since 1789, that the French had found enormously difficulty to achieve in practice, with Britain's appeal to its ancient constitution and the historic rights of Britons that had been secured in reality. It was widely claimed that Britain had established the rule of law, protected property, and secured a wide range of civil liberties by peaceful, pragmatic, and evolutionary means since its own more moderate revolution in 1688-89. The French had made great claims for their Declaration of the Rights of Man and the Citizen of 1789, but the French Revolution of 1789 had not been able to implement these rights at that time and had struggled ever since to establish a stable political regime which actually defended all these rights. It was firmly believed in Britain that more civil and political rights had been achieved there by peaceful stages since 1689 and, moreover, Britain was steadily progressing in a similar evolutionary manner towards an ever more democratic political system.[82] This encouraged politicians and political commentators to believe that the British had discovered the secret of how to promote democracy and safeguard personal liberty while preserving stability. They took enormous pride in this. They sometimes expressed the hope that their constitutional principles and political practices might be copied by other nations, but they often doubted if the people of other lands possessed the required national characteristics or personal qualities. They looked askance, in particular, at the way France struggled to establish a stable

---

[82]   G. Best, "The French Revolution and Human Rights," in *The Permanent Revolution: The French Revolution and its Legacy*, ed. G. Best. pp. 101-127.

political system.[83] There was much stress on Burke's expressed beliefs that a reliance on experience, tradition, and practical wisdom was preferable to an attachment to abstract rational theories of government, that justice and the rule of law were more important benefits than the right to exercise political power, and that citizens had duties as well as rights. When they considered the Russian and the Chinese Revolutions of the twentieth century, they believed that the follies and crimes of the French Terror of the 1790s were being repeated on a larger scale. It was not entirely surprising therefore that when Roger Scruton, the British philosopher and conservative political commentator, was asked to write an essay marking the bicentenary of the French Revolution in 1989, he chose to praise Edmund Burke's critique of this revolution and to make direct comparisons between the mistakes made after 1789 with the even more alarming totalitarian experiments of the twentieth century.[84]

*****

Today, it is clear that the French Revolution still attracts considerable interest from informed Britons, who recognise it as a dramatic and fascinating series of events of major importance in world history. It

---

83   G. Varouxakis, *Victorian Political Thought on France and the French* (Basingstoke: Palgrave Macmillan, 2002).

84   R. Scruton, "Man's Second Disobedience: a Vindication of Burke," in *The French Revolution and British Culture*, ed. C. Crossley and I. Small, pp. 187-222.

continues to be the case, however, that it is seen very differently by those in Britain who approach it from different perspectives and for different reasons. Academic historians and advanced students are particularly aware of its complexity, recognise that it must be studied from a variety of angles and methodologies, know that it can be interpreted in very different ways, and appreciate that it had a profound impact not only on those who lived through it and faced its challenges, but on subsequent French, European, and even world history. It has also assisted informed Britons to understand important issues that affect all mankind, such as the nature of revolutions and counter-revolutions, the strength of the commitment to human rights, the competing interests of the individual and the state, the growth of nationalism, the conflict between religion and secularism, and the comparative influence on human actions of political ideas and material interests.[85] In popular culture, however, the image of the French Revolution so far as it impacts on the British public is very much more restricted. The average Briton, asked to offer a view on the French Revolution, is likely to focus overwhelmingly on the violence and anarchy in Paris, referring to mobs on the streets, the Terror, and the excessive use of the guillotine.[86] There would be little recognition of the positive and

---

85   See, for example, the essays in *The Permanent Revolution: The French Revolution and its Legacy*, ed. G. Best.

86   See, for example, the works of Graeme Fife, a man deeply interested in France. He has written two recent histories of the French Revolution aimed at the general reader: *The Terror: The Shadow of the Guillotine, France 1792-1794* (London: Piatkus Books, 2004) and *Angel of the Assassination* (London: Merit Publishing Int'l, 2009), which is a study of Charlotte

constructive features of the French Revolution or awareness of the impact on the development of the Revolution of internal and external counter-revolutionary forces. Many British politicians and political commentators probably share this restricted vision of the French Revolution, but they are likely to be less fascinated by the drama, excitement, and horror of the Terror, and more convinced that Britain has wisely learned political lessons from it. Their view of the Revolution is likely to persuade them that Britain has been well advised to avoid using violence to overthrow established institutions and attempting to replace them with new ones based on abstract rational principles. They may well believe that Britain has sensibly adopted a pragmatic, gradual, and evolutionary approach to political and constitutional changes that has secured civil liberty and democratic processes by much more peaceful means. They may hold this view, despite Britain's real political difficulties with how to reform its voting system, how to revise its second legislative chamber, and how to combine a deep attachment to the sovereignty of the Westminster Parliament with the claims of devolved legislatures in Scotland, Wales and Northern Ireland and with the authority wielded by the institutions of the European Union.

Corday's murder of Marat; and also a play, *The Great French Revolution Show* (1984); and several BBC radio scripts such as *Revolutionary Portraits, A Breath of Fresh Air*, and *The Whisper of the Axe*, all dealing with the French Terror.

晚近對法國大革命的反省

摘要

　　起於1789年的法國大革命，對英國有極深刻的影響。它使英國菁英甚至一般人分成雀躍與同情革命理想，以及反對與對革命理念抱持戒慎恐懼的兩群人。在思想上最爲深刻，影響最爲深遠的保守反省是1790年柏克所出版的《法國大革命的反思》。許多史家也仔細分析了從大革命伊始到拿破崙戰爭結束 (1815) 的時期。本文突破前人範疇，試圖對1815至2015兩百年的大革命反思做一鳥瞰，分析其中三個面向。一，從1815以來法國大革命歷史解釋的變化；二，英國詩人、小說家、劇作家，導演等對法國大革命的文化詮釋；三，大革命對英國左、中、右政黨政治理念的衝擊。

關鍵詞：史考特、卡萊爾、柯立茲、華茲華斯、雪萊、珍奧斯汀、狄更斯、輝格、托利

《新青年》的數位人文研究

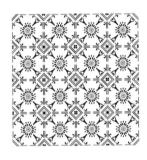

金觀濤、劉青峰、邱偉雲

一、大數據和觀念史研究

　　2015年是兩件重要事情的一百年，一是愛因斯坦（Albert Einstein, 1879-1955）提出廣義相對論，另外一件事是陳獨秀（1879-1942）創立了《新青年》雜誌。廣義相對論對科學具有重大意義，這一百年來已經被證明，而由《新青年》所開啓的現代思想轉型，雖然也已被諸多學者所證實與肯定，但我們認爲《新青年》之中，還有一個尚未被發掘的意義。這即是它對於今天正在興起的數位人文研究而言，具有作爲最佳實驗場域的重要性。近幾年來，政治大學歷史與思想數位人文實驗室（Digital Lab for History and Thoughts）團隊，不斷地以《新青年》作爲研究樣本，進行各種數位人文的探索，使得《新青年》此一重要報刊，因爲新方法的出現，而有了新問題、新探索以及新的挑戰。本文將從政大團隊的研究經驗作爲基礎，除了介紹我們過去以數位人文方法對《新青年》所作過的研究工作之外，還將展望未來數位人文的發展，以此繼往開來的分享，作爲《新青年》發刊屆滿百年之紀念。

　　在本文開始前，我們先說明有關政治大學歷史與思想數位人文實驗室團隊的成立緣起與背景，這還要從我們在香港中文大學的工作講起。自1990年代以來，開始出現了將大量文本進行數位化的潮流，其中包含影像典藏與文字數位化工程，憑藉數位化後的文字語料，研究者可以計算與分析文本中的大量關鍵詞頻率及意義，進而宏觀地觀察歷史上的思想演變。站在這一浪潮的灘頭，從1997年開始在一系列研究課題計劃的支持下，我和青峰在香港中文大學中國文化研究所逐步建立了一個包含有一億兩千萬字的「中國近現代思想史數據庫」，這一數據庫收錄了從1830年到1930年的六類重要政治思想文

獻，[1]同時我們運用上述數據庫資料，進行了諸多現代政治術語形成之考察。[2]根據這些研究，我們發現中國思想從傳統到當代，可歸納出經歷了三個演變階段，而我們提出的三階段論，則與以往思想史研究有所不同。

我們認為中國近代思想史轉型時代的第一個階段是在十九世紀中葉以後，即洋務運動到1895年甲午戰爭之際。這個階段的特點是，當時中國人會用傳統儒學思想，選擇性地吸收現代西方觀念，如果西方現代觀念跟中國儒學思想是相親和的，那麼中國人就接納，如果是不親和的就拒絕。我們在對中國近代諸多重要政治關鍵詞／觀念的分析中，可以清楚地看到這一點。但是在1895年以後到1915年，這二十年中間卻又發生了一個很重要的變化，即中國的儒學本位主義開始動搖。在這一階段中，我們可以看見，雖然一方面在私領域中，中國人仍在家族內部堅持儒學的價值，但另一方面在公領域中，卻開始學習和大量引進西方的現代觀念，這一變化在中國近現代關鍵詞研究上是非常明顯的，而且很容易被觀察到。我們把這二十年定名為中國現代思想的形成階段，或者說，是中國以比較開放的心態學習西方現代觀念的階段，我們稱這第二階段形成的思想為中國「現代」思想。而自1915年《新青年》創辦，新文化運動開始之後，則進入了中國近現代思想轉型的第三階段。

1 計有清末民初近代期刊、晚清檔案資料、清季經世文編、清末民初士大夫著述、晚清來華外人中文著譯、西學教科書等六大類文獻，詳細書目參見金觀濤、劉青峰：〈附錄一「中國近現代思想史專業數據庫」（1830～1930）文獻目錄〉，《觀念史研究：中國現代重要政治術語的形成》（香港：中文大學出版社，2008），頁461-477。

2 相關研究成果，發表於各期刊，後收錄於金觀濤、劉青峰：《觀念史研究：中國現代重要政治術語的形成》一書，餘例不詳舉。

　　我們認爲第三階段的主要工作，是對第二階段學習的成果進行重構。爲什麼呢？因爲我們發現，在這一階段中，一部分從西方學來的近代詞彙，其意義本身發生了重要變化，另外一部分的新觀念，則受到強調和重視，中國人開始接受更激進的西方觀念，但是在思想的結構上面，我們卻看到了向傳統的回歸，並不是回歸儒學，而是回歸中國傳統的深層思維方式。[3] 上述所言的三個階段，是我和青峰通過中國近現代思想史數據庫（1830-1930）中諸多重要關鍵詞彙的研究後發現的。而《新青年》雜誌的重要性，即在於它的起迄年代，正契合於第三階段，故研究《新青年》，可以幫助我們理解第三階段是怎麼發生的？也就是說，有助於我們理解中國人在一百年前的新文化運動中，是怎麼開始思想重構運動的。所謂重構運動，就是把從西方學來的現代觀念轉化爲中國式的現代觀念，而且這些現代觀念至今爲止還統治著中國人的思想，故我們稱之爲當代思想。因此，分析《新青年》的文本，對於我們研究思想重構運動而言，實具有其重大的意義。爲甚麼這樣講？因爲《新青年》文本有一個特點，它的刊行時間是從1915年到1926年，而它的分卷是在當時就依出刊時序定下來的，被編成11卷，並非後人重編的。而這11卷的內容，非常自然地契合著中國思潮變化最快、對後世影響最大的這十年的觀念轉化歷程，所以《新青年》此一文本，非常適合作爲分析這十年間思想演變內在邏輯機制的基本素材。

3　關於以上中國近代思想史轉型時代的三階段說，可詳參金觀濤、劉青峰著：〈導論：爲甚麼從思想史轉向觀念史？〉，《觀念史研究：中國現代重要政治術語的形成》，頁7-8。

二、《新青年》和中國當代觀念的形成

我們舉一個例子，1895年以後，中國人曾經接受西方的共和觀念，它曾對應著儒家道德菁英學習西方共和政治，呈現爲從清末立憲到民初共和的嘗試。但是在統計《新青年》十一卷文本中「共和」一詞的使用情況時，我們看到了什麼情況呢？我們看見「民主」對「共和」的取代。圖一中「菱形點」代表的是「共和」、「方型點」代表的是「民主」，兩條線代表著「民主」與「共和」二詞歷年使用的頻度與分布變化情況。從圖一中可以看到在1918年之際，兩個關鍵詞的詞頻高低分布趨勢調換過來了。根據我們過去研究可知，在1915年前「民主」這個詞，比較接近中國的「民作主」或「全民政治」這樣的觀念，但是1915年前主導社會行動的主要觀念是「共和」而不

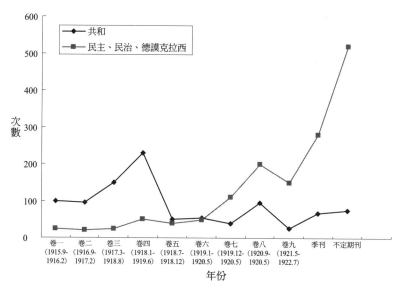

圖一　《新青年》中「共和」、「民主」的使用次數

是「民主」。當時「共和」觀念的內涵，是指由一群道德菁英分子進行立憲，建立共和國，然「共和」觀念卻在共和國建立後被「民主」取代，我們在《新青年》中即可看到「民主」取代「共和」的歷史線索，這不正是中國當代思想形成的過程嗎？

今天「共和」這個詞／概念，除了在中華民國的英文翻譯Republic of China和中華人民共和國的國號裡面使用外，在中國的政治語彙裡已很少使用，人們更多地用「民主」表達自己的政治訴求。而「民主」是什麼意思呢？在大陸很多人仍將其理解為「民作主」，而在台灣就是選舉主義。《新青年》的關鍵詞統計表明，「民主」取代「共和」是發生在馬列主義和三民主義形成之前，或者說這一取代現象，正是新道德意識型態形成的重要前提之一。[4]

另外一個例子是「真理」取代「公理」。「真理」和「公理」這兩個詞古已有之，「真理」來自於佛教，「公理」的意義是公共領域之理和普遍之理。我們知道，儒家倫理打通公和私兩個領域，例如孝道即是貫通公私兩個領域的觀念，是普遍之理，但不是公共領域之理。由於「公理」觀念和儒家倫理不甚切合，因此歷史上很少用。傳統文獻中作為正當性論證詞彙的是「天理」或「實理」，基本上不使用「公理」。「公理」一詞的勃興，是從1895年以後開始到1915年之間，它指的是中西公共之理，即不同於私領域的公共領域之理。「公理觀」也是中國文化現代轉型第二階段的產物，它的內涵可以是指「共和主義」、「競爭」，也可以是指「人權」等等現代價值。但是就在《新青年》雜誌中，「公理」卻被另外一個詞取代了，這個詞就是

4　以上研究詳參金觀濤、劉青峰：〈從「共和」到「民主」—中國對西方現代政治觀念的選擇性吸收和重構〉，收於《觀念史研究：中國現代重要政治術語的形成》，頁247-282。

我們今天仍然在用的「眞理」一詞。「眞理」跟「公理」有什麼不一樣呢？「公理」是公共領域的道理，代表共和、人權、競爭等等；而「眞理」則是連通私領域的家庭與公領域乃至宇宙規律之理。1978年中國大陸改革開放時，即提出「實踐是檢驗眞理的唯一標準」，政治制度正當性基礎是「眞理」，到今天仍是如此，今日中國人用「眞理」這個詞的時候，仍然並沒有區分公領域跟私領域。「眞理」取代「公理」是什麼時候？就是在新文化運動中，我們從圖二《新青年》雜誌中「眞理」和「公理」二詞的歷年詞頻變化圖的統計中，即可以看見「眞理」壓倒了「公理」的現象。[5]

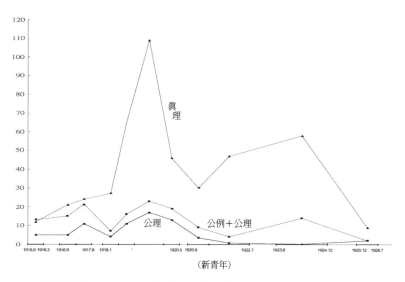

圖二 《新青年》中「真理」、「公理」、「公例＋公理」的使用次數

5 以上研究詳參金觀濤、劉青峰：〈「天理」、「公理」和「眞理」——中國文化合理性論證以及正當性標準的思想史研究〉，《觀念史研究：中國現代重要政治術語的形成》，頁27-67。

　　由上可見，《新青年》是一個很好的範本，能夠讓我們看見當時一些重要觀念的轉折是在何時發生、又是怎麼發生的。除了上述例子外，我們還曾研究過主義觀。眾所周知，中國當代思想形成的中心指標是「主義」的興起。中國的傳統儒家文化是一種道德意識型態，但不叫「主義」；中國近現代思想轉型的第二階段亦沒有一統天下的「主義」，正是通過「新文化運動」中《新青年》與《建設》等雜誌思想的傳播，馬列主義跟三民主義這兩種新道德意識型態最後才會確立，既然「主義」觀如此重要，則《新青年》中「主義」的統計分析就成為研究中國當代思想形成的關鍵，而正是在該研究中，數位人文學的重要性就順勢凸顯了出來。

三、處理海量數據的困難

　　我和青峰在香港中文大學時，也想用前面那種研究「民主」、「共和」觀念時的方法，試圖找到「主義」觀念的轉化機制，但是卻發生了極大的困難。我們提取出「中國近現代思想史專業數據庫（1830-1930）」裡含「主義」的句子，一看有五萬多條。我們很想研究「主義」的種類，但卻不知如何處理這五萬多條數據。第一，無法統計有過多少種主義，數完了這個忘了那個；第二，無從了解這些種類的主義在歷史上是怎麼分布的。我們怎麼能知道某個時期有哪些主義興起？又有哪些主義衰亡？也許今天看來，五萬多條句子不算大數據，但我們當時已經感到處理海量數據時可能會碰到的困難了。

　　2008年我們來到政治大學工作，在從事觀念史研究時開始和資科學者結合，建立了研究團隊。我們把這個問題交給了剛建立的政治大學數位人文研究團隊。政大團隊裡面有資科學者，他們採用人機互動的方法，設計相關程式，計算並解決了上述的問題，終於第一次搞

清楚了中國歷史上有過多少種主義。「主義」這個詞基本上是1890年代後期才有的，和道德價值指向直接相關。大家可以猜一下中國曾出現過多少種主義？大概猜不到吧，總共有1680多種！這麼多種類的「主義」中，哪些年新增的「主義」類型最多呢？這就更難推測了。我們做思想史研究的人往往認為，大概是1903年拒俄運動以後，隨著革命思潮的勃興「主義」種類才多起來的？或者是1905年後當《民報》和《新民叢報》就民族主義大論戰後，「主義」才開始勃興的？答案都不確切！

　　圖三是用數位方法所得到的結果，這是從1896年到1928年「主義」種類使用數量的分布曲線，[6] 在每一年都有新的「主義」產生，每

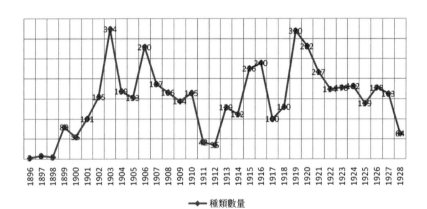

圖三　「中國近現代思想史專業數據庫（1830-1930）」中「主義」類型數量的歷年分布圖

6　凡此以下有關「主義」相關研究，可詳參詹筌亦、王乃昕：〈「主義」的數位人文研究〉，收入項潔等主編：《數位人文在歷史學研究的應用》（臺北：台灣大學出版中心，2011），頁219-245。

年出現的主義種類數如圖所示。大家可以看到，從1896年以後，中國就有了一個全民族的渴望「主義」的思想運動，每年都有各式各樣新的「主義」被提出來。換言之，1896年之際儒學開始解體後，中國人就希望能用另外一種意識型態去代替儒家道德意識型態，這就是尋找「主義」運動背後的思想機制。[7] 上述關於主義種類數量的分布結果表明，尋找主義的動力貫穿中國近現代思想轉型的第二、第三階段。第二階段的「主義」是多元化的，而要等到第三階段才會趨於集中，代表的正是新道德意識型態的形成，上述現象可以從「主義」使用的總數量看出。

　　在使用數位方法前，我們已經從「中國近現代思想史專業數據庫（1830-1930）」中得到每年「主義」一詞的使用量，我們可以看到圖四中有兩個高峰，一個是1903年以後隨著拒俄運動出現的高峰，另外一個是1919年以後的高峰，我們還可以看到這兩個高峰之間有一個低峰，這個低峰時期對應著中國進行立憲運動到中華民國建立時期。上述的歷年詞頻統計雖然有用，但在用數位方法得到「主義」種類以前，是無法進一步分析新主義形成過程的。

　　唯有明確掌握「主義」的種類數，才可以統計各類主義歷年出現頻度，進而把不斷增加的那些「主義」類型找出來，最後勾勒出新「主義」形成的宏觀圖象。我們找到二十種頻次最高的「主義」，畫出其年頻度曲線，圖五是「帝國主義」、「社會主義」、「資本主義」……等二十種「主義」歷年使用頻度。這二十種「主義」的消長，明確表明馬列主義和三民主義是在社會主義勃興，走向反對帝國

7　關於中國近代所凸顯的主義化趨勢特徵，王汎森先生也曾進行過深入研究，可詳參王汎森：〈「主義時代」的來臨—中國近代思想史的一個關鍵發展〉，《東亞觀念史集刊》第4期（2013年6月），頁3-90。

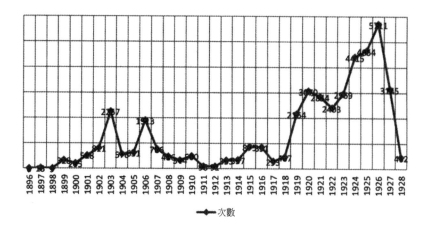

圖四　「中國近現代思想史專業數據庫（1830-1930）」中「主義」詞頻的歷年分布圖

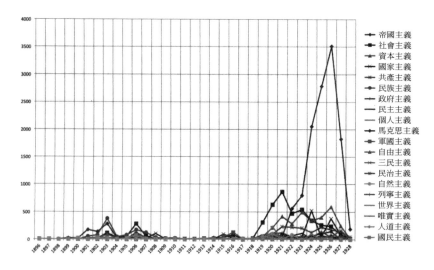

圖五　「中國近現代思想史專業數據庫（1830-1930）」中使用數量前20種主義在每年的使用頻度

主義的思潮中形成的。

這裡，除了各種主義歷年使用頻度外，我們還需要通過統計方法，知道兩種主義歷時聚合關係。圖六是用 CUSUM（Cumulative proportion chart over period）基礎統計方法對「社會主義」跟「無政府主義」進行數據處理的結果：[8]

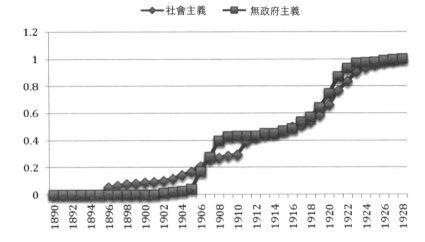

圖六 「中國近現代思想史專業數據庫（1830-1930）」中「社會主義」與「無政府主義」歷年使用頻度比例累加圖

8　本處採用的是 CUSUM 基礎統計法，如圖六中「社會主義」的 CUSUM 曲線，實際計算方式即是先把 1890-1928 年每一年的「社會主義」的詞頻統計出來後，再計算出每一年詞頻占 1890-1928 年總詞頻的比例，而後把歷年「社會主義」詞頻比例累加計算，即可得出圖六中「社會主義」的 CUSUM 曲線。CUSUM 為一簡單的統計方法，在工業上已有固定定義，全稱為 Cumulative sum control chart，但我們此處所使用之 CUSUM 意義與之不同，我們所使用 CUSUM 全稱為 Cumulative proportion chart over

　　圖六中的正方型線段是代表無政府主義，菱形線段則是社會主義，當這兩條線的分布曲線接近的時候，表明這兩個觀念在該階段使用頻度相近；當這兩個拉開的時候，表明它們在該階段使用頻度相遠。從圖六中可以看到，在早期，1896年到1910年間，社會主義跟無政府主義產生的時候，當時「社會主義」一詞用的多，而「無政府主義」一詞用的少，表示在該階段中這兩個觀念是不一樣的，才有獨自高頻使用的時期，但是到了在新文化運動中間，這兩個觀念使用頻度是一致的，沒有特別強調哪一個觀念，表示並未認為這兩個觀念有巨大的不同，因此不需要特別使用以強調之。由此線索可見，中國的無政府主義最後很容易傾向於社會主義、共產主義。再比如說，我們再來看看「馬列主義」跟「三民主義」。我們知道馬列主義跟三民主義早期是同源的，但什麼時候分開的呢？在下圖七裡很清楚，三民主義應是從1920年以後與馬克思主義分開，因為在1920年後，馬克思主義的急遽使用現象，代表著此一主義正在被問題化與定義之中，因此才會出現高頻使用階段；而1924年以後列寧主義才開始被大量使用，這意味著此一主義被獨立地意識到其內涵，而與三民主義有明確

---

period，因為我們主要是用在進行觀念詞頻成長比例的歷時性變化觀察之上，由於我們採用的CUSUM橫軸為時間，故稱為Cumulative proportion chart over period。基本上累加的概念在量化研究中並不少見，例如，累加機率函數（Cumulative Probability Density Function）、工業統計的CUSUM控制圖（Cumulative Sum Control Chart）都利用了累加的特性，而CUSUM圖呈現即是累積相對頻次，其作法是將一般頻次，按時間累加其頻率的比例而成，由於CUSUM圖的線條只上下下，此做法可減少頻次圖的線條交錯，使得圖表呈現會比一般頻次圖簡潔，便利於人文研究者進行讀圖分析。由於CUSUM圖是已被大量利用的圖表形式與計算方法，故其作法在基本統計教科書中幾乎都被提及，此處不詳述，有興趣者可參見可參見Altman, Douglas G.,Practical Statistics for Medical Research（Taylor & Francis, 1991），pp.29-31。

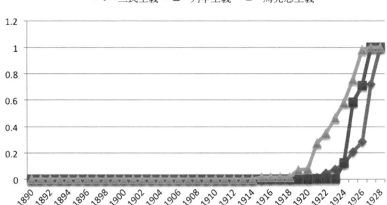

圖七　「中國近現代思想史專業數據庫（1830-1930）」中「三民主義」與「馬克思主義」、「列寧主義」歷年使用頻度比例累加圖

的區隔，或者講的更清楚一點，是1925年國民革命運動起來以後，才促使三民主義與馬列主義明確劃分的。

　　在研究「主義」的嘗試中獲得如上成果，令我們非常開心，當天就開了香檳慶祝，認為這將會催生一門新的數位人文學學科。我們認為，人文問題有兩種，第一種是我們熟悉的，僅靠人文學者個人研究即可，不太需要用到電腦，即使需要簡單的統計，亦可人工計數；但還有另外一種人文問題，如果沒有電腦輔助，人文學者個人是無法進行研究的，這時就需要有資科或統計學者的參與。雖然在「主義」研究中，我們僅僅使用了最簡單的資科技術與統計方法，但它已經解決了我們過去無法著手研究的問題，這就足以表明它代表著一個新方向的開始。那天大概是2011年的年末，也就是三、四年以前的事情

了。我們曾跟項潔先生講過，從第二種人文問題出發，以後光是人文研究者就無法獨立進行研究了，必須依賴數位學者跟人文學者的結合才能進行。

四、數位人文研究的重要性

　　2011 年之前我們仍然是用比較簡單的數位人文方法進行研究，由人文學者人工挑選關鍵詞後再向資訊、統計學者提出要求，由他們設計程序和進行複雜的計算與建立模型。雖然上述方法亦具有成效，可解答不少人文問題，但是卻有一個問題仍然存在，即我們仍是不可避免地要先由人文學者做出主觀認定、只能觀察到對任一人文學者自身而言覺得重要的關鍵詞分析結果，這樣的研究路徑，仍然被限制在人文學者主觀單一的視野中。後來，更多的 IT 和數學研究者加入了我們研究團隊，在合作過程中，因為他們時常處於跨領域研究時必定會面臨到的「專業落差」中，即：他們並不了解歷史上有哪些詞可以作為關鍵詞，因此，他們提出一個有趣且意義深遠的問題，即：我們是否有可能用電腦自動地、比較客觀地找到文本中的重要關鍵詞？也就是說，這些詞並非由人文學者主觀挑選，而是基於某些客觀的數學原理、統計方法所挑選出來的關鍵詞，也許還可能有人文學者原先不知道的關鍵詞呢？這樣的提問著實非常具有吸引力，但對人文學者來說卻是不可能做到、而且非常麻煩的事情。因為，目前人文學者使用電腦，通常都是做查詢或驗證的工作，針對我們已知觀念進行檢索與簡單統計，分析它們的某種歷史發展趨勢，怎麼可能不先主觀設定關鍵詞、由電腦技術找到某種未知的重要關鍵詞呢？

　　在上述問題意識下，我們開啟了尋找一種客觀給出關鍵詞方法的

研究道路。首先我們的第一個嘗試是20世紀30年代語言學中的「齊夫定律」（Zipf's Law）。所謂「齊夫定律」其實很簡單，它講的是一般語言學現象，即在一個5000字以上的文本中，一個詞使用的頻度跟它的使用頻度的排序之間具有某種關係性（兩者相乘爲常數）。經改進後的「齊夫定律」可表達爲如Zipf-Mandelbrot公式：

$$p(R=r)\ \alpha\ \frac{1}{(r+b)^a}, r=1,...,k \ ; \ a,b>0,$$

或者可寫爲：

$$p(R=r)=\frac{1}{c(r+b)^a}, \ c=\sum_{r}^{k}\frac{1}{r^a}$$

R爲一服從Zip'f-Mandelbrot定律之隨機變數。而$p(R=r)$爲一個離散的機率分配（Probability mass function）。其中，r是字的排序，k爲最大的字排序，a,b爲該機率分配的參數。根據該公式，排序越後面的字，出現的機率會迅速下降。

現在「齊夫定律」的應用已非常廣泛，而我們將之引入客觀尋找關鍵詞方法的研究中。我們根據以往的研究經驗發現一個有趣的現象：假定某一文本是要表達某一中心思想，那麼與該思想相應的關鍵詞，往往是對齊夫定律的理論值而言具有最大偏差值的詞。我們想驗證和檢驗這樣的猜想，顯而易見，最好的試驗文本就是《新青年》。這是因爲，第一，它對應著某一群特定主體，每一卷都存在著想要表達的主要思想觀念；第二，思想史學者對《新青年》各卷的研究已經很深入了，我們可以用來檢驗電腦技術得到的結果。

但是如何計算文本中的詞彙對齊夫定律的偏離值呢？我們的研究

團隊有位學統計學的年輕人，他說可以用統計學方法來計算出《新青年》裡面的每一個詞，對應於齊夫定律的理論值偏差有多少，他與人文學者合作，經過計算而得到每個詞相對於齊夫定律的偏離值。大家知道，十一卷的《新青年》雜誌約五百萬字，對每一個詞進行計算是人力所不可為的。但只要用電腦，根據統計學公式編排程序進行計算，卻可以很快地完成。後來，憑藉著電腦程序和給定的統計方法，我們將五百萬字的《新青年》中每一個詞進行自動計算，比對其詞頻與排序和齊夫定律理論值曲線的偏差狀況。當計算結果擺在我們人文學者面前的時候，我們嚇了一跳，這個結果如圖八。

圖八的結果叫盒狀圖（Boxplot）。這是什麼意思呢？圖中越遠離0的點就是與齊夫定律理論值偏差越多的點，每一個點都代表一個詞

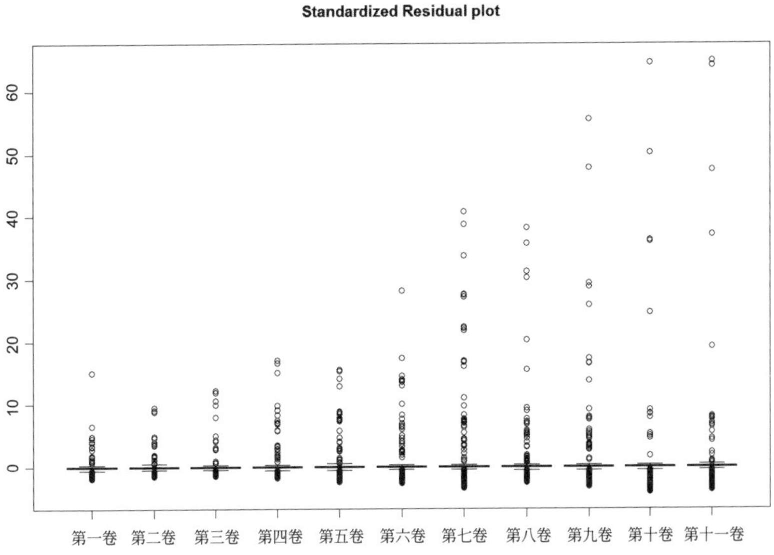

圖八 《新青年》中詞彙詞頻與排序與齊夫定律理論曲線偏差值盒狀圖

彙，跳出來的點就是偏差值越大的關鍵詞。根據這個計算，我們就可以把《新青年》十一卷中各卷具有最大偏差值的詞彙列舉出來，如表一：

表一　《新青年》十一卷中最大偏離段的關鍵詞詞表

卷一	國家、政府
卷二	青年
卷三	文學、中國、社會
卷四	娜拉、文學、中國、社會、我們
卷五	中國、我們、他們
卷六	社會、我們、他們、主義
卷七	中國、社會、我們、他們
卷八	社會、我們、他們、資本、階級
卷九	社會、我們、他們、資本、階級、革命、（資、無）產階（級）
卷十	社會、我們、資本、階級、革命、（資、無）產階（級）
卷十一	社會、我們、資本、階級、革命、（資、無）產階（級）

　　大家可以看見，第一卷中最大偏差的是兩個詞，一個是「國家」，第二個是「政府」。第二卷中最大偏差的就是一個詞，是「青年」。第三卷中最大偏差的是三個詞，即「文學」、「中國」跟「社會」，不是「青年」了。第四卷中具有最大偏差值的詞彙中，「娜拉」加進來了，除了「娜拉」外，還有「文學」、「中國」、「社會」跟「我們」，在第四卷中「我們」一詞跳出來成為具有最大偏差值的關鍵詞了。諸如上述《新青年》十一卷各卷之最大偏差值關鍵詞，是電腦自己找到的，已不需要人文研究者的預先選擇。

　　我們一看到這個結果，一下就呆住了。爲什麼呆住了呢？因爲我們在香港中文大學時曾經與復旦大學歷史系師生合作，就是想用文本分析的方法找到《新青年》中每一卷的主導觀念傾向。花了一年多時間，結果卻差強人意。因爲《新青年》雜誌很複雜，意義變化很大，每個研究者在閱讀和分析文本時，不可避免地會帶入各自的主觀性。現在，通過齊夫定律的計算後所列出的十一卷中最大偏差值關鍵詞表，竟跟我們長期以來研究《新青年》後的感覺居然是一模一樣的。

　　眾所周知，《新青年》的創辦人之所以要創辦這個刊物，是出於對民初政治的失望和反省。在其初辦時，主張不談時政，而要從當時最普遍的弊病中尋找文化根源，而在這樣的辦刊宗旨下，就不可避免地會涉及到與國家、政府觀念相關理論的介紹與思考，「國家」、「政府」就成爲第一卷中最大偏離的重要關鍵詞。而到第二卷的時候，「青年」一詞成爲最大偏離段中的關鍵詞，這表明思考文化問題的主體是青年。人文學者早就知曉，《新青年》主體意識凸現是從第二卷開始的，「青年」成爲最大偏離使我們感到有點神奇，因爲這與過去人文研究結果若合符節。第三卷則進入到文學革命時期，因此「文學」一詞跳出來，這是意料之中的。接著是第四卷，「娜拉」作爲一個文學革命中個人主體性的引導詞跳出來了。然後第五卷出現了代表青年主體的「我們」一詞，接著出現了跟「我們」對立的「他們」。「他們」是誰？就是梁啓超（1873-1929）所代表的那幫紳士。第八卷以後，這個「我們」、「他們」的對立就變成「階級」對立，「資本」、「革命」等關鍵詞也隨之成爲最大偏離了。[9]

9　關於齊夫定律、偏離值計算方式、《新青年》十一卷中具有最大偏差值的關鍵詞表，可詳參金觀濤、梁穎誼、姚育松、劉昭麟：〈統計偏離值分析於人文研究上的應用——以《新青年》爲例〉，《東亞觀念史集刊》

　　上述工作意味著，原來人文學者認爲一些不可逾越的障礙是可以克服的。因爲上述研究表明了，過去人文研究者通過閱讀都不一定能找到的文本主導觀念，竟然可以用數位辦法做到。當然，這種方法是否適用於其他文本，還有待於檢驗，也許是我們運氣好，碰巧用到《新青年》這樣一個適合進行研究的文本。目前這樣一個方法的有效性有多廣泛，是不是適合於處理所有報刊，我們尚不知道，但是在《新青年》上，我們的確做到了。即使上述方法有限制，只適合某一類文本，但這也不要緊，因爲它開創了一個可能性。現在我們已經把計算偏離，通過盒狀圖尋找關鍵詞的程序標準作業化了，即在人工閱讀文本前，已可以先自動計算任何一個文本，客觀地計算文本中詞彙使用對齊夫定律的偏離度，提供給人文學者參考。

五、如何研究觀念系統的變遷

　　以上講的是我們在2012年的工作，2014年我們又往前進了一步。由於《新青年》文本表達的內容代表的是一個知識群體觀念體系變遷的過程，我們想是否有可能用數位方法去揭示《新青年》知識群體的觀念體系是怎樣變化的呢？觀念系統是觀念的集合，如果關鍵詞代表觀念，那麼，觀念系統也可以用關鍵詞互相聯繫的網絡來表示。於是，我們想到社會網絡分析技術（Social Network　Analysis），它是否可以運用到觀念體系的研究上呢？

　　在嘗試使用網絡分析技術處理《新青年》時，我們發現到另一種

第6期（2014年6月），頁327-366，此文原發表於「第四屆數位典藏與數位人文國際研討會」，國立台灣大學數位典藏研究發展中心、國立台灣大學圖書館主辦，2012年11月29-30日。

挑選文本關鍵詞的方法，而這方法與前面講到的用對齊夫定律最大偏離值所選出來的關鍵詞不同，網絡分析技術可以找到另外一類，具有可呈顯詞彙之間意義關聯度之重要性的關鍵詞彙。而且，第二類網絡關鍵詞與第一類偏離值關鍵詞並不一致。由高度偏離齊夫定律理論曲線選出的第一類關鍵詞，主要意義為對所對應觀念強調的程度；而用觀念節點的分析方法所找到的第二類關鍵詞，則可以揭示觀念系統變遷的機制。這裡，關鍵是要確定代表不同觀念的詞彙之間的聯繫，算出不同關鍵詞之間的聯繫度，畫出相應網絡。[10]這樣的網絡結點圖有助於揭示文本中複雜的意義結構。

前面所列表一，是我們已討論過偏離齊夫定律值最大的詞彙表，是第一類關鍵詞，代表的是某一卷的文本要表達的中心觀念。現在，我們用網絡分析技術來分析一批「高詞頻」關鍵詞之間的關聯度，即它們之間的相關性，它們之間有多近？有多少聯繫？我們先用相關性計算得到這一批關鍵詞之間的整體聯繫，而後依計算結果將其畫出來，這些網絡圖就是代表著觀念系統結構的網絡。圖九是《新青年》第一卷高頻詞之間的聯繫網絡，其計算步驟是，先選出《新青年》第一卷中20個高頻的關鍵詞，接著用概念關係性計算公式，算出這20

10　在實際計算方法與步驟上，簡單的說首先是先採用N-Gram程式，擷取出《新青年》每卷前20個高頻關鍵詞作為網絡節點；其次，以「篇」為節點的關聯單位，以Phi coefficient為關聯性計算公式，並設定Phi coefficient的檢定門檻值為0.005，計算這20個高頻關鍵詞的兩兩相關性；其三，最後以前20%為共現頻率門檻值，畫出20個高頻關鍵詞節點的相關性網絡，完成概念網絡圖的繪製。關於詳細計算公式與過程以及以下研究論述，可詳參金觀濤、邱偉雲、梁穎誼、陳柏聿、沈錳坤、劉青峰：〈觀念群變化的數位人文研究－以《新青年》為例〉，「2014第五屆數位典藏與數位人文國際研討會」，中研院數位文化中心、臺大數位人文研究中心，2014年12月1日至2日。

個關鍵詞之間的關係係數，然後再依照係數強弱，進行概念節點之間
的網絡連結，最後繪製成圖九：

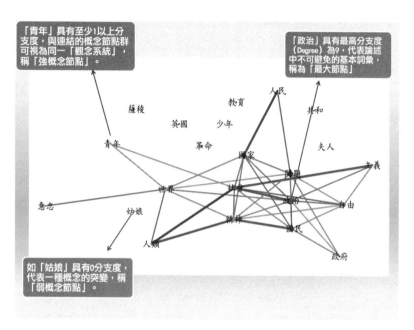

圖九　《新青年》第一卷概念網絡圖

　　圖九中有的概念節點是與其他概念節點具有網絡關係的，但有些
沒有。譬如說「姑娘」這個詞在第一卷中使用頻度很高，屬高頻詞集
合的元素，但它跟其他概念節點卻沒有產生關係，我們把它稱為「弱
概念節點」。再如「青年」這個詞，它與其他概念節點具有網絡連
結，我們把它稱為「強概念節點」。而「政治」這個詞既是高頻詞，
同時又與九個概念節點具有關係連結，可以視為第一卷概念網絡的中

心，我們可稱爲「最大節點」。另外，「社會」、「國家」、「國民」是「次最大節點」，它們和「最大節點」構成某種核心式的關係結構群。

我們可以根據上述方法，把《新青年》每一卷的網絡都畫出來。下面的圖十、圖十一和圖十二，分別是第二卷、第三卷和第四卷的網絡概念節點圖。

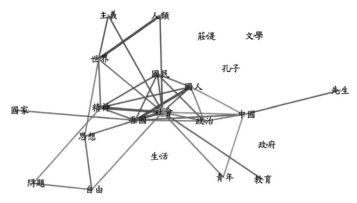

圖十　《新青年》中第二卷概念網絡圖

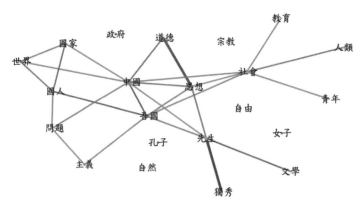

圖十一　《新青年》中第三卷概念網絡圖

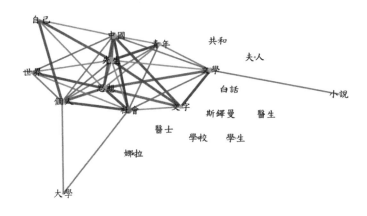

圖十二　《新青年》中第四卷概念網絡圖

　　圖十表明，第二卷的「最大節點」是「社會」，「次最大節點」是「精神」、「國民」、「吾國」。圖十一表明，在第三卷中「中國」和「思想」成為「最大節點」及「次最大節點」，與此相關的主要觀念是「文學」、「先生」、「社會」，「文學」等。

　　圖十二是第四卷的網絡節點圖，非常有意思的是，跳出一個「娜拉」這樣一個「弱概念節點」。重大結點則是「先生」、「思想」「中國」、「社會」等，而「文學」、「個人」、「世界」等主要觀念也已被交織到新的網絡中。依次，我們可以作出《新青年》11卷各卷的最大節點分布圖。

　　如果各卷只選出一個最大節點，可以得出圖十三：

　　現在，我們來對比表一和圖十三列出的詞彙，非常有意思的是，由齊夫定律算出的最大偏離值的第一類關鍵詞，與網絡分析技術算出來的最大節點的第二類關鍵詞並不一致。我們可以看到，表一中，第一卷中第一類核心觀念的兩個關鍵詞是「國家」和「政府」，而在圖

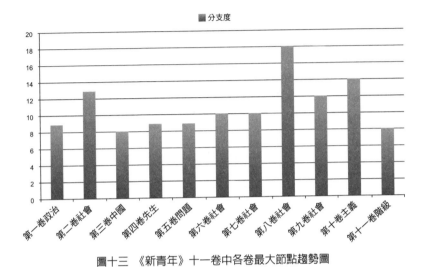

圖十三 《新青年》十一卷中各卷最大節點趨勢圖

九中它們只是「強概念節點」和「次最大節點」，還不是「最大節點」，最大節點是「政治」。這顯示出在1915-1916年時，刊物的內容，包括第一類關鍵詞「國家」和「政府」所代表的論述，無論任何論述主題皆與「政治」密切相關，即「政治」觀念雖具有普遍性，但不似「國家」與「政府」具有強調性，這正呈現出《新青年》從創刊開始就是以「政治」為主要辦報宗旨。第二卷最大節點為「社會」一詞，這顯示出五四青年的論述中心開始從「政治」問題導向「社會」。第三卷中的最大節點從「社會」成了「中國」，這代表著當時論述主題都圍繞在「中國」。第四卷的最大節點是「先生」，與這一卷的內容多是論戰文字相關，「先生」乃是論戰雙方對對手的尊稱。第五卷「問題」是最大節點，這表明刊物內容有「問題化」的趨勢，討論政治問題、社會問題、貞操問題、教育問題等各種問題。這時，

意識形態語言尚不占主導。第六、第七、第八到第九卷的最大節點都是「社會」，說明刊物內容一直是在關注中國社會的重建。第十卷的「主義」、第十一卷的「階級」成為最大節點，則表明了《新青年》已有明顯的馬列主義政治傾向。也就是說，網絡節點圖可以更清楚地揭示《新青年》群體的思想體系具有如下兩個特點：一，高度關心政治和社會；二，逐漸趨向馬列主義意識形態。

我們想強調的是，概念網絡圖中最重要的節點，跟齊夫定律的最大偏離關鍵詞可以基本一致，也可能不一致。「最大節點」代表觀念系統的核心，具有普遍性，抓住它就能看到以它為中心的觀念系統之觀念網絡。我們透過數位人文技術，給出了《新青年》十一卷中概念網絡形成演變的軌跡，跟我們人文學者藉由文本分析研究所得出的結論，可以說是非常吻合的。

需要指出的是，這只是我們應用數位方法的一個嘗試，尚不成熟，難免有不少問題，需要不斷嘗試和改進，這個嘗試直到現在還在持續進行。儘管如此，我們發現，數位人文方法確實可以幫助人文學者解決過去某些無法回答與解決的問題。比如說，我們團隊中有的學者正在用數位人文方法研究文言轉白話的發展轉軌，這個研究才剛開始；[11]又比如說，我們還嘗試進行中文音譯詞的擷取工作，[12]當然這樣的工作是離不開一個大團隊的。

近幾年，在我們與資科學者、統計學者、數學家合作的數位人文

---

[11]　詳參何立行、余清祥、鄭文惠：〈從文言到白話：《新青年》雜誌語言變化統計研究〉，《東亞觀念史集刊》第 7 期（2014 年 12 月），頁 427-454。

[12]　參見王昱鈞、呂翊瑄、蔡宗翰、劉青峰、金觀濤及劉昭麟：〈漢文文獻之外來語音譯詞擷取方法〉，收於項潔編：《數位人文研究與技藝》（臺北：台灣大學出版中心，2014 年 4 月），頁 121 137。

研究過程中，一方面我們深感數位人文是一個大有發展前途的新興學科，另一方面，更需要強調的一點是，數位人文研究必定是以人文問題爲中心的。只有當遇到某種非借助電腦否則不能回答的問題時，或者借助電腦可以幫助人文學者更爲省時省力時，才需要使用數位技術與統計方法；而且，並不一定要使用越複雜的技術與方法就表示越有用，某些在數位學者看來非常簡單的工具和方法，只要對解決人文學者的問題非常有用，就可以與人文學者合作。所以數位人文的研究工作，乃是以人文的研究爲中心的，以人文的問題意識爲中心的，以人文的判據意義分析爲中心的，這是電腦所不能代替的。因此在整個數位人文分析經驗中，我們覺得一個最重要的主軸與方向，就是以人文爲核心，充分依靠大數據的處理技術，讓數位跟人文相結合，以解釋思想史變化的內在理念。

我們相信數位人文研究的工作才剛剛開始，而《新青年》是一個很特別的刊物，得以適當地讓我們結合資科統計技術與人文分析工作，而這些嘗試正揭示著一個新的方向的產生，我們認爲這就是數位人文學的發展方向，期待有更多人文與數位研究者投入，共同推進數位人文學的發展，這是我們衷心的期盼。

Talks at "New Reflections on *New Youth*: Liberalism and Radicalism in Modern China"

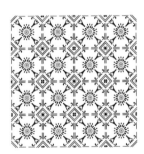

David Der-wei Wang

---

* Edited transcript of Dr. David Der-wei Wang's talk at the 2015 AAS-in-Asia Roundtable "New Reflections on New Youth: Liberalism and Radicalism in Modern China"

Good morning everybody. I want to first thank Dr. Huang Ke-wu 黃克武 for his invitation to be part of this panel, particularly to be on the same panel with the much-respected Prof. Jin Guantao 金觀濤. I will speak bilingually regarding this topic of "youth" and the making of modern Chinese culture at large. For my fifteen minutes I would like to make two points, basically. First, I will argue that "youth"—the discovery, or even invention of "youth"— represented one of the most important phenomena in the making of Chinese modernity. And second, I want to argue that, from my perspective as a literature student, that "youth" has exerted a tremendous imaginative power, particularly in terms of Chinese literary publications that have affected all dimensions of modern Chinese experience.

I'd like to make a few observations and comments with regard to these two points I am trying to make. But to begin with, just a very familiar quote for everybody, that is the essay "Warning to Youth" 敬告青年 by Chen Duxiu 陳獨秀 in the first issue of *Youth Magazine* 青年雜誌. The time was 1915. In "Warning to Youth"—I suppose this is a passage which is very familiar to everybody, but particularly allow me here to call your attention to the imagistic power of the passage I am quoting here. I am reading in Chinese:

「青年如初春，如朝日，如百卉之萌動，如利刃之新發于硎，人生最寶貴之時期也。」This, in a way, is very poetic—polemical and poetic. It really suggests that we need some rhetorical force; only after instilling this kind of rhetorical power into our statement could we really generate this imaginative or even imaginary power with regard to the promise, or the prospect of youth.

「青年之於社會，猶新鮮活潑細胞…」 Here we have a kind of medical or a biological reference. 「…細胞之在人身。」

「予所欲涕泣陳詞者，」 Now here we have the effective emission of tears and cries—吶喊的聲音…

「惟獨望於新鮮活潑之青年。」 So 「青年」 is now being packaged as something almost like a product, like a very wonderful product—新鮮的、很活潑的…「以自覺而奮鬥。」

This is of course the beginning moment of the invocation of the image or imaginary of 「青年」（youth）at the beginning of the modern century.

And here I have two images: on the left side is the inaugural issue of the *La Jeunesse*《青年》雜誌—the original title of this magazine—the time again was 1915. And then of course next year, as a result of the controversy over the property right of the title of the journal, the journal was renamed *New Youth* 新青年. Not just 「青年」 but now 「新青年」: new, renewed youth. So this really even doubled or compounded the effect of the power of the provocative publication of the concept of 「青年」.

What I am saying here is that the whole genealogy of 「青年」 is implicated not only in the 1915 statement made by Chen Duxiu, but actually could be traced back to the turn of the 21st century. For example, in the year 1900 (actually, 陰曆的一月、元月—the beginning of the year in the lunar calendar）Liang Qichao 梁啓超 in his famous *Ode to a Young China* 少年中國說, for the first time in the twentieth century writes: 「吾心目中有一少年中國在。」

So again 「青年」、「少年」 and so forth—are all being summoned as

the new and the generative force in the making of Chinese modernity. And of course "young China"「少年中國」was eventually taken up by scholars and intellectuals such as Huang Yuanyong 黃遠庸 and Wang Guangqi 王光祈 to become a campaign on behalf of this new aspiration for young China. In 1912, the newspaper or journal *Young China* 少年中國 was founded.

Another interesting point for our thinking about "youth" is the year 1916. Li Dazhao 李大釗 in his famous essay "Youth" 青春 wrote:「惟眞知愛青春者，乃能識宇宙有無盡之青春。」Here「青春」is associated with the cosmic—immense cosmic movement—which could mobilize the whole Chinese soul and the mind toward the right direction of modernity.「惟眞能識宇宙有無盡之青春者⋯」This is the immense, continuously generating sources or resources of youth propelling the progress of Chinese modernization project.「乃能具此種精神與氣魄。」Here, echoing Fansen's 汎森 observation of such terms as「以太」(ether),「精神」(spirit) and「氣魄」(vigor), we can highlight both modern and archaic elements in the Chinese language reference.「惟眞有此種精神與氣魄者，乃能永享宇宙無盡之青春。」So「青春」was actually being first evoked as a temporal register in terms of the progression of time, and then being transcended into something eternal and immense— 無盡, infinite. So that's a really a kind of ironic bracketing of the progression of the recently gained awareness of time and temporality.

Arguing that throughout the whole twentieth century,「青春」on the one hand is acutely a temporal awareness, and on the other hand「青春」easily was being rarified, mystified, to become something transcendental, something endowed with mythological power, something almost a-temporal. So this combination is something for us to think about at the beginning of another century.

Lu Xun 魯迅 in 1925 was also echoing this nation-wide aspiration for a kind of source of「青春」by writing「因為身外的青春倘一消滅，我身中的遲暮也即凋零了。」That's 1925. And not only that, even Chiang Kai-shek reflects this language. I mean「青春」, by the 1930s, was being politicized and was being taken up as a kind of political propaganda. Chiang Kai-shek was talking about「青年是國家的主人，是民族的生命，也是革命的後備。國家和民族，一切艱難巨大的責任」等等等等 … and so forth, all associated with「青春」.

As time moved on, of course you have notions such as political force being associated with「青春」like「十萬青年十萬軍」during the War of Resistance period. "Young" or "youth expedition army" was being sent down to the southwestern China and Southeast Asia to fight the holy crusade against Japan, young Bolsheviks, and so on, while the leftwing was being mobilized to fight for the new cause of revolution. Down to 1957, Mao Zedong was in Moscow addressing a group of young Chinese—*young Chinese*—in Moscow. This is a famous line:「你們青年人朝氣蓬勃，正在興旺時期，好像早晨八、九點鍾的太陽，希望寄託在你們身上。」And so forth.

So again and again what I am trying to say is that we are talking about different kinds of concepts of temporaries implied in this discourse of「青春」.

The sense of urgency and a sense of eternity are being brought together as it were to formulate an actually paradoxical logic in the twentieth century evocation of「青春」.

Returning to the historical dimension, we probably can observe certain so-called key moments when「青春」was being foregrounded as the propelling force for a new campaign, a new ideology, and so forth.

Meanwhile, I would like to just mention a few literary titles for your consideration as to how literature could be brought to bear upon this kind of massive propagation and massive propaganda in the name of「青春」. In the May Fourth movement 1919, everybody is familiar with the 青年的運動 and the like. Ba Jin, in 1931, wrote *Family*: that kind of hallmark representing the sentiment of one whole generation of readers in celebration of this kind of literary articulation of the power of youth. And then 1949, another moment in which「青春」was being invoked in association with the rebirth of yet another new China. And at the same time, writers were engaged in writing so as to bear witness to this discourse or aspiration for a new politicized「青春」. Here two examples for your consideration.

On the one hand, Yang Zhu's *A Song of Youth*—《青春之歌》— a title which seems to best embody the spirit of the time. The author was Yang Zhu 楊沫, a woman author, and the novel was about 一二九運動 of 1935, recalling the past, and anticipating the future –「無盡的青春　無限的青春不斷地在湧向。」And of course in just eight years Yang Zhu was going to find herself condemned as a representative of the "not youth" but the older generation, destined to be eradicated from the continued current of discovery the youth. That time was the Cultural Revolution.

On the other hand, you have *Long Live Youth*. Wang Meng 王蒙 is of course one the most famous figures in Chinese cultural politics in the second half of the twentieth century. He wrote《青春萬歲》when he was only 19-years-old, and the time [was] 1953. And yet this《青春萬歲》was regarded as so politically *incorrect* that this 組織部來的年輕人 —Wang Meng—after 1956 faced massive condemnation and eventually was exiled to Xinjiang for 22 years.《青春萬歲》was not being rehabilitated, so to speak, and published until 1979; at that time Wang Meng was no longer young.

So the struggle between various kinds of representatives of「青春」—「誰有青春的發言人？」— seems to be an intriguing question in this new regime. On the one hand, Chairman Mao was talking about youth as「八、九點鍾的太陽」, and truly in 1966, 紅太陽又升起了; one million Chinese youths were being summoned to Tiananmen Square to salute the saint of the Chinese Revolution. On the other hand, we may wonder whether this「青春」was being truly called forth or being enshrined, or even enshrouded by a different kind of ideology not necessarily on behalf of the spirit of youth or「青春」.

Perhaps the last time we saw「青春」being associated with both political power and literary power was in 1989—when, again, on Tiananmen Square, millions of Chinese youth came to celebrate their own power and actually imaginary legitimacy on behalf of themselves, on behalf of the nation, though of course what they were to be faced with was the crackdown of this so-called power of youth. This is the historical moment everybody remembers and is familiar with.

I would like to end with two images talking about how this「青春」power works as kind of literary and artistic source of inspiration and affection, and conclude with a thought about how this invocation is being associated with the so-called spirit of the time. First, *Children of Troubled Time* 風云兒女 — 1935. For those who are familiar with this movie surely know that the theme song for this movie was no other than「義勇軍進行曲」and the composer was Nie Er 聶耳, who composed this song at the age of twenty-three. And Nie Er was soon going to be drowned—next year actually; he died in a swimming accident. But《風云兒女》depicts a「大時代」, representing the time, representing that kind of yearning for the rejuvenation of new China. And that was 1935.

And second, now 80 years later, what we are having is《小時代》, and here we are celebrating another kind of youth, represented by a young man who is now not too young anymore. When he was first discovered at the end of the twentieth century he was 17, 18 years old. Now we can call him a young entrepreneur — 年輕創業家. And《小時代》—this is our time. I wonder what the young revolutionaries, idealists and romantics in the 1920s and 30s when they were dedicating their dreams and their youth to a cause of a new nation, would think of today's generation of Chinese youth who can't wait to consume yet another production in the name of youth. Are we in a「小時代」？ What kind of「青春」are we talking about?

To conclude, let me just make the following observations for general discussion. Are we talking about「青春」as a kind of physiological or psychological status or stature in terms of the imaginary of Chinese modernity? Second, are we talking about「青春」as a kind of temporal factor which has helped define our understanding of China at different stages of modernity? And third, is 「青春」a kind of aesthetic image being continuously invoked, almost taking a dimension of an a-temporal kind of awareness? Or is 「青春」a kind of political interpellation, a kind political momentum and, particularly, is it a kind of calling—「青春」、「青年」? We can perhaps see that it is a kind of discursive power, as we are gathering together for two hours to discuss it. Is it an effective sort of source for our discussion? Or finally, is 「青春」merely a myth or mythology representing twentieth century China of a certain kind? Clearly, numerous kinds of dimensions and questions can be raised as we reflect on the causes and the consequences of the whole discourse of 「青春」.

But my final question is meant to be polemical or provocative. When we talk about 青春, usually we are talking about the positive side of 「青春」. 青年的力量通常是關於進步的、關於激情的、關於年輕人的, inventive power and so forth. Can we also, besides talking about the liberating and the liberal implications of 「青春」, think of 「青春」as something imposing, sometimes even coercive, and sometimes a kind of surveillance power? It does have that kind of implication; we need to at least ponder the implications of this side of "youth." I am saying this not just because I am getting really old; I am thinking of the other side of the dialogic of 「青春」, so I am throwing out these questions for general comment.

Thank you very much.

Political Ideals of *New Youth*:
Chen Duxiu and Republicanism

Yoshizawa Seiichio

---

*   Edited transcript of Dr. Yoshizawa Seiichio's talk at the 2015 AAS-in-Asia Roundtable "New Reflections on New Youth: Liberalism and Radicalism in Modern China"

New Youth's attitudes toward discussing political issues

This paper reexamines *New Youth* Magazine's attitudes toward politics, especially in its early volumes. Many scholars have pointed out that the editorial policy of *New Youth* was to avoid discussion of current political problems, suggesting its apparent apolitical character.[1] As evidence for that view, they cite an editor's words published in the correspondence section of the opening issue of *Youth Magazine*. An editor of the magazine, probably Chen Duxiu, clearly declared, "To reform young people's thinking and to cultivate young people's morality is this magazine's main aim. To criticize current political issues is not our business."[2]

I think this phrase deserves a closer analysis to understand the magazine's basic attitudes toward political discussion.[3] The phrase cited above is a portion of the reply to a letter written by a man named Wang Yonggong. It is unclear who Wang Yonggong was. If Wang did exist, the name was likely a pseudonym. Wang warned that some people had inaugurated a group named "Chouan hui" with the intension of abolishing

---

1   Lin Yü-sheng, *The Crisis of Chinese Consciousness: Radical Antitraditionalism in the May Fourth Era* (Madison, 1979), p. 64. Nomura Kōichi, *Kindai Chūgoko no shisō sekai: Sin seinen no Gunzō* (Tokyo, 1999), pp. 10-46.

2   "Tongxin," *Qingnian zazhi* vol. 1, no. 1 (Sept. 1915).

3   Wang Qisheng has pointed out that the *Youth Magazine*'s professed a-political stance represented its original nature as a common journal for youth. Wang Qisheng, *Geming yu fan-geming: shehui wenhua shiye-xia de minguo zhengzhi* (Beijing, 2010), pp. 2-3.

the republican regime and restoring an imperial system. He also pointed out that the Japanese people had a keen eye to take advantage of an unstable situation. Wang thus requested that the magazine caution the Chinese people against the coming dangers.

In the reply to Wang's letter, the editor also criticized the Chouan hui and contested its grounds for supporting an imperial regime. Nevertheless, the editor did not wish to argue against the people who were trying to restore an imperial system. This was, as cited above, because the purpose of the magazine was not to engage in current politics but to enlighten young people. The editor gave a supplementary explanation for his reluctance to engage in politics. Since the consciousness of the Chinese people, he observed, had not awakened totally, there was no good reason to blame the government. He concluded pessimistically that the Chinese people showed no interest in politics, and that, since even the ultimatum delivered by Japan had not been enough to awake them, a mere essay in his magazine would have no effect.

Here, he is referring to the humiliation caused by the so-called "twenty-one demands," which, in February 1915, the Japanese government presented to the Chinese government. After unfruitful negotiations, in May, Japan delivered an ultimatum to settle the dispute with China. This reply to Wang Yonggong is well known as a clear-cut manifestation of *New Youth*'s editorial policy. However, it is not easy to understand what this short reply really meant. Regarding this reply as an expression of *New Youth*'s apolitical stance, some scholars might conclude that *New Youth* had intentionally avoided political discussion and concentrated on reforming Chinese culture. As such, *New Youth* was considered the most important media outlet in the New Culture Movement. In this kind of analysis, the dichotomy between politics and culture plays an important role.

It is, however, uncertain whether this dichotomy reflected the original intent of the editor, Chen Duxiu.[4] To reconsider this question, we will first examine the political situation and atmosphere at the time. Then, we will try to understand why Chen Duxiu sought to enlighten young people.

A Political Crisis and Apathy in 1915

Japan's twenty-one demands aroused dramatic indignation throughout China. In many cities, people boycotted Japanese goods to express their objection to the oppressive demands and collected money to support national defense. President Yuan Shikai intentionally maneuvered the negotiation with Japan into a prolonged deadlock. But after Japan delivered the ultimatum, the Chinese government accepted many of the demands. With historical hindsight, we may say that the Chinese government did not compromise without forethought and managed to protect national interests as much as possible. However, at the time, many felt that the Chinese government had yielded to the ultimatum. As a result, disappointment and apathy became prevalent in Chinese society.

---

4   Of course, this dichotomy may be useful in a wider perspective. See Wang Hui, "Wenhua yu zhengzhi de bianzou: zhanzheng, geming yu 1910 niandai de "sixiang-zhan," *Zhongguo shehui kexue* no.4 (2009).

Therefore, for some intellectuals, revitalizing patriotism was very important. Liang Qichao vigorously criticized the Chinese government on the grounds that its self-justifying attitude was hurting the trust of the people and making patriotic sentiments meaningless.[5] Liang Qichao's essay contained a response to an article written by Chen Duxiu in 1914. In this controversial article "Patriotism and Self-Consciousness," Chen pointed out that patriotism could lead to great danger. For Chen, self-consciousness working with reason was indispensable to wholesome patriotism. Chen was, however, skeptical about the ability of the Chinese people to maintain their own state.[6]

Although Chen wrote the article before the twenty-one demands problem began, it received some responses after the Chinese government accepted the Japanese ultimatum in May 1915. Li Dazhao was worried that Chen's essay might make the people become desperate. Li was very anxious about national pessimism and the increasing suicide rate at that time, and he warned of the danger that self-consciousness might bring, specifically in total disillusion to politics. To overcome that kind of risky trend, Li was eager to remake a state that deserved to be an object of patriotism.[7]

Furthermore, Zhang Shizhao, an influential intellectual and an editor,

---

[5]   Liang Qichao, "Tong dingzui yan," *Da Zhonghua* vol. 1, no. 6 (June 1915).

[6]   Duxiu, "Aiguoxin yu zijuexin," *Jiayin zazh*, vol.1, no. 4 (Nov. 1914).

[7]   Li Dazhao, "Yanshixin yu zijuexin," *Jiayin zazhi* vol. 1, no. 8 (Aug. 1915). On this controversy, see Maurice Meisner, *Li Ta-chao and the Origins of Chinese Marxism* (Cambridge, Mass., 1967), pp. 21-26.

criticized both Chen Duxiu and Liang Qichao. According to Zhang, the political situation in the summer of 1915 was discouraging young people. Zhang thus suggested that they should rebuild the state by using self-consciousness.[8]

This was the intellectual atmosphere in 1915.[9] Even if there was some disagreement among these intellectuals, they had a common concern in mind: with the depressed national mood following from the political situation, the Chinese, particularly youngsters, were falling into desperate apathy. The most significant factor behind the national mood was the twenty-one demands problem and its humiliating settlement.

The chief editor of *Dongfang zazhi*, Du Yaquan, also pointed out that, in the autumn of 1915, almost everyone in China was pessimistic. For Du Yaquan, the most meaningful way to recover from that sentiment was encourage each person to pursue his or her own business and to foster desires.[10]

Thus, we can determine that Chen Duxiu sought to confront the disappointed atmosphere of the time when he inaugurated *Youth Magazine*. Overcoming the political apathy of the people, especially youth, was a very important theme of the magazine. In order to approach that goal,

---

8   Qiutong (Zhang Shizhao), "Guojia yu wo," *Jiayin zazhi* vol.1, no. 8 (Aug. 1915).

9   In detail, see Luo Zhitian, *Luanshi qianliu: minzu zhuyi yu minguo zhengzhi* (Shanghai, 2001), pp. 60-108.

10   Gaolao (Du Yaquan), "Wuren jinhou zhi zijue," *Dongfang zazhi* vol. 12, no. 10 (Oct. 1915).

Chen had to choose a detour route. Even if Chen declared, "to criticize current political issues is not our business," he was very concerned with encouraging young people to take part in politics. Now the question is, what kind of ideal vision of the polity did he have in mind?

Chen Duxiu's Commitment to Republican Ideals

It is well known that Chen Duxiu uncompromisingly advocated for the rights of individuals. For example, in the opening essay of the first issue of *Youth Magazine* "Call to Youth," Chen advised young people "to be independent, not to be slavish." He asserted that everyone should strive to uphold his or her independence and freedom. We can cite many more quotes to show that Chen always insisted on the value of individualism. However, that is only one side of Chen's concern. According to him, the most successful nations in the world gradually shifted from a scattered society toward greater and greater social cohesion. After building a state at last, an advanced nation found a way to control it democratically. As a result, even some kingdoms, such as Great Britain and Belgium, adopted republican politics. Chen concluded that a true state in the modern age should be democratic, and, in contrast, totally refused to accept that a state should consist of slavish people.[11] Of course, Chen's argument was greatly influenced by social Darwinist views. Nevertheless, here we can also find his eagerness for republicanism; only independent individuals could

---

11   Chen Duxiu, "Jinri zhi jiaoyu fangzhen," *Qingnian zazhi* vol. 1, no. 2 (Oct. 1915).

actively participate in democratic politics. In other words, if people were in a condition of slavery, they could not unite with each other to make a republican state.

In the history of Western political thought, classical republicanism had its origins in ancient Greece and was revived in Renaissance Italy. According to an influential study by J. G. A. Pocock, republican values played a very important role in early modern Britain and the United States. In that case, the republican vocabulary contended that a human being, namely a political animal, was so constituted that his nature was completed only in an active life practiced in a civic life.[12]

I think Chen Duxiu was fascinated with republican ideas like that. In his article "Our Last Awaking," he demanded that Chinese youth regard politics as their own business and take part in politics. According to Chen's observation, most people in China showed no interest in politics and would not involve themselves in it. Chen criticized, "they do not know that the state is the public property of the people; neither do they know that human beings are political animals." Therefore, he could not help asserting that whether a constitutional government or the government of the people would come about depended upon the awakened people of the nation who were entitled to be the host of the state. Therefore, in his opinion, if a republic with a constitutional government had not been built on the basis of the positive participation of the people, it should be called a false

---

[12]   J. G. A. Pocock, *Virtue, Commerce, and History* (Cambridge, 1985), pp. 40-41.

republic.[13]

He also published an essay titled "1916" to give three pieces of advice to "the youth in 1916." The first was "Hold the position of a conqueror. Do not be conquered." Secondly, he admonished them to respect individuality. His third piece of advice to youth was "Participate in the national movement. Do not get involved in a party movement." This piece of advice seems to have appeared out of context. As Chen explained, political parties had lost their meaning when the year 1915 came to an end. Furthermore, although there had been a party movement in China, the national movement had not yet begun. In conclusion, he declared, "If you are proud to be young men and women in 1916, make every effort to be a powerful citizen of the nation and change the party movement into a national movement."[14]

When he wrote another essay "Patriotism in My View," he insisted that the reason China was suffering from an aristocratic government and foreign invasion was that the public virtue and private virtue of the nation had been severely corrupted. Therefore, he called for youth to cultivate six kinds of moral principles: diligence (*qin*), frugality (*jian*), unselfishness (*lian*), cleanness (*jie*), honesty (*cheng*), and trust (*xin*).[15] Although preaching these morals may be seen as an effort to reform national culture, it should be noted that, for Chen, these were indispensable ethics to

---

[13]   Chen Duxiu, "Wuren zuihou zhi juewu," *Qingnian zazhi* vol.1, no. 6 (Feb. 1916).

[14]   Chne Duxiu, "Yijiuyiliu nian," *Qingnian zazhi* vol. 1, no. 5 (Jan. 1916).

[15]   Chen Duxiu, "Wo zhi aiguo zhuyi," *Xin Qingnian* vol. 2, no. 2 (Oct. 1916).

remake China, and therefore he referred to them as a path to patriotism and an ideal polity.

Concluding Remarks

It is well known that Chen Duxiu harshly criticized Kang Youwei, who was trying to establish Confucianism as a state religion. Chen's attack on Confucianism seems a good example of what Lin Yü-sheng called his attitude of "iconoclastic totalism."[16] However, we can say that his ideal of republicanism *per se* was of a totalistic nature. In his belief, all individuals should be awoken and should struggle for a republican state. True, as the dispute over a state religion became harsh, his explicit mention of the republican ideal decreased. Nevertheless, we can understand that he unchangingly expected youth to hold to republican virtue.

Then, we must ask, where did he find these republican ideals? I cannot explore this question here. In the late Qing period, Liang Qichao already outlined the people's virtue in his series of essays *Xinmin shuo* (Discourse on the New Citizen).[17] It is probable that the influence of Liang and other intellectuals guided Chen on his quest for the civic virtues of the Chinese. Seen from a wider point of view, Chen's eagerness for republican ideas may be understood as one expression of "the Rousseau strain" that

---

16 Lin Yü-sheng, *The Crisis of Chinese Consciousness*, pp. 56-81.
17 Hazama Naoki, "On Liang Qichao's Conceptions of *Gong* and *Si*: "Civic Virtue" and "Personal Virtue in the *Xinmin shuo*," in *The Role of Japan in Liang Qichao's Introduction of Modern Western Civilization to China*, ed. Joshua A. Fogel (Berkeley, 2004).

Benjamin Schwartz found in the history of the twentieth century.[18]

---

18   Benjamin I. Schwartz, *China and Other Matters* (Cambridge, Mass., 1996), pp. 208-226.

Scientific Life View: Personal or Human

 Jeu Jenq Yuann

Professor of Philosophy, National Taiwan University

---

* Edited transcript of Dr. Jeu Jenq Yuann's talk at the 2015 AAS-in-Asia Roundtable "New Reflections on New Youth: Liberalism and Radicalism in Modern China"

At this centenary of the New Culture Movement, dated from the birth of *Le Jeunesse* in 1915, I am very grateful to have this opportunity to say something on this significant occasion. The New Culture Movement was labeled as a movement of promoting science and democracy. The former was relatively easy to apprehend in terms of its application while the latter has turned out to be a long pursuit, not merely for China but also for many countries around the world. So, my question is this: what is the relationship between science and democracy, after a hundred years of their long march?

To answer this question, I will take advantage of the 40th anniversary of the publication of P. Feyerabend's *Against Method* (London: Verso, 1975). This book is known for its thesis of epistemological anarchism ("anything goes"), and it holds the view that there is no common method referring to the essential nature of science running through all of its practices. In the erstwhile popular view of anti-positivism, Feyerabend's claims raised attention of many sides. His methodology of democratic pluralism is one among many.

Feyerabend thinks that as there is no clear-cut way to define science by the application of any method in particular and that we have to admit that the current view of revering science as the master knowledge is not only misleading but also damaging to democracy. What we should now do is precisely what we did in the past by separating religion from politics, taking the influences of science out of the realm of politics. The right thing to do in politics today is let diverse cultures including science juxtapose and compete with each other, and eventually one of them will prevail.

Through the process of competition, there should be no employment of force (that would be non-democratic). Propaganda and persuasion are the means of democracy to achieve a tentative consensus. This describes Hu Shi's position during the debates of science and metaphysics in 1923.

In 1923, when Zhang Junmai (Carson Chang) delivered a talk at Tsing Hua University on the topic "Concerning the Problem of Life View, Science is Useless" (人生觀問題解決，絕非科學所能為力), it led to a series of debates regarding "life view." The debates were labeled "polemics between science and metaphysics" and actually they were all about life views, referring to a comprehensive outlook about what humanity should stand for. At the time, a lot of people thought that the side supporting a scientific life view got the upper hand. However, this is not accurate, as the criteria needed to compare life views were completely lacking. Even among the group supporting the scientific life view, mainly represented by Hu Shi and Chen Duxiu, prominent supporters could not definitively repudiate the other side in debates by proofs.

The lack of proof in repudiating the holders of the traditional life view was, however, not considered a problem at the time. It was explained away by accusing the traditionalists of holding an obstinate and conservative nature. This was naturally a pre-determined stance, which precluded the reasonableness of any life views other than those of science. Therefore, even in the face of the triumphant feeling of the scientific side, the debates were never concluded with successful persuasion.

We now know very well that the open-ended result of the debates refers to their metaphysical nature; all talks concerning the formation of all life views are metaphysical in the sense that they transcend experience. The supporters of scientific life views confused two distinct things and then ignored this fact. It was one thing to urge people to believe the prevalence of science, but it was quite another thing to hold that science could therefore extend its validity beyond experience to become the supervisory approach to an entire life. Both Hu Shi and Chen Duxiu claimed their belief in science, but they failed to notice science, by its nature, limits its validity to that of experiences.

Bearing this confusion in mind, the value of the debates would seem to be undermined. However, things are more complicated. Hu Shi and Chen Duxiu themselves did not agree on the way through which the scientific life view should be put forward. To us today, their difference is crucial, as it refers to the basic ideas of democracy, one of the two major objectives of the New Culture Movement.

Hu Shi sternly advocated the scientific life view, but he somehow noticed that before anything else, two questions needed to be addressed. First, how do we connect science to the scientific life view? And second, why is the scientific life view necessarily better than all other life views? To these two questions, Hu thought the scientific life view stood in a position scarcely different from the acceptance of scientific knowledge tout court, which defined the universe including life. Hu listed ten points regarding the comprehensive accumulation of scientific knowledge of all sorts.[1]

---

[1]   The 10 points are the following: 1. We know the infinitude of space according

In fact, Hu, though implicitly, admitted the fact that both questions are extremely hard to answer explicitly. Even though we hold all modern science true, we fail to link the correctness of science with a correct life view. Hu and Chen were by no means exceptions, and for this reason they both admitted that cherishing the scientific life view was carried out under this belief. So, the problem for both of them was how to convince people who did not share the same belief. The distinct approaches they took to convincing people to accept their belief reflected fundamental differences in their implicit views of the nature of democracy.

The difference between Hu and Chen lay in their attitudes toward the following two questions. First, to whom (personal or all humans?) does the scientific life view belong? And second, what is the utility (accidental or necessary?) of the scientific life view? Hu thought that the life views were changeable throughout history, so a person can change his or her life view through thinking. And also, since the change can be good, as when one becomes, enlightened, it is conducted under the principle of progress.

Chen. however. held an entirely different attitude. While Hu paid attention to propaganda and education in order to let the change of life view take place and hence select the scientific one, Chen paid attention to order and norms. The scientific life view is valuable as a matter of historical necessity and it stands there not as one alternative among many acceptable possiblities. Rather, it is the single correct course for all human beings; no exceptions are allowed. Moreover, promoting the scientific life view is not for any specific purpose, as the job itself is not purposive, but obligatory. To Chen, this position stands exactly like the recognition of truth, which has to be unique. We need to relinquish our previous faults by admitting a new life.

Being a pragmatist, Hu was willing to accept that in the long run people would change their life view as there was no way to convince people instantly. He even exemplified his position by taking the instances of Copernicus and Darwin into account. He thought that the scientific revolution that had once changed Europe's life view would also take place in China if our means of propaganda and education worked. He would not even deny the means was something similar to preaching a new religion representing the current truth. Chen criticized Hu for being subjective, and he insisted that an objective approach was needed and science needed to be demonstrated as a kind of knowledge with authority to supersede everything non-scientific.

The difference between Hu and Chen was crucial. Their difference was not only concerned with the positions of being right or left in politics;

---

to physics; 2. We know the infinitude of time according to pale biology; 3. We know that all changes are natural according to scientific naturalism; 4. We know the cruelty of survival according to biology; 5. According to physiological knowledge, humans are one of the animals; 6. According to anthropology, human societal development is a consequence of evolution; 7. According to psychology, all human psychological phenomena are causal; 8. According to sociology, human morality is mutable; 9. According to physics and chemistry, matter are living not mortal {??matter itself cannot die but is immortal'??}, dynamic not static; 10. According to the combination of sociology and biology, individuals are mortal, but humanity is immortal. Finally, Hu felt that if the term "scientific life view" sounded inadequate, then he would accept the title "naturalistic life view."

it was the difference between being democratic or authoritarian. After all, even in Europe, evaluations concerning the value, essence, and superiority of science needed to be considered in very long duration in order to let the massive consensus arise. To this regard, we have to admit that Hu was indeed a democrat, even in the twenty-first century, the era of post-modernity.

《思想史》稿約

1. 舉凡歷史上有關思想、概念、價值、理念、文化創造及其反思、甚至對制度設計、音樂、藝術作品、工藝器具等之歷史理解與詮釋，都在歡迎之列。

2. 發表園地全面公開，竭誠歡迎海內外學者賜稿。

3. 本學報爲半年刊，每年三月及九月出版，歡迎隨時賜稿。來稿將由本學報編輯委員會初審後，再送交至少二位專家學者評審。評審人寫出審稿意見書後，再由編委會逐一討論是否採用。審查探雙匿名方式，作者與評審人之姓名互不透露。

4. 本學報兼收中（繁或簡體）英文稿，來稿請務必按照本刊〈撰稿格式〉寫作。中文論文以二萬至四萬字爲原則，英文論文以十五頁至四十頁打字稿爲原則，格式請參考 *Modern Intellectual History*。其他各類文稿，中文請勿超過一萬字，英文請勿超過十五頁。特約稿件則不在此限。

5. 請勿一稿兩投。來稿以未曾發表者爲限，會議論文請查明該會議無出版論文集計畫。本學報當儘速通知作者審查結果，然恕不退還來稿。

6. 論文中牽涉版權部分（如圖片及較長之引文），請事先取得原作者或出版者書面同意，本學報不負版權責任。

7. 來稿刊出之後，不付稿酬，一律贈送作者抽印本30本、當期學報2本。

8. 來稿請務必包含中英文篇名、投稿者之中英文姓名。論著稿請附中、英文提要各約五百字、中英文關鍵詞至多五個；中文書評請加附該書作者及書名之英譯。

9. 來稿請用真實姓名，並附工作單位、職稱、通訊地址、電話、電子郵件信箱地址與傳真號碼。

10. 投稿及聯絡電子郵件帳號：intellectual.history2013@gmail.com。

《思想史》撰稿格式

（2013/08 修訂）

1. 橫式（由左至右）寫作。

2. 請用新式標點符號。「 」用於平常引號，『 』用於引號內之引號；《 》用於書名，〈 〉用於論文及篇名；英文書名用 Italic；論文篇名用 " "；古籍之書名與篇名連用時，可省略篇名符號，如《史記‧刺客列傳》。

3. 獨立引文每行低三格（楷書）；不必加引號。

4. 年代、計數，請使用阿拉伯數字。

5. 圖表照片請注明資料來源，並以阿拉伯數字編號，引用時請注明編號，勿使用 "如前圖"、"見右表" 等表示方法。

6. 請勿使用："同上"、"同前引書"、"同前書"、"同前揭書"、"同注幾引書"，"ibid.,""Op. cit.,""loc. cit.,""idem" 等。

7. 引用專書或論文，請依序注明作者、書名（或篇名）、出版項。

   A. 中日文專書：作者，《書名》（出版地：出版者，年份），頁碼。

   　　如：余英時，《中國文化史通釋》（香港：牛津大學出版社，2010），頁 1-12。

   　　如：林毓生，〈史華慈思想史學的意義〉，收入許紀霖等編，《史華慈論中國》（北京：新星出版社，2006），頁 237-246。

   B. 引用原版或影印版古籍，請注明版本與卷頁。

如：王鳴盛，《十七史商榷》（臺北：樂天出版社，1972），卷12，頁1。

　　如：王道，《王文定公遺書》（明萬曆己酉朱延禧南京刊本，臺北國家圖書館藏），卷1，頁2a。

C. 引用叢書古籍：作者，《書名》，收入《叢書名》冊數（出版地：出版者，年份），卷數，〈篇名〉，頁碼。

　　如：袁甫，《蒙齋集》，收入《景印文淵閣四庫全書》第1175冊（臺北：臺灣商務印書館，1983），卷5，〈論史宅之奏〉，頁11a。

D. 中日韓文論文：作者，〈篇名〉，《期刊名稱》，卷：期（出版地，年份），頁碼。

　　如：王德權，〈「核心集團與核心區」理論的檢討〉，《政治大學歷史學報》，25（臺北，2006），頁147-176，引自頁147-151。

　　如：桑兵，〈民國學界的老輩〉，《歷史研究》，2005：6（北京，2005），頁3-24，引自頁3-4。

E. 西文專書：作者—書名—出版地點—出版公司—出版年分。

　　如：Samuel P. Huntington, *Political Order in Changing Societies* (New Haven: Yale University Press, 1968), pp. 102-103.

F. 西文論文：作者—篇名—期刊卷期—年月—頁碼。

　　如：Hoyt Tillman, "A New Direction in Confucian Scholarship: Approaches to Examining the Differences between Neo-Confucianism and Tao-hsüeh," *Philosophy East and West*, 42:3 (July 1992), pp. 455-474.

G. 報紙：〈標題〉—《報紙名稱》（出版地）—年月日—版頁。

　　〈要聞：副總統嚴禁祕密結社之條件〉，《時報》（上海），2922號，1912年8月4日，3版。

"Auditorium to Present Special Holiday Program," *The China Press* (Shanghai), 4 Jul. 1930, p. 7.

H. 網路資源：作者—《網頁標題》—《網站發行機構／網站名》—發行日期／最後更新日期—網址（查詢日期）。

倪孟安等，〈學人專訪：司徒琳教授訪談錄〉，《明清研究通訊》第5期，發行日期2010/03/15，http://mingching.sinica.edu.tw/newsletter/005/interview-lynn.htm (2013/07/30)。

8. 本刊之漢字拼音方式，以尊重作者所使用者為原則。

9. 本刊為雙匿名審稿制，故來稿不可有「拙作」一類可使審查者得知作者身分的敘述。

《思想史》購買與訂閱辦法

（2014/3/31修訂）

一、零售價格：每冊新臺幣480元。主要經銷處：聯經出版公司官網、門市與全省各大實體書店、網路書店。

二、國內訂閱(全年二冊/3、9月出版)：

機關訂戶，新臺幣960元；個人訂戶，新臺幣760元；學生訂戶，新臺幣720元。郵政劃撥帳戶「聯經出版公司」，帳號01005593。

三、海外訂閱(全年二冊/3、9月出版)：

港澳/大陸地區——航空每年訂費NT$2200元（US$78），
　　　　　　　　海運每年訂費1972元（US$70）

亞洲/大洋洲地區—航空每年訂費NT$2342元（US$82），
　　　　　　　　海運每年訂費2086元（US$74）

歐美/非洲地區——航空每年訂費NT$2542元（US$90），
　　　　　　　　海運每年訂費2086元（US$74）

若需掛號，全年另加US$5

請將費用以美金即期支票寄至：

臺北市大安區新生南路三段94號1樓　聯經出版公司

1F., No.94, Sec. 3, Xinsheng S. Rd., Da'an Dist., Taipei City 106, Taiwan (R.O.C.)

TEL：886-2-23620308

Subscription

A. List price: (surface postage included)

Hong Kong, Macao, China US$70 per issue; Asia, Oceania, America, Europe, Australia and Other Areas US$74. (Add US$5 for registered mail)

B. List price: (air mail)

Hong Kong, Macao, China: US$78 per issue; Asia and Oceania Areas US$82 per issue;

America, Europe, Australia and Other Areas: US$90. (Add US$5 for registered mail)

C. Subscription Rate: (2 issues per year)

Please pay by money order made payable to:

Thoughts History, 1F., No.94, Sec. 3, Xinsheng S. Rd., Taipei City 106, Taiwan (R.O.C.)

E-mail：lkstore2@udngroup.com

TEL：886-2-23620308

FAX：886-2-23620137

聯 經 出 版 事 業 公 司

《思想史》期刊　信用卡訂閱單

訂 購 人 姓 名：＿＿＿＿＿＿＿＿＿＿＿＿＿＿＿

訂 購 日 期：＿＿＿年＿＿＿月＿＿＿日

信 用 卡 別：□VISA CARD　□MASTER CARD

信 用 卡 號：＿＿＿＿＿＿＿＿＿（卡片背面簽名欄後三碼）＿＿＿必填

信用卡有效期限：＿＿＿月＿＿＿年

信 用 卡 簽 名：＿＿＿＿＿＿＿＿＿＿＿＿＿（與信用卡上簽名同）

聯 絡 電 話：日(O)：＿＿＿＿＿＿＿＿＿夜(H)：＿＿＿＿＿＿＿＿

傳 眞 號 碼：＿＿＿＿＿＿＿＿＿＿＿＿＿

聯 絡 地 址：＿＿＿＿＿＿＿＿＿＿＿＿＿＿＿＿＿＿

訂 購 金 額：NT$＿＿＿＿＿＿＿＿＿＿＿元整

發　　　　票：□二聯式　□三聯式

統 一 編 號：＿＿＿＿＿＿＿＿＿＿＿＿＿＿

發 票 抬 頭：＿＿＿＿＿＿＿＿＿＿＿＿＿

◎若收件人或收件地不同時，請另加填！

收 件 人 姓 名：□同上＿＿＿＿＿＿＿＿＿＿＿＿□先生　□小姐

收 件 人 地 址：□同上＿＿＿＿＿＿＿＿＿＿＿＿＿＿＿＿

收 件 人 電 話：□同上 日(O)：＿＿＿＿＿＿　夜(H)：＿＿＿＿＿＿

※ 茲訂購下列書籍，帳款由本人信用卡帳戶支付

訂閱書名	年 / 期數	寄送	掛號	金額
《思想史》	訂閱＿＿＿年	□ 航空 □ 海運	□ 是 □ 否	NT$

訂閱單填妥後

1. 直接傳眞 FAX：886-2-23620137

2. 寄臺北市大安區新生南路三段94號1樓　聯經出版公司 收

　TEL：886-2-23620308

思想史
思想史 5

2015年9月初版　　　　　　　　　　　　　　定價：新臺幣480元
有著作權・翻印必究
Printed in Taiwan.

編　　　著	思想史編委會
總　編　輯	胡　金　倫
總　經　理	羅　國　俊
發　行　人	林　載　爵

出　版　者	聯經出版事業股份有限公司	叢書主編	陳　逸　達
地　　　址	台北市基隆路一段180號4樓	封面設計	沈　佳　德
編輯部地址	台北市基隆路一段180號4樓
叢書主編電話	(0 2) 8 7 8 7 6 2 4 2 轉 2 2 5
台北聯經書房	台北市新生南路三段94號
電　　　話	(0 2) 2 3 6 2 0 3 0 8
台中分公司	台中市北區崇德路一段198號
暨門市電話	(0 4) 2 2 3 1 2 0 2 3
台中電子信箱	e-mail：linking2@ms42.hinet.net
郵政劃撥帳戶第	0 1 0 0 5 5 9 - 3 號
郵撥電話	(0 2) 2 3 6 2 0 3 0 8
印　刷　者	世和印製企業有限公司
總　經　銷	聯合發行股份有限公司
發　行　所	新北市新店區寶橋路235巷6弄6號2樓
電　　　話	(0 2) 2 9 1 7 8 0 2 2

行政院新聞局出版事業登記證局版臺業字第0130號

國家圖書館出版品預行編目資料

思想史　5/思想史編委會編著 . 初版 . 臺北市 .
聯經 . 2015年9月（民104年）. 352面 . 14.8×
21公分（思想史：5）
ISBN　978-957-08-4641-6（平裝）

1.思想史　2.文集

110.7　　　　　　　　　　　　104021777